Great
RUSSIAN
Short Stories
of the Twentieth Century

A DUAL-LANGUAGE BOOK

Замечательный
РУССКИЙ
короткий рассказ
двадцатого века

Edited and Translated by
YELENA P. FRANCIS

DOVER PUBLICATIONS
Garden City, New York

ACKNOWLEDGMENTS: SEE PAGE xi.

Copyright

Bibliographical Note

Great Russian Short Stories of the Twentieth Century / Замечательный русский короткий рассказ двадцатого века: *A Dual-Language Book*, first published by Dover Publications in 2013, is a new selection of Russian stories reprinted from standard Russian texts and accompanied by new English translations prepared for the Dover edition by Yelena Francis, who also made the selection and wrote the Introduction and author biographies.

Library of Congress Cataloging-in-Publication Data

Great Russian short stories of the twentieth century : a dual language book Замечательный русский короткий рассказ двадцатого века / edited and translated by Yelena P. Francis.
  p. cm. — (Dual-language book)
Selection of Russian stories, reprinted from standard Russian texts, accompanied by new English translations.
  ISBN-13: 978-0-486-48873-8
  ISBN-10: 0-486-48873-X
  1. Short stories, Russian—20th century—Translations into English. I. Francis, Yelena P., editor, translator. II. Title: 880-01 Замечательный русский короткий рассказ двадцатого века. III. Series: Dual-language book.

PG3286.G75 2013
891.73' 0108—dc23

                                                                    2012040309

Manufactured in the United States of America
48873X08   2021
www.doverpublications.com

CONTENTS

INTRODUCTION

Russian literature of the twentieth century grew out of the rich and fertile soil of its nineteenth-century predecessors. Among them are such important names in the high art of narrative as the national geniuses Alexander Pushkin, Nikolai Gogol, Mikhail Lermontov, Ivan Turgenev, Ivan Goncharov, Nikolai Leskov, Feodor Dostoevsky, and Leo Tolstoy. This epoch is traditionally called the "Golden Age" of Russian literature, when the native literature, gradually following along the paths of the European literary trends, evolved from sentimentalism, through romanticism, to the mature realist masterpieces filled with profound original philosophy and deep psychological analysis, as well as the stunning literary landscape depicting Russian nature.

Then, trouble appeared on the horizon. It looked like a sad paradox, but the first signs of the coming storms showed up during the period of serious positive domestic political changes called the "Great Reforms." Alexander II liberated the serfs in 1861 and introduced drastic improvements in education, army service, legislation, local administration, and other areas. These reforms endowed the society with a notably higher degree of freedom, making life less suffocating. At the same time, those steps towards a more civilized society were accompanied with the blind cruelty of the terrorists' attacks. The leftists' movements tried to hasten a social revolution and to prevent the changes by peaceful reforms. Intensification of technological progress, and the beginning of industrial capitalism, with all its senseless exploitation of the masses of unqualified, cheap and voiceless workers, caused a sharp contrast between the rich and the poor. That, in turn, quickly caused a split within the society.

These developments, these new conditions, brought forth a new type of social and interpersonal dynamics—both in the society and within families—new attitudes to life, and new values.

In addition to the already drastically new "ways," the Russian Empire was still on the threshold of even more important changes. They came later, after Alexander's reforms, and approached closer and closer like a roaring thunderstorm. The trigger was the assassination of Alexander II. After that, the shameful defeat in the Russo-Japanese War, like a domino effect, brought forth the Revolution of 1905. The events of World War I became the last lightning strike, after which the Empire, covering one-sixth of the globe, collapsed like a house of cards. The Revolution of 1917 followed. The October Proletarian Revolution triggered the fratricidal, bloody Civil War that inflicted enormous casualties on Russia, resulting in the establishment of the Soviet power. The Communist regime was born, with the creation of the USSR and Stalin's purges. Then another disaster was looming—World War II.

All these catastrophic events followed each other in close sequence. One can hear a similar "scenario" in Russian folklore:

"When one trouble is coming,
It is bringing another."

All that history was reflected, as in a mirror, in Russian art in various forms. The twentieth century, in spite of all the ordeals, enriched Russian literature with many outstanding artists of the narrative form—in particular, the short story genre.

* * *

The "Great Reforms" of the second part of the nineteenth century resulted in a developing economy, and there also was much more ideological freedom in the society than before. There was an astonishing flourishing of Russian art: philosophy, painting, poetry and literature, music, and theater. It was the time of the modernist movement, and in Russian art another term was coined—"the Silver Age." There were different

art groups, literary salons and manifestos, many discussions, and numerous experiments in form and language, in poetry as well as fiction. This epoch of Russian art is famous for the profusion of outstanding poets and writers.

Then, after the Revolution of 1917, these art movements gradually began to die down. The reason for that lies within the new ideological policies and the censorship instituted by the Communist regime. Those who were not able to collaborate fled the country. Those who wanted to stay, to try to write and to survive, played "Russian roulette," uncertain where they would find themselves next morning—at home or in the prison of the secret police.

Many artists who in the past had been involved in the revolutionary movement still nourished their illusions, dreaming about building a new type of society never before seen in the history of mankind. This new group of writers came on stage. Most of them had a dream about a new world, built on the foundation similar to the original Christian ideas. They were aware of all the difficulties and injustice of that time, but they thought that all of the troubles were only temporary phenomena. Those people were artists, strictly controlled and often directly told by the Communists how and what to write. But even under that enormous pressure, the writers managed to create beautifully written, profound fiction, which contained deep philosophy, subtle lyricism, and interesting original characters.

The writers selected for the present collection of Russian short stories are representative of the "threshold," of the "transition" period in literature linking the twilight of classical mature realism and the birth of modernism, as well as the beginning of Soviet literature.

The reader will find classical examples of realist style in the writings of Dmitry Mamin-Sibiryak, Vladimir Gilyarovsky, Aleksandr Kuprin, and Skitalets.

Dmitry Mamin-Sibiryak is known for looking at the characters in his stories through the eyes of an ethnographer and an admirer of the Urals and Siberia, and for his "animated" descriptions of nature.

His exotic personality is credited for Vladimir Gilyarovsky's status as a celebrity of his time, as well as a "Renaissance Man." He was a person of a great positive aura, loved by everyone; an incredibly popular journalist, a good athlete, an adventurer in the style of Jack London's characters, an able poet, memoirist, and a gifted writer. His narratives are well written and sometimes touching, with their combination of social protest and romanticism, an echo of his life-long attraction to poetry.

Skitalets, as a writer (unjustly forgotten), is close to Gilyarovsky's slightly sentimental style, his light shades of romanticism, and his compassion for the poor. His originality lies in his interest in depicting eccentric artistic characters.

Aleksandr Kuprin is still one of the most popular writers among the Russian reading public. His fiction expresses sadness for the suffering of the people. Readers like his tender love stories and his kind fiction for children. He was among the first to rise up passionately in protest against the wave of Jewish pogroms of those times, writing about them with bitterness towards the society that tolerated such atrocities. He also was one of the first who touched the hidden and shameful subject of prostitution, writing with compassion about these women.

Leonid Andreev's short stories were loved by readers in the past and still are popular today. In spite of his reputation as a modernist, many of his narratives are written in the classical "Golden Age" tradition. It is a balanced combination of subtle psychological insight and an attempt to understand and forgive. One can feel as if God were permanently watching his characters and measuring mercifully both their sins and their virtues.

It is impossible not to include in this collection fiction by the beloved Anton Chekhov, with his profound psychological analysis and the melancholy and penetrating gaze of a wise doctor.

The icon of Soviet literature, essentially canonized by the Communist regime, Maxim Gorky is a special case in this

group. He stands apart with his passion for revolutionary changes, his love for strong and independent characters, and his romanticizing of that bloody epoch. He is close to classical realism with his detailed descriptions of characters and their surroundings, and his desire to find harmony in interaction between man and nature in his original narrative.

Another group of writers included in this collection are luminous representatives of the "Silver Age"—Modernism. One of these is the leader of Russian Symbolism, Valery Bryusov; another is known for her brave experiments with an alloy of narrative and poetry, Lydia Zinovieva-Annibal.

It was impossible, in this respect, to pass over such an outstanding figure as Yevgeny Zamyatin. He is the nonconformist author and creator of the social anti-utopia titled *We*—a warning to mankind. He wrote numerous short stories in an extremely original style, reminding one of avant-garde canvases by his predilection for the metaphorical.

Due to his original experiments with humorous fiction, the famous humor writer Ilya Ilf is included into the same group. In his young years he wrote blank verse, and in his stories one can see beautiful layers of poetry among the foundation of the quite realistic fiction, mixed with subtle irony.

Among the group of talented Soviet writers, Aleksandr Grin and Arkady Gaidar are known for their romanticism. Aleksandr Grin is still very popular, especially among young readers, for the fantastic magical worlds that his characters inhabit, for his positive vision, and for the confidence that even in the most difficult situation there is always "a light at the end of the tunnel."

Arkady Gaidar, another writer who created popular tales and stories after the Civil War, was so influential that his books started a charitable movement among teenagers, similar in principle to the Boy Scouts. The hallmark of his artistic originality is his fresh and childlike vision of the world.

The most beloved, the most famous, and the most quoted Russian Soviet writer, Mikhail Bulgakov, could be called a cult author. He is admired for his novels and dramas, his fiction, and

his film scripts. The story chosen for this collection is a miniature *chef-d'oeuvre*. It is a subtle mixture of narrative and drama that creates a unique feeling of personal presence at the beginning of a romance.

So, the reader interested in Russian life and history, the Russian mentality, and the Russian soul, will find here a great deal of material for reflection, and, at the same time, an opportunity to enjoy a wide variety of styles, original characters, and situations. A *Notes* section with sources and details on the stories appears at the end of the book.

I would like to thank Rochelle Kronzek and Janet Kopito, my editors at Dover Publications, and Richard Pierre, the book's proofreader, for their assistance.

Finally, I would like to thank my husband, Sven, for his patience and support during my work on this project.

ACKNOWLEDGMENTS

Vasily Grossman, "From the Bus Window": © The Estate of Vasily Grossman, ИЗ ОКНА АВТОБУСА (FROM THE BUS WINDOW) by Vasily Grossman, first published in 1967. ДОБРО ВАМ (GOOD TO YOU). МОСКВА (MOSCOW). СОВЕТСКИЙ ПИСАТЕЛЬ (SOVIET WRITER).

Great Russian
Short Stories of the
Twentieth Century

Замечательный
русский
короткий рассказ
двадцатого века

A DUAL-LANGUAGE BOOK

Maxim Gorky
(Aleksei Maximovich Peshkov)
Сирота / The Orphan

Николай Александрович Ярошенко (1846–1898). Мальчик в саду. 1892.
[Мемориальный музей-усадьба художника Н. Ярошенко. Кисловодск]

Nikolai A. Yaroshenko. *The Boy in the Garden*. 1892.
[The Memorial Museum of N. Yaroshenko. Kislovodsk]

MAXIM GORKY
(ALEKSEI MAXIMOVICH PESHKOV)

1868–1936

Gorky was, for almost a century, the most glorified Soviet writer, and, according to one of his most popular poems— "A Stormy Petrel of Revolution." He is likely the most controversial personality of Russian literature of the twentieth century. Gorky was a very prolific writer and a playwright. His oeuvre contains numerous stories, essays, novels, plays, as well as poetry. He truly was an original fiction writer judging by his style, language, his philosophy, and his vision of Russia and Russian national character.

On the one hand, in Stalin's times, Gorky became almost "a living classical genius" and a literary icon of the time. He was extremely powerful: the Soviet leaders—the deities of the new Communist Russia, Stalin and the chiefs of the secret police among them—would frequently come to his house to have dinner and tea. Gorky was idolized, called the "Founder of Socialist Realism" and a "Great Proletarian Writer." The circulation of his books was enormous. In the city Nizhni Novgorod, where Gorky lived, numerous squares, streets, monuments, parks, libraries, and other objects were named after him. Dozens of screen versions of his fiction were produced. Gorky also was a writer of great authority, who, like a savior, could often protect many colleagues suffering from the Communist regime and persecuted by Soviet propaganda and censorship. To do justice to him, he really saved a lot of them, and for many he was a guardian angel.

In Perestroika times, after the collapse of the Soviet Union, the pendulum of the public opinion and media swung in the opposite direction. Gorky was blamed for being an anti-Russian supporter of the Communist regime. Even the city of Gorky, named after him, was reunited with its former name of Nizhny Novgorod. As wisdom would have it, the truth is to be found somewhere in the middle. There is no reason to create an icon of this original and gifted man, just as there is no one to blame him for all the crimes of the oppressive Soviet regime and Stalin's Purges.

The life of this writer was extremely difficult, and this was the reason that Aleksei Maximovich Peshkov accepted the pen name "Gorky," which in Russian means "bitter." He did not want to use his real last name, Peshkov, considering it not significant or serious (in the Russian language, "peshka" means "pawn"). He described his life in detail in his trilogy *Childhood*, *My Apprenticeship*, and *My Universities*, as well as in many stories. In general, Gorky's narrative is autobiographical. It is natural that the first impressions in childhood are the most influential, molding one's personality and forming an outlook on life. Having lost his father in his early childhood, he had to live with his mother and his grandparents in Nizhny Novgorod. His childhood was horrifying: the permanent humiliation, physical punishment, the greediness of relatives and rudeness and cruelty towards each other. Everything created an atmosphere of permanent terror—the thick darkness of life, hopelessness and a dead end. When the boy was about eleven, his grandfather ordered him to leave home and start earning a living. Without education, support or any professional skills, he had to try an endless list of jobs, from dishwasher to baker's assistant. For a while, Gorky even was a hobo traveling all over Russia, and as a logical result of his personal experiences he joined the leftist political movement and became a Bolshevik Party member. Many events followed: successful writings, glory, traveling abroad, friendship with not only world famous writers, like Leo Tolstoy and Anton Chekhov, but with the "Leader of the World

Proletariat," Vladimir Lenin. At first, there was Gorky's enthusiastic support, followed with a bitter disappointment in the results of the October Revolution of 1917. He lived abroad, almost in exile, came back to Soviet Russia, and later died under quite suspicious circumstances.

Among Gorky's fiction, the short story "The Orphan" continues a "series" of his writings about children (the most well-known is his *Childhood*). Like many of them, it is recognizably autobiographical. Gorky was raised by his grandparents, and the only support and love in the family he received was from his grandmother—a very kind, gifted and wise woman. She was the center of the family and the center of his universe. He knew what it meant to lose his only close friend, as happened to a young character in the story. As for Gorky himself, it was likely not a coincidence that he tried to commit suicide a few months after his grandmother's death.

In this story, written so passionately and with such commiseration, one can feel the grieving of the little boy as if it were taking place in front of our very eyes. In Gorky's stories, nature plays an important role, framing the events and almost performing a certain melody "backstage." One can see this in the monotonous, gloomy, cold rain, the poor cemetery, and the little boy in the middle of the space surrounded by the crosses and graves. Even the sky is crying along with the orphan, who has lost his home. He feels, but cannot express, his helplessness and hopelessness, his defenselessness and solitude in the hostile world around him.

МАКСИМ ГОРЬКИЙ

Сирота

В туманный и дождливый день у ворот кладбища маленькая группа людей, стоя в луже грязи, торговалась с извозчиками.

— Пятиалтынный! — густым басом восклицал высокий и тучный священник в ответ на дружные крики извозчиков, просивших по четвертаку.

— Ах, какие вы бесстыжие! — укоряла их одна из четырёх женщин, окружавших священника. Она держала зонт над его головой и сама плотно жалась к его боку, стараясь укрыться от дождя, мелкого, как пыль.

— Погоди, мать, не толкайся! — говорил священник, внушительно приподнимая кверху правую руку. — Ну, за пятиалтынный везёте?

— Ах, какие вы жадные! — огорчённо восклицала матушка, нетерпеливо переступая по грязи с ноги на ногу. На её худом лице с большими круглыми глазами пылало негодование, и она, высоко подобрав свою юбку, так нетерпеливо дёргала её, точно хотела бежать.

— Далеко ли тут? — говорила она, убедительно качая головой. — Вы подумайте — далеко ли?

Но извозчики не хотели думать. Ожесточённо дёргая вожжами и раскачиваясь на козлах, они кричали, перебивая друг друга:

— Помилуйте, батюшка! Не торгуйтесь, матушка! Пожалуйте! Притом же — за упокой души…

Дьякон, псаломщик с крестом в руках и ещё три женщины, укутанные в большие платки, тоже возмущались

MAXIM GORKY

The Orphan

On a foggy and rainy day, by the cemetery gate, a small group of people standing in a muddy puddle were bargaining with the cabmen.

"Fifteen kopeks!" The tall and heavy-set priest exclaimed in a deep bass, in response to the cabman's shouts asking for twenty-five kopecks.

"Oh, shame on you!" One of the four women surrounding the priest was reproaching them. Holding an umbrella above his head, she was drawing tightly close to his side, trying to hide from the drizzling dust-like rain.

"Hold on, Mother, don't push me!" the priest said, raising his right hand impressively. "Well, will you drive for fifteen kopecks?"

"Oh, how greedy you are!" the priest's wife exclaimed in distress, impatiently shifting from one foot to another in the dirt. Her bony face, with big round eyes, was burning with indignation, and she, picking up her skirt high, was pulling at it so impatiently as if she wanted to run.

"Is it so far from here?" she was saying, convincingly shaking her head. "Think, if it is really so far?"

But the cabmen did not want to think. Fiercely jerking the reins and swaying on the boxes, they were shouting, interrupting each other:

"For goodness sake, Father! Don't bargain, Mother! Get in! Besides, it is for the peace of a soul..."

The Deacon, the psalm reader, holding a cross, and three more women, wrapped in big shawls, were also outraged with

7

жадностью извозчиков и ревностно поддерживали оживление торга. Они очень шумели пред входом в обитель вечного покоя, и холодный ветер, точно желая скорее прогнать их, сбрасывал им на плечи крупные капли дождя с ветвей берёз и лип, уныло осенявших каменную ограду кладбища…

Нищие, в грязных и мокрых лохмотьях, окружали этих людей и, разбрызгивая грязь своей тяжёлой обувью, болезненно и назойливо ныли:

— Подайте Христа-а ра-ади…

— Копеечку за упокой её душеньки — пода-айте!

— Поминаючи усопшую…

— Фу, какие ненасытные! — кричала матушка, высовывая голову из-под зонта. — Да ведь вам уже подали… ведь получили вы по баранке… Ай-я-яй! Как вам не стыдно!

Понуро опустив головы, четыре лошади вздрагивали, стряхивая с себя воду, и покорными глазами косились на своих хозяев, ожидая привычного окрика или удара кнутом.

— Батюшка! — решительно воскликнул один извозчик, — желаете поехать за двугривенный?

— Пятиалтынный… — отрицательно качнул головой батюшка.

— Боже мой, какие…

Но прежде чем попадья кончила начатый упрёк, извозчик озлобленно хлестнул лошадь кнутом и поехал прочь. Другие извозчики тоже задёргали вожжами…

— Ну, ладно! Ну — давай! — махнул рукой священник. — За двугривенный — давай! Садись, мать, на этого… полезай, отец дьякон! Садитесь все… Пошёл с богом!.. Стой, стой! А где… внук?

— Ай матушки! Где он? — пугливо воскликнула попадья.

— Извозчик — стой! Отец дьякон, а? Бабы, вы как же это? Чего вы смотрите? — строго спрашивал священник.

Женщины, уже сидевшие на пролётках, стали слезать в грязь, растерянно бормоча что-то.

the greediness of the cabmen and ardently kept up the bargaining. They made a lot of noise by the gate to the dwelling of eternal peace, and the cold wind, as if it was eager to chase them away faster, threw heavy drops of rain on their shoulders from birch and linden trees, dolefully overhanging the stone cemetery wall...

The beggars, in dirty and wet rags, surrounded those people, and, splashing mud with their heavy shoes, painfully whined:

"Give alms, for Chri-i-i-st's sa-a-a-ke..."

"A kopeck for the peace of her soul, gi-i-ive!"

"Praying for the deceased woman..."

"Ugh, so insatiable you are!" The priest's wife was shouting, sticking her head out of the umbrella. "You have already been given alms, haven't you...You have already gotten a baranka each, haven't you... Ooh, ooh! You ought to be ashamed!"

Hanging their heads, the four horses were quivering, shaking off water, and looking sideways at their owners, expecting the usual shouts or strikes with a whip.

"Father!" one cabman resolutely exclaimed, "Would you like to go for twenty kopecks?"

"Fifteen kopecks..." the priest shook his head.

"My Lord, what people..."

But before the priest's wife finished the reproach she had already started, the cabman whipped spitefully at his horse and started driving away. Other cabmen also pulled their reins...

"Well, all right! Well—very well!" the priest waved his hand. "Let's go then for twenty kopecks! Mother, get on this one... climb, Father Deacon! Everyone get on... Let's go, with God's blessing!.. Stop, stop! And where is... the grandchild?"

"Oh, my God! Where is he?" the priest's wife timidly exclaimed.

"Cabman, stop! Father Deacon, oh! Women, what are you thinking about? What are you waiting for?" the priest was angrily asking.

The women, already sitting in cabs, started stepping down to the mud, murmuring something in embarrassment.

— Экий какой... шельмец! — угрюмо ворчал дьякон, тоже спрыгивая с пролётки. — У могилы остался, видно... Вы, отец Яков, поезжайте, не беспокойтесь, а я с Кириллом останусь... мы привезём мальчонку...

И, подобрав рясу, дьякон пошёл к воротам кладбища, внимательно глядя себе под ноги.

— Да, да — как же? — говорил священник, усаживаясь на пролётке и следя, чтоб широкие одежды его не попали в колесо. — Надо его найти... он мне поручен... и прочее такое! Извозчик — трогай! На могиле, отец дьякон, ищи его... на могиле!

Две пролётки с дребезгом поехали. На передней сидел священник с женой, на второй — три женщины, а третья — со псаломщиком — осталась у ворот. Псаломщик поставил большой крест себе в ноги, обнял его руками, прижал к груди, а потом засунул руки в рукава пальто и наклонил голову на левое плечо, чтоб защитить от дождя щёку. Нищие исчезли как-то вдруг, точно грязь поглотила их и они растворились в ней.

— Вот торговались, небойсь... а теперь я стой и дожидайся чего-то... — сказал извозчик, глядя вслед уехавшим. Псаломщик, тоже недовольный этим ожиданием под дождём, промолчал.

— Кого потеряли-то? — подождав, спросил извозчик.

— А тебе что?

— Мне-то? А ничего... только вот — жду я...

— И подождёшь! — хмуро сказал псаломщик.

— Известно — подожду... Однако у старухи-то, у покойной, слышь, деньги были...

— Ну?

— Кому же это она их определила?

— Не тебе...

— Известно, не мне... Кабы мне — я бы и не спрашивал... а я спрашиваю — на церковь, мол, или как?

— На воспитание её внука священнику нашему, — сообщил псаломщик, ёжась от дождя, попадавшего ему за воротник пальто.

"What an... imp!" the Deacon was muttering gloomily, also jumping down from the cab. "He remained by the grave, I think... You, Father Yakov, go, don't worry, and I will stay with Kirill... We will bring the kid..."

And, picking up his cassock, the Deacon headed towards the cemetery gate, attentively looking at the road.

"Yes, yes—how is that?" the priest was saying, taking a seat in the cab and making sure not to get his loose clothes stuck in the wheel. "You should find him... He was entrusted to me... and so on! Cabman—let's go! On the grave, Father Deacon, look for him... on the grave!"

Two cabs left with a tinkling sound. On the front one, the priest was sitting with his wife, on the second were three women, and the third one, with the psalm reader, remained by the gate. The psalm reader put a big cross down by his feet, embraced it with both arms, pressed it against his chest, then put his hands into his coat pockets, and bent his head to his left shoulder to protect his cheek from the rain. Somehow, the beggars suddenly disappeared, as if the mud swallowed them and they dissolved in it.

"You see, we bargained... and now I should be here and wait for God knows what...," the cabman said, following the departing cabs with his eyes. The psalm reader, also unhappy with waiting in the rain, said nothing.

"Whom did you lose, eh?" the cabman paused and asked.

"Why do you ask?"

"Me? For no reason... only here...I am waiting..."

"And you will be waiting!" the psalm reader answered gloomily.

"Of course, I will wait... Though, the old woman, the deceased, listen, had money..."

"So?"

"Whom did she leave it to?"

"Not to you..."

"Of course, not to me... If to me, I would not ask... And I am asking if she left it to the church or to whom?"

"To our priest to raise her grandson," the psalm reader said shivering from the rain, getting under his coat collar.

— Та-ак! — сказал извозчик. Потом он спросил, велик ли внук и сколько осталось денег, но псаломщик уже не отвечал ему.

— Стало быть, невелик он, внук-то, коли некуда его девать, кроме как на воспитание, — вслух умозаключил извозчик. Его лошадь взмахнула хвостом — он обругал её, ударил вожжами и умолк. Дождь сыпался беззвучно, а голые и мокрые ветви деревьев, качаясь под ударами ветра, вздыхали и стонали.

А на кладбище, под одним из бесчисленных крестов его, стоял маленький мальчик с лицом, распухшим от слёз. Он съёжился в чёрный комок и молча смотрел на бугор земли пред ним — свежий, только что утрамбованный лопатами бугор мокрой глины. Часто с вершины бугра, бесшумно скользя по его боку, сползал к ногам мальчика комок земли. Мальчик следил за его движением светлыми и печальными глазами и вздыхал тихонько. В одном углу кладбища хоронили бедных, тут не было ни одного памятника из камня, не было и деревьев вокруг мальчика; стояли только одни деревянные, простые, чёрные, зелёные, белые, неокрашенные, гнилые и искривлённые кресты — все мокрые от дождя и красноречивые в своём торжественном молчании. Мальчик стоял, прислонясь к большому чёрному кресту, упорно смотрел на новую могилу и не видел ничего, кроме этого мокрого коричневого бугра, таявшего под дождём.

На чёрном мохнатом пальто мальчика осели мелкие серебристые капельки дождя, и тоскливое лицо его тоже было мокро. Он держал руки в карманах и голову склонил на грудь. Из-под круглой шапки выбилась прядь рыжеватых волос и прилипла к его правому виску. И, одинокий среди множества крестов, символов страдания, он своим белым и печальным личиком тронул сердце дьякона, подошедшего к нему с раздражением за прогулку среди могил по грязи и под дождём.

— Ну, чего же ты стоишь тут, Петрунька? — сказал дьякон, взяв его за руку. — А мы тебя ищем... все уже уехали. Пойдём...

"So-o-o!" the cabman said. Then he asked how old the grandson was, and how much money was left, but the psalm reader did not answer him anymore.

"So, I see that the grandson is not big enough, so nothing can be done with him except sending him for adoption," the cabman concluded out loud. His horse waved its tail, and he cursed it, struck it with the reins, and fell silent. It was raining, noiselessly, and naked wet branches of trees were waving, struck by the wind, sighing and moaning.

And in the cemetery, under one of its countless crosses, a small boy was standing with his face swollen from tears. He shriveled into a black lump and in silence was watching the small heap of ground in front of him, a fresh one, a heap of clay, just rammed with spades. Often, a lump from the top of the grave slid silently down, crawling to the boy's feet. The boy watched its movement with his bright sad eyes and sighed quietly. In this corner of the cemetery, the poor were buried, there were no tombstones; there were no trees around the boy; only wooden, simple, black, green, white, undyed, rotten and curved crosses—all wet from the rain and eloquent with their grand silence. The boy was standing, leaning against the big black cross and was not able to tear himself away from the fresh grave, and did not see anything except that wet brown heap melting under the rain.

Tiny silver drops of rain were covering the boy's black furry coat, and his sad face was also wet. He kept his hands in the pockets, and hung his head. A lock of reddish hair came out from under his round hat, and stuck to his right temple. And, so lonely, with his sad white face, surrounded by numerous crosses, the symbols of suffering, he touched the heart of the Deacon, who was coming to him annoyed, because he had to walk among the graves, through the mud, under the rain.

"Well, why are you standing here, Petrunka?" the Deacon said holding his hand. "We have been looking for you... Everybody has already left... Let's go..."

— Куда? — тихо спросил мальчик.

— К отцу Якову… ты у него жить будешь теперь… ты не плачь… это воля Божия. Господь может прогневаться на тебя за слёзы твои… И опять же — ведь она старая была у тебя, бабушка-то, а все люди — смертны. Все умрут в час свой… и я и ты — все умрут!

Он вёл мальчика за руку и следил за тем, чтоб не потерять своих галош в грязи. Он хотел говорить ласково, но говорил озабоченно, потому что боязнь потерять галоши мешала ему быть ласковым с сиротой. Мальчик закусил губу, удерживая рыдания, разбуженные угрюмыми словами, и почти бежал за дьяконом, шагавшим широко и быстро.

— Ничего! — сказал дьякон, мельком взглянув в его лицо.

— Отец Яков — хороший человек… ты будешь играть с Мишуткой и Зоей… заживёшь весело… да!

Мальчик представил себе Зою, смуглую и бойкую девочку с чёрными глазами. Она прыгает пред ним, показывая ему нос, и дразнит его, распевая злым голосом:

— «Рыжий от грыжи, рыжий от пропажи, рыжий свечи зажигать, рыжий трубы затыкать…»

— Я не люблю Зою… — печально сказал он.

— Ну, это пустяки!.. Полюбишь, в одной комнате жить-то будете…

— Я не буду…

— А… нельзя этого…

Мальчик тихо заплакал.

— Эх ты… сиротина! — вздохнул дьякон, глядя на него.

Когда дошли до извозчика, дьякон заботливо усадил его в ноги псаломщику и поощрительно сказал:

— Сиди крепче!.. Приедем — чай будем пить…

— Ну-у, жаба! — крикнул извозчик на лошадь.

Пролётка запрыгала по мостовой сквозь серую завесу дождя и тумана. Из тумана выдвигались дома, и, казалось, они тихо и молчаливо плывут куда-то, оглядывая мальчика большими и бесцветными глазами. В груди мальчика было холодно и тесно для сердца.

"Where?" the boy asked quietly.

"To Father Yakov... You are going to live in his place now... Don't cry... This is God's will. God can get angry with you for your tears... And also, she was old, your grandmother, and all men are mortal. Everyone will die in their time... both you and I—everybody will die!"

He held the boy by his hand and kept his eyes on his galoshes, so as not to lose them in the dirt. He wanted to speak tenderly, but spoke anxiously, because his fear of losing his water-proof shoes prevented him from being tender with the orphan. The boy bit his lip, holding back his sobbing, awakened with gloomy words, and was almost running behind the Deacon who walked wide and fast.

"It is all right!" the Deacon said, casting a cursory glance at his face. "Father Yakov is a good man... you will play with Mishutka and Zoya.., you will live jolly... yes!"

The boy imagined Zoya, a swarthy and glib girl with black eyes. She is jumping in front of him cocking a snook at him and teasing him, singing with a mean voice:

"Red from a small-pox, red like a fox, red to start a fire, red to hang on wire..."

"I don't like Zoya..." he said sadly.

"Well, this is a trifle!.. You will like her; you will share the room..."

"I will not..."

"Oh...You should not..."

The boy began to cry quietly.

"Oh... You are an orphan!" the Deacon sighed looking at him.

When they came to the cabman, the Deacon carefully sat him by the psalm reader's feet and said encouragingly:

"Hold on well!... We will come and drink tea..."

"Come on, toad!" the cabman shouted at his horse.

The cab jumped across cobblestones through the gray curtain of rain and mist. Out of the fog, the houses floated into sight, and it seemed as if they were swimming somewhere quietly in silence, looking over the boy with their large colorless eyes. The boy felt his heart growing cold and tight.

Anton Pavlovich Chekhov
На Святках / On Christmastide

Исаак Левитан (1860–1900). Деревенька под снегом. 1985.

I. Levitan. *Small Village Under the Snow.* 1885.

ANTON PAVLOVICH CHEKHOV

1860–1904

There are Russian writers who are extremely difficult to write about. What new things can we write about the classics of Russian literature, of its "Golden Age" in its full bloom, like Feodor Dostoevsky, Leo Tolstoy and Anton Chekhov? Long ago, even during their lifetime, they became "living icons." Both in the past and nowadays, people either love or hate them with an equal degree of passion. They read and reread their writings, write stage and screen adaptations, try to imitate them, follow their teachings—the philosophy expressed in their fictions—and write parodies. Certainly, there is a great deal of research, from books to articles, dedicated to those "Gods of Literature," describing their style, vocabulary selection, vision, ideas about the world and the human condition, religious and philosophical views, and many other "facets" of their legacy.

In this short introduction, it would be reasonable to remind the reader about some more important biographical Rubicons in the life of Anton Chekhov and to present the reasons for choosing the story "On Christmastide" for this collection.

Anton Pavlovich Chekhov, a renowned writer, is the author of about 900 works of literature. He produced short stories, tales, and plays. He was born into a family of a not-too-well-off merchant, in the small southern Russian city of Taganrog. As a high school student, Anton Chekhov wrote short humorous stories and dramatic episodes. In 1879, he moved to Moscow and became a student at the Department of Medicine of

Moscow University; after graduation he began to work as a physician in small towns near Moscow. Chekhov was a good doctor, but his passion for writing was at least as strong, even at that time. As a student, he published many short humorous stories in numerous magazines. He sometimes wrote a story every day.

Then, Chekhov's stories became longer and more serious. He gained some valuable experience traveling around Russia and beyond: Siberia and the Far East, sailing through the Indian Ocean, Ceylon, and coming back to Russia. Based on these impressions, he wrote the book *Sakhalin Island*.

In spite of quite a successful medical practice and some good prospects, Chekhov decided to devote his life to the career of a writer, although he never stopped offering medical help to people, especially the poor, and volunteering for charity work. At the same time, this work as a doctor, especially in the Russian provinces, enriched his life experience and vision, and knowledge of people and their psychology provided him with unique material for his narratives and dramas.

There were many years of hard, fruitful work—in Moscow, in his estate nearby, and in his Crimean house where Chekhov had to live because of its favorable climate (the writer suffered from tuberculosis; he died of it at forty-four).

In Chekhov's life, there were years of incredible popularity and severe criticism. At first, the public did not like and did not understand his innovative plays (the premiere of *The Seagull* failed), but later it was praised and included in the golden set of world dramatic art together with *Uncle Vanya, The Cherry Orchard*, and *Three Sisters*.

Like most outstanding writers, Chekhov went through a chain of transformations, different stages of development of his style and approach, from his early, sparkling, funny stories to his later ones, with depictions of characters and their inner philosophy that are psychologically profound and complex, but at the same time simple in narrative and plot composition.

The story "On Christmastide" (1900) is one of the later stories, created by Chekhov about four years before his death. In

this story, Chekhov again touched on a motif of a message of desperation and hope sent by people separated by destiny. He first flirted with a similar theme in his famous miniature with an unhappy ending, "Vanka Zhukov" (1886).

In his later narrative pieces, which often are called miniature novels, Chekhov perfected his skills as a mature author. His art of depicting the development of the plot and philosophically psychological "portraits" of the characters is brilliant. His approach to showing the lives of his characters was most convincing, profound, and realistic. He expressed in them his ideas about life and death, the loneliness of a person in this world, the sense of life, the family ties and importance of mercy and kindness, and the bitter power of cruel circumstances and insensitive people in charge, ruining human life, and true values of human relations. These features of Chekhov's late narratives can be easily seen in the story "On Christmastide," combining deep emotional depiction and profound psychological analysis.

АНТОН ПАВЛОВИЧ ЧЕХОВ

На Святках

I

— Что писать? — спросил Егор и умокнул перо.

Василиса не виделась со своею дочерью уже четыре года. Дочь Ефимья после свадьбы уехала с мужем в Петербург, прислала два письма и потом как в воду канула: ни слуху ни духу. И доила ли старуха корову на рассвете, топила ли печку, дремала ли ночью — и всё думала об одном: как-то там Ефимья, жива ли. Надо бы послать письмо, но старик писать не умел, а попросить было некого.

Но вот пришли Святки, и Василиса не вытерпела и пошла в трактир к Егору, хозяйкиному брату, который, как пришёл со службы, так и сидел всё дома, в трактире, и ничего не делал; про него говорили, что он может хорошо писать письма, ежели ему заплатить как следует. Василиса поговорила в трактире с кухаркой, потом с хозяйкой, потом с самим Егором. Сошлись на пятиалтынном.

И теперь — это происходило на второй день праздника в трактире, в кухне — Егор сидел за столом и держал перо в руке. Василиса стояла перед ним, задумавшись, с выражением заботы и скорби на лице. С нею пришёл и Пётр, её старик, очень худой, высокий, с коричневой лысиной; он стоял и глядел неподвижно и прямо, как слепой. На плите в кастрюле жарилась свинина; она шипела, и фыркала, и как будто даже говорила: «флю-флю-флю». Было душно.

— Что писать? — спросил опять Егор.

ANTON PAVLOVICH CHEKHOV

On Christmastide

I

"What to write?" Yegor asked and dipped the pen.

Vasilisa had not seen her daughter for four years already. After the wedding, her daughter, Yefimia, left for Petersburg with her husband, sent two letters and then vanished without a trace, nothing was heard from her. And whether the old woman was milking a cow at dawn, or was stoking a stove, or dozing at night—she was thinking only one thought: how Yefimia was doing and if she was still alive. They should have sent her a letter, but the old man could not write, and there was no one to ask about that.

But Christmastide came, and Vasilisa was not able to bear it anymore, and went to the tavern to Yegor, the owner's wife's brother, who, since he returned from service, was sitting at home, in the tavern, doing nothing. People were saying that he could write letters well if he was paid well. Vasilisa talked to the tavern cook, then with the owner's wife, then with Yegor himself. They agreed on fifteen kopecks for the job.

And now—it was going to be the second day of the Christmastide—in the kitchen of the tavern, Yegor was sitting at the table holding a pen in his hand. Vasilisa was standing in front of him, plunged deep in her thoughts, with an expression of concern and sorrow on her face. Petr, her old man, came with her; he was very thin, tall, with a brown bald head; he was standing motionless and looking straight in front, like a blind man. On the stove, pork was frying in a pan; it was sizzling and snorting, as if it were saying: "Flyu-flyu-flyu." It was stifling hot.

"What to write?" Yegor asked again.

— Чего! — сказала Василиса, глядя на него сердито и подозрительно. — Не гони! Небось не задаром пишешь, за деньги! Ну, пиши. Любезному нашему зятю Андрею Хрисанфычу и единственной нашей любимой дочери Ефимье Петровне с любовью низкий поклон и благословение родительское навеки нерушимо.

— Есть. Стреляй дальше.

— А ещё поздравляем с праздником Рождества Христова, мы живы и здоровы, чего и вам желаем от Господа… Царя Небесного.

Василиса подумала и переглянулась со стариком.

— Чего и вам желаем от Господа… Царя Небесного… — повторила она и заплакала.

Больше ничего она не могла сказать. А раньше, когда она по ночам думала, то ей казалось, что всего не поместить и в десяти письмах. С того времени, как уехали дочь с мужем, утекло в море много воды, старики жили, как сироты, и тяжко вздыхали по ночам, точно похоронили дочь. А сколько за это время было в деревне всяких происшествий, сколько свадеб, смертей. Какие были длинные зимы! Какие длинные ночи!

— Жарко! — проговорил Егор, расстёгивая жилет. — Должно, градусов семьдесят будит. Что же ещё? — спросил он.

Старики молчали.

— Чем твой зять там занимается? — спросил Егор.

— Он из солдат, батюшка, тебе известно, — ответил слабым голосом старик. — В одно время с тобой со службы пришёл. Был солдат, а теперь, значит, в Петербурге в водоцелебном заведении. Доктор больных водой пользует. Так он, значит, у доктора в швейцарах.

— Вот тут написано… — сказала старуха, вынимая из платочка письмо. — От Ефимьи получили, ещё бог знает когда. Может, их уж и на свете нет.

Егор подумал немного и стал быстро писать.

«В настоящее время, — писал он, — как судба ваша через себе определила на Военое Попрыще, то мы Вам советуем заглянуть в Устав Дисцыплинарных Взысканий

"What!" Vasilisa said, looking at him angrily and suspiciously. "Don't rush! You don't write for free, but surely for money! Well, write. 'To our dear son-in-law, Andrei Khrisanfych, and our only beloved daughter, Yefimia Petrovna, with love and a low bow, and from us, your parents, our unbroken blessings forever."

"Here it is. Shoot further."

"And also we wish you Happy Holy Christmas, we are alive and healthy, and wish you the same from Our Lord... Heavenly Father."

Vasilisa thought and exchanged glances with the old man.

"And we wish you the same from Our Lord... Heavenly Father..." she repeated and began to cry.

She could not say anything else. And before, when she had been thinking at night, it had seemed to her that she would not be able to express everything even in ten letters. Since that time, when her daughter left with her husband, a lot of water had passed under the bridge, and the old people lived like orphans, and sighed heavily at night, as if they had buried their daughter. And how many events had happened in the village during that time! How many marriages, and deaths! What long winters there were! What long nights!

"It is hot!" Yegor said, unbuttoning his vest. "Must be about seventy degrees. Anything else?" he asked.

The old people kept silence.

"What does your son-in-law do there?" Yegor asked.

"He is from soldiers, my dear fellow, you know," the old man answered with his weak voice. "He returned from the army the same time as you did. He was a soldier, and now, so, he is in Petersburg, in a hydropathical clinic. The doctor treats patients with water. So, he is a doorman at the doctor's."

"Here it is written...," the old woman said, taking out the letter from a small kerchief. "We received it from Yefimia, only God knows how long ago. Maybe they are not in this world anymore."

Yegor thought a little and started writing fast.

"*This time,*" he was writing, "*because you destiny, through itself, appointed you to the Amy Servis, we wuld advice you to look at the Regulating of Disciplinary Punishment and Criminal*

и Уголовных Законов Военного Ведомства, и Вы усмотрите в оном Законе цывилизацию Чинов Военного Ведомства».

Он писал и прочитывал вслух написанное, а Василиса соображала о том, что надо бы написать, какая в прошлом году была нужда, не хватило хлеба даже до Святок, пришлось продать корову. Надо бы попросить денег, надо бы написать, что старик часто похварывает и скоро, должно быть, отдаст богу душу... Но как выразить это на словах? Что сказать прежде и что после?

«Обратите внемание, — продолжал Егор писать, — в 5 томе Военых Постановлений. Солдат есть Имя обчшее, Знаменитое. Солдатом называется Перьвейшый Генерал и последней Рядовой...».

Старик пошевелил губами и сказал тихо:

— Внучат поглядеть, оно бы ничего.

— Каких внучат? — спросила старуха и поглядела на него сердито. — Да, может, их и нету!

— Внучат-то? А может, и есть. Кто их знает!

«И поэтому Вы можете судить, — торопился Егор, — какой есть враг Иноземный и какой Внутреный. Перьвейшый наш Внутреный Враг есть: Бахус».

Перо скрипело, выделывая на бумаге завитушки, похожие на рыболовные крючки. Егор спешил и прочитывал каждую строчку по нескольку раз. Он сидел на табурете, раскинув широко ноги под столом, сытый, здоровый, мордатый, с красным затылком. Это была сама пошлость, грубая, надменная, непобедимая, гордая тем, что она родилась и выросла в трактире, и Василиса хорошо понимала, что тут пошлость, но не могла выразить на словах, а только глядела на Егора сердито и подозрительно. От его голоса, непонятных слов, от жара и духоты у неё разболелась голова, запутались мысли, и она уже ничего не говорила, не думала и ждала только, когда он кончит скрипеть. А старик глядел с полным доверием. Он верил и старухе, которая его привела сюда, и Егору; и когда упомянул давеча о водолечебном заведении,

Laws of the Military Deportment, and you will see in that Law the Rule the Ditermination of the Ranks of the Military Diportment."

He was writing and reading what he had written aloud, and Vasilisa was thinking that they should write about the deprivations they had been experiencing last year, they did not have enough bread even till Christmastide, and so they had to sell their cow. They ought to ask for money, they should write that the old man often gets sick, and soon, probably, would meet his Maker... But how to express this in words? What to say before and what after?

"*Pay attantion,*" Yegor continued to write, "*that the volume 5 of the Army Enactments. A Soldier is geniral name, a famous one. Both best General and list Private can be called a Soldier...*"

The old man moved his lips and said quietly:

"To see the grandchildren, it would be good."

"What grandchildren?" the old woman asked and looked at him angrily. "Maybe there are none!"

"Grandchildren? Maybe there are some. Who knows!"

"*And therefore, you can judge,*" Yegor was in a hurry, "*which enemy is Forign, and which is Damestic. First our Damestic enemy is Bacchus.*"

The pen was squeaking, making curlicues on paper, looking like fishing hooks. Yegor hurried and read each line a few times. He was sitting on a stool, spreading his legs under the table, full, healthy, mug-faced, with a red back of a head. It was insensitivity itself, rude, arrogant, invincible, and proud of being born and raised in the tavern, and Vasilisa understood well that here it was vulgarity, however she was not able to express herself in words, but was only looking at Yegor angrily and suspiciously. From his voice, the obscure words, the heat and stuffiness, her head started aching. Her thoughts became mixed up, and she was not saying anything, and only longing for him to stop squeaking. But the old man was looking on with full trust. He believed both the old woman, who had brought him there, and Yegor; and, when he

то видно было по лицу, что он верил и в заведение, и в целебную силу воды.

Кончив писать, Егор встал и прочёл всё письмо сначала. Старик не понял, но доверчиво закивал головой.

— Ничего, гладко... — сказал он, — дай Бог здоровья. Ничего...

Положили на стол три пятака и вышли из трактира; старик глядел неподвижно и прямо, как слепой, и на лице его было написано полное доверие, а Василиса, когда выходили из трактира, замахнулась на собаку и сказала сердито:

— У-у, язва!

Всю ночь старуха не спала, беспокоили её мысли, а на рассвете она встала, помолилась и пошла на станцию, чтобы послать письмо.

До станции было одиннадцать вёрст.

II

Водолечебница доктора Б. О. Мозельвейзера работала и на Новый год так же, как в обыкновенные дни, и только на швейцаре Андрее Хрисанфыче был мундир с новыми галунами, блестели как-то особенно сапоги, и всех приходивших он поздравлял с Новым годом, с новым счастьем.

Было утро. Андрей Хрисанфыч стоял у двери и читал газету. Ровно в десять часов вошёл генерал, знакомый, один из обычных посетителей, а вслед за ним — почтальон. Андрей Хрисанфыч снял с генерала шинель и сказал:

— С Новым годом, с новым счастьем, ваше превосходительство!

— Спасибо, любезный. И тебя также.

И, идя вверх по лестнице, генерал кивнул на дверь и спросил (он каждый день спрашивал и всякий раз потом забывал):

— А в этой комнате что?

— Кабинет для массажа, ваше превосходительство!

Когда шаги генерала затихли, Андрей Хрисанфыч осмотрел полученную почту и нашёл одно письмо на своё

mentioned the clinic, it was clear from his face, that he believed both in the clinic, and in the healing power of water.

Having finished writing, Yegor stood up and read the whole letter from the beginning. The old man did not understand, but trustfully nodded his head.

"That's good, smooth," he said. "Let God give you health. It's good..."

They put three five-kopeck coins on the table, and left the tavern; the old man was looking motionless and straight, like a blind man, and one could see complete trust in his face, but Vasilisa, leaving the tavern, raised her hand against the dog, and said angrily:

"Oh, evil!"

For the whole night, she could not fall asleep, the thoughts bothered her, and at dawn, she got up, said a prayer, and went to the station to send the letter.

There were over seven miles to walk to the station.

II

The hydropathical clinic of the doctor B.O. Mozelveizer was also open on New Year's Day, as on weekdays. And the doorman, Andrei Khrisanfych, was wearing the uniform with new silver lace, and his boots were especially shiny; and he wished all visitors a Happy New Year and New Year Happiness.

It was morning. Andrei Khrisanfych was standing by the door and reading a newspaper. At exactly ten, a familiar general, one of the usual visitors, came in, and after him – a mailman. Andrei Khrisanfych took the general's overcoat and said:

"Happy New Year, New Year Happiness, Your Excellency!"

"Thank you, my friend. The same to you."

And, going up the stairs, the general nodded towards the door and asked (he asked about that every day, and then every time he forgot):

"And what is in this room?"

"The room is for the massage, Your Excellency!"

When the general's steps faded away, Andrei Khrisanfych looked through the received mail and found one letter addressed

имя. Он распечатал, прочёл несколько строк, потом не спеша, глядя в газету, пошёл к себе в свою комнату, которая была тут же внизу, в конце коридора. Жена его Ефимья сидела на кровати и кормила ребёнка; другой ребёнок, самый старший, стоял возле, положив кудрявую голову ей на колени, третий спал на кровати.

Войдя в свою комнатку, Андрей подал жене письмо и сказал:

— До́лжно, из деревни.

Затем он вышел, не отрывая глаз от газеты, и остановился в коридоре, недалеко от своей двери. Ему было слышно, как Ефимья дрожащим голосом прочла первые строки. Прочла и уж больше не могла; для неё было довольно и этих строк, она залилась слезами и, обнимая своего старшенького, целуя его, стала говорить, и нельзя было понять, плачет она или смеётся.

— Это от бабушки, от дедушки... — говорила она. — Из деревни... Царица Небесная, святители-угодники. Там теперь снегу навалило под крыши... деревья белые-белые. Ребятки на махоньких саночках... И дедушка лысенький на печке... и собачка жёлтенькая... Голубчики мои родные!

Андрей Хрисанфыч, слушая это, вспомнил, что раза три или четыре жена давала ему письма, просила послать в деревню, но мешали какие-то важные дела: он не послал, письма где-то завалялись.

— А в поле зайчики бегают, — причитывала Ефимья, обливаясь слезами, целуя своего мальчика. — Дедушка тихий, добрый, бабушка тоже добрая, жалосливая. В деревне душевно живут, бога боятся... И церковочка в селе, мужички на клиросе поют. Унесла бы нас отсюда Царица Небесная, Заступница-Матушка!

Андрей Хрисанфыч вернулся к себе в комнатку, чтобы покурить, пока кто не пришёл, и Ефимья вдруг замолчала, притихла и вытерла глаза, и только губы у неё дрожали. Она его очень боялась, ах, как боялась! Трепетала, приходила

to him. He opened it, read a few lines, and then, leisurely, looking at the newspaper, headed to his room, which was in the same place, downstairs, at the end of the corridor. His wife, Yefimia, was sitting on the bed feeding a baby; the other child, the eldest, was standing by her side, putting his curly head on her lap, and the third one was sleeping on the bed.

Coming into his small room, Andrei gave his wife the letter and said:

"It must be from the village."

After that, he left, not tearing himself away from the newspaper, and stopped in the corridor, not far from the door. He could hear how Yefimia was reading the first lines with a trembling voice. She read them and could not any more; even those lines were enough for her, and she burst into tears, and hugging her eldest child and kissing him, she began to talk, and it was impossible to understand if she was crying or laughing.

"This is from grandmother and grandfather...," she was saying. "From the village... Holy Queen of Heaven, Holy Saints. There has been snow piling up to the roofs... the trees are white... Little children are on tiny sleds... And the bald grandpa by the stove, and the yellow doggy... Oh, my dear, beloved!"

Andrei Khrisanfych, listening to it, remembered that three or four times his wife had given him letters and asked to send them to the village, but some important business always prevented him from that. He had not sent anything, and the letters had been misplaced somewhere.

"And small hares are running in the field," Yefimia was lamenting, melting into tears, and kissing her little boy. "Grandpa is quiet, kind, and grandma is also kind and compassionate. People in the village live openheartedly, and fear God... And in the village there is a small church, and the peasants sing in the church choir. I wish our Holy Queen of Heaven would take us away from here, our Mother-Patron!"

Andrei Khrisanfych returned to his little room to smoke before anyone arrived, and Yefimia fell silent right away, quieted down, and wiped her eyes, and only her lips were trembling. She was

в ужас от его шагов, от его взгляда, не смела сказать при нём ни одного слова.

Андрей Хрисанфыч закурил, но как раз в это время наверху позвонили. Он потушил папиросу и, сделав очень серьёзное лицо, побежал к своей парадной двери.

Сверху спускался генерал, розовый, свежий от ванны.

— А в этой комнате что? — спросил он, указывая на дверь.

Андрей Хрисанфыч вытянулся, руки по швам, и произнес громко:

— Душ Шарко, ваше превосходительство!

afraid of him, oh, so much afraid! She shuddered with horror at the sound of his steps, his look, and did not dare say a word in his presence.

Andrei Khrisanfych lit a cigarette, but exactly at that moment, someone called him from upstairs. He put out the cigarette and, making a very serious face, ran to the front door.

The general was coming downstairs, pink and fresh after his bath.

"And what is in this room?" he asked pointing at the door.

Andrei Khrisanfych stood erect and at attention, and said loudly:

"Charcot shower, Your Excellency!"

Leonid Nikolaevich Andreev
Гостинец / The Present

Н. А. Ярошенко (1846–1898). Якуб.
[Государственный Русский музей. Санкт-Петербург]

N. Yaroshenko. Yakub.
[The State Russian Museum. St. Petersburg]

LEONID NIKOLAEVICH ANDREEV

1871–1919

Leonid Nikolaevich Andreev is an outstanding representative of the "Silver Age" period of Russian literature. Since his childhood he liked to read, and as to his personality, he had a penchant for behaving in a somewhat extraordinary manner. This strange inclination would, for example, push him towards some shocking acts, such as placing himself in front of an approaching train in order to check his strength of will (according to some other versions, because of an unrequited love). Another peculiar move in his student years was his attempted suicide after an unhappy love affair. Probably, this was an expression of Andreev's extreme sensitivity and the urge towards poignancy of feelings. These contrasting traits of behavior led him to choose to constantly live on the edge of an emotional and physical abyss, and coexisted with the writer's deep religious faith.

Andreev's first story was published in 1898, and soon, only a couple of years later, in 1901, his first success arrived. His early stories were realistic, filled with melancholy to the degree of being gloomy, usually very pessimistic (among his favorite writers were Feodor Dostoevsky and Anton Chekhov, whose influence could be seen in Andreev's narratives), and often with a touch of sentimentality (probably the influence of his favorite English writer, Charles Dickens). The most interesting subjects for Andreev were death and solitude, the most distinguishing features of his tragic perception of the world.

In his stories, Andreev was very attentive to the psychological evolution of a character, and not as much to the events of the plot. And due to the usual dramatic content, the reader always gets a feeling of an approaching thunderstorm or a catastrophe. The writer describes a common person suffering from the humiliation of everyday poverty and the necessity to struggle in order to survive, and at the same time—the torment of realizing one's own unworthiness and sinfulness.

Andreev, though, would always give his characters a chance for spiritual resurrection, repentance, and forgiveness. This indulgence is clearly seen in his first successful short story, "Bargamot and Garaska," which brought him fame in 1898. The action in it takes place on the Easter holiday, as in his other well-known "Easter" story, included in the present volume. The choice of "The Present" for this collection was due to the fact that in it the reader can find the best example of Andreev's talent as an artist-psychologist, filled with compassion for and understanding of the character. He said, "The choice of the character is not that important to me—a priest, a clerk, a good-hearted man, or a swine. The only thing that is important to me, is that he is a human being, and that is why he carries the burdens of life... All live creatures have a soul, all suffer from the same pains, and in the great indifference and equality they blend together confronting the terrifying forces of existence."

For some period, the writer was involved in revolutionary activities, for which he was arrested and sent to prison, and this was why he had to live abroad for a time. Later, Andreev became disillusioned with the revolutionary ideas and preferred to live as an immigrant in Finland.

The story "The Present" was first published in the newspaper *The Kurier* of 1901, and later, in 1902, under the title "The Easter Present"—in the magazine *Narodnoye Blago*, as well as in a separate collection of the writer's stories that came out in 1904. Leo Tolstoy, after reading the story, underlined some episodes and made a note in the margin—"5," which meant "excellent" in the Russian grading system.

ЛЕОНИД НИКОЛАЕВИЧ АНДРЕЕВ

Гостинец

I

— Так ты приходи! — в третий раз попросил Сениста, и в третий раз Сазонка торопливо ответил:

— Приду, приду, ты не бойся. Ещё бы не прийти, конечно, приду.

И снова они замолчали. Сениста лежал на спине, до подбородка укрытый серым больничным одеялом, и упорно смотрел на Сазонку; ему хотелось, чтобы Сазонка подольше не уходил из больницы и чтобы своим ответным взглядом он ещё раз подтвердил обещание не оставлять его в жертву одиночеству, болезни и страху. Сазонке же хотелось уйти, но он не знал, как сделать это без обиды для мальчика, шмурыгал носом, почти сползал со стула и опять садился плотно и решительно, как будто навсегда. Он бы ещё посидел, если бы было о чём говорить; но говорить было не о чем, и мысли приходили глупые, от которых становилось смешно и стыдно. Так, его всё время тянуло называть Сенисту по имени и отчеству — Семёном Ерофеевичем, что было отчаянно нелепо: Сениста был мальчишка-подмастерье, а Сазонка был солидным мастером и пьяницей, и Сазонкой звался только по привычке. И ещё двух недель не прошло с тех пор, как он дал Сенисте последний подзатыльник, и это было очень дурно, но и об этом говорить тоже нельзя.

Сазонка решительно начал сползать со стула, но, не доведя дело до половины, так же решительно всполз назад и сказал не то в виде укоризны, не то утешения:

LEONID NIKOLAEVICH ANDREEV

The Present

I

"So, do come!"—asked Senista for the third time, and for the third time Sazonka hurriedly answered:

"I will come. Go, don't be afraid. How can I not come—surely, I will come."

And they fell silent again. Senista was lying on his back, covered to his chin with a gray hospital blanket, and looking persistently at Sazonka. He would like Sazonka to linger longer in the hospital, and confirm one more time with his eyes his promise not to leave him as a sacrifice to loneliness, sickness, and fear. But Sazonka wanted to leave, though he did not know how to do this without hurting the boy: he was sniffing, almost slipping down the chair, and then pulling himself up again sitting down and leaning tight to the back decisively, as if forever. He would stay longer if they had anything to talk about; but there was nothing to say, and his thoughts were so stupid that he felt funny and ashamed. For example, he was longing to call Senista by his first name and patronymic – Semyon Yerofeevich, which was horribly ridiculous: Senista was a boy-apprentice, and Sazonka was an experienced tailor and a drunkard, and was called Sazonka only by force of habit. Two weeks had not passed since he had given a rap on the back of the boy's head, but that was very bad, and he could not mention that either.

Sazonka decisively started slipping down the chair, but after half way down, he resolutely climbed back up, and said as either a reproach or a comfort:

— Так вот какие дела. Болит, а?

Сениста утвердительно качнул головой и тихо ответил:

— Ну, ступай. А то он бранить будет.

— Это верно, — обрадовался Сазонка предлогу. — Он и то приказывал: ты, говорит, поскорее. Отвезёшь — и той же минутой назад. И чтобы водки ни-ни. Вот чёрт!

Но вместе с сознанием, что он может теперь уйти каждую минуту, в сердце Сазонки вошла острая жалость к большеголовому Сенисте. К жалости призывала вся необычная обстановка: тесный ряд кроватей с бледными, хмурыми людьми; воздух, до последней частицы испорченный запахом лекарств и испарениями больного человеческого тела; чувство собственной силы и здоровья. И, уже не избегая просительного взгляда, Сазонка наклонился к Сенисте и твёрдо повторил:

— Ты, Семён… Сеня, не бойся. Приду. Как ослобонюсь, так и к тебе. Разве мы не люди? Господи! Тоже и у нас понятие есть. Милый! Веришь мне аль нет?

И с улыбкой на почерневших, запёкшихся губах Сениста отвечал:

— Верю.

— Вот! — торжествовал Сазонка.

Теперь ему было легко и приятно, и он мог уже поговорить о подзатыльнике, случайно данном две недели назад. И он осторожно намекнул, касаясь пальцем Сенина плеча:

— А ежели тебя по голове кто бил, так разве это со зла? Господи! Голова у тебя очень такая удобная: большая да стриженая.

Сениста опять улыбнулся, и Сазонка поднялся со стула. Ростом он был очень высок, волосы его, все в мелких кудряшках, расчёсанные частой гребёнкой, подымались пышной и весёлой шапкой, и серые припухшие глаза искрились и безотчётно улыбались.

— Ну, прощевай! — сказал он, но не тронулся с места.

Он нарочно сказал «прощевай», а не «прощай», потому что так выходило душевнее, но теперь ему показалось этого

"These are the things. Does it hurt, ah?"

Senista nodded assent and quietly replied, "Well, go. Or he will scold you."

"That's right." Sazonka was glad to get a reason for leaving. "The master had ordered me: 'You', he said, 'go faster. As soon as you get him there, the same minute come back. And not a drop of vodka.' What a devil!"

But with this thought that he could leave any minute, Sazonka felt a sharp pain of pity in his heart towards the large-headed Senista. All the unusual surroundings here inspired pity: tight rows of beds with pale gloomy people; the air poisoned to its last particle with the smell of medicines and fumes of a sick human body; and his own feeling of strength and health. And now not avoiding the begging look, Sazonka bent to Senista and firmly repeated:

"You, Semyon, Senya, don't be afraid. I will come. As soon as I get free—right away to you. Are we not humans? God, our Savior! We have some understanding too. Dear! Do you believe me or not?"

And smiling with his blackening parched lips, Senista answered: "I believe."

"You see!" said Sazonka, exultantly.

Now it was easy and pleasant to him, and he already could talk about a rap on the back of head he had given the boy by accident two weeks ago. And lightly touching Senista's shoulder he hinted: "And if someone hit you on your head, it was not because of meanness. Jesus! Your head is so handy: big and shorthaired."

Senista smiled again, and Sazonka got up off the chair.

He was very tall, his hair, all in ringlets brushed with a fine-tooth comb, rose fluffy like a jolly shock, and his gray, slightly swollen eyes could not stop sparkling with a smile.

"Well, bye for now!" He said, but did not move.

He said "Bye for now!" not "Good-bye," because it sounded heartier, but now it did not feel hearty enough. He needed to do something even more heart-felt and good, such a thing after which Senista would lay in the hospital happily,

мало. Нужно было сделать что-то ещё более душевное и хорошее, такое, после которого Сенисте весело было бы лежать в больнице, а ему легко было бы уйти. И он неловко топтался на месте, смешной в своём детском смущении, когда Сениста опять вывел его из затруднения.

— Прощай! — сказал он своим детским, тоненьким голоском, за который его дразнили «гуслями», и совсем просто, как взрослый, высвободил руку из-под одеяла и, как равный, протянул её Сазонке.

И Сазонка, чувствуя, что это именно то, чего не хватало ему для полного спокойствия, почтительно охватил тонкие пальчики своей здоровенной лапищей, подержал их и со вздохом отпустил. Было что-то печальное и загадочное в прикосновении тонких горячих пальчиков: как будто Сениста был не только равным всем людям на свете, но и выше всех и всех свободнее, и происходило это оттого, что принадлежал он теперь неведомому, но грозному и могучему хозяину. Теперь его можно было назвать Семёном Ерофеевичем.

— Так приходи же, — в четвёртый раз попросил Сениста, и эта просьба прогнала то страшное и величавое, что на миг осенило его своими бесшумными крылами.

Он снова стал мальчиком, больным и страдающим, и снова стало жаль его, — очень жаль.

Когда Сазонка вышел из больницы, за ним долго ещё гнался запах лекарств и просящий голос:

— Приходи же!

И, разводя руками, Сазонка отвечал:

— Милый! Да разве мы не люди?

II

Подходила Пасха и портновской работы было так много, что только один раз в воскресенье вечером Сазонке удалось напиться, да и то не допьяна. Целые дни, по-весеннему светлые и длинные, от петухов до петухов, он сидел на подмостках у своего окна, по-турецки поджав под себя ноги, хмурясь и неодобрительно посвистывая. С утра окно находилось в тени, и в разошедшиеся пазы тянуло

and he could leave easier. And he was awkwardly dawdling, funny in his childish confusion, when Senista again helped him out of the trouble.

"Farewell," he said with his child-like falsetto, for which he was teased a "psaltery," and simply, like an adult, stretched his hand out of the blanket and reached it out to Sazonka's, as an equal.

And Sazonka, feeling that it was exactly what he was lacking for a full peace of mind, respectfully wrung the thin fingers with his huge paw, held them for a moment and released them with a sigh. There was something sad and mysterious in the touch of the thin hot fingers: as if Senista was not only equal to all people in the world, but higher than they, freer than everyone, and the reason was that now he belonged to the unknown, but terrifying and mighty Master. And now one could call him Semyon Yerofeevich.

"So, do come," asked Senista for the fourth time, and this request chased away from him that awful and majestic Something, which had spread above him its noiseless wings for an instant.

And then Senista again turned into a boy, sick and suffering, and again Sazonka was sorry for him, very sorry.

When Sazonka left the hospital, the smell of medicines and the begging voice: "Do come" were following him for a long time.

And, spreading his hands aside, Sazonka was questioning: "Dear me! Are we not humans?"

II

Easter was coming, and there was so much work for tailors that only one Sunday evening Sazonka managed to get drunk, and not even dead drunk. All these days, long and filled with the spring-time light, from cockcrows to cockcrows, he was sitting cross-legged on his bench by the window, straining his eyes, and disapprovingly whistling. In the morning, the window was in the shade, and a chilly draft was sneaking through the loosened cracks in the walls, but by midday, the sun was shin-

холодком, но к полудню солнце прорезывало узенькую жёлтую полоску, в которой светящимися точками играла приподнятая пыль. А через полчаса уже весь подоконник с набросанными на нём обрезками материй и ножницами горел ослепительным светом, и становилось так жарко, что нужно было, как летом, распахнуть окно. И вместе с волной свежего, крепкого воздуха, пропитанного запахом преющего навоза, подсыхающей грязи и распускающихся почек, в окно влетала шальная, ещё слабосильная муха и приносился разноголосый шум улицы. Внизу у завалинки рылись куры и блаженно кудахтали, нежась в круглых ямках; на противоположной, уже просохшей стороне улицы играли в бабки ребята, и их пёстрый, звонкий крик и удары чугунных плит о костяшки звучали задором и свежестью. Езды по улице, находившейся на окраине Орла, было совсем мало, и только изредка шажком проезжал пригородный мужик; телега подпрыгивала в глубоких колеях, ещё полных жидкой грязи, и все части её стучали деревянным стуком, напоминающим лето и простор полей.

Когда у Сазонки начинало ломить поясницу и одеревеневшие пальцы не держали иглы, он босиком и без подпояски, как был, выскакивал на улицу, гигантскими скачками перелетал лужи и присоединялся к играющим ребятам.

— Ну-ка, дай ударить, — просил он, и десяток грязных рук протягивали ему плиты, и десяток голосов просили:

— За меня! Сазонка, за меня!

Сазонка выбирал плиту поувесистее, засучивал рукав и, приняв позу атлета, мечущего диск, измерял прищуренным глазом расстояние. С лёгким свистом плита вырывалась из его руки и, волнообразно подскакивая, скользящим ударом врывалась в средину длинного кона, и пёстрым дождём рассыпались бабки, и таким же пёстрым криком отвечали на удар ребята. После нескольких ударов Сазонка отдыхал и говорил ребятам:

— А Сениста-то ещё в больнице, ребята.

ing through as a narrow yellow stripe, in which the slightly agitated plume of dust was playing as shiny dots. And half an hour later, the whole windowsill would be covered with pieces of fabric and scissors, shining from the dazzling sunlight, and it was getting so hot that they had to open the window wide as in summertime. And together with the wave of fresh, strong air, filled with the smell of damp manure, drying dirt and discarded cigarette butts, a stray, still weak fly was flying through the window, and the discordant noise was heard from the outside. Down, by the outer wall bench, the hens were digging and blissfully cackling, coddling themselves in round holes; on the other, already dried side of the street, kids were playing knucklebones; and their discordant, ringing shouting, and strikes of cast-iron plates hitting bones, sounded with fervor and freshness. There was very little traffic on the street in this Orel suburb, and occasionally, a peasant from the outskirts slowly drove by; his wagon jumped in deep gouges, still full with liquid dirt, and all its wooden parts rumbled, with the sound reminiscent of summer and the spaciousness of the fields.

When Sazonka felt pain in his back, sore from sitting for too long, and his numbed fingers could not hold the needle, barefoot and without a gird, as he was, he rushed outside making giant leaps over the puddles and joined the playing children.

"Well, let me hit." he asked, and a dozen of dirty hands handled him the plates, and a dozen of voices asked,

"For me! Sazonka, for me!"

Sazonka chose a heavier plate, rolled up his sleeve, posed as a discus-thrower, and measured the distance by a squinting eye. With a light whistling, the plate flew off his hand, and with a wavy jumping up movement, and a sliding hit, dug itself into the middle of the long line of bones. They scattered as a motley rain, and the kids rejoiced with the same excited screams. After a few hits, Sazonka rested and said to the children:

"And Senista is still in the hospital, guys."

Но, занятые своим интересным делом, ребята принимали известие холодно и равнодушно.

— Надобно ему гостинца отнести. Вот ужо отнесу, — продолжал Сазонка.

На слово «гостинец» отозвались многие. Мишка Поросёнок подёргивал одной рукой штанишки — другая держала в подоле рубахи бабки — и серьёзно советовал:

— Ты ему гривенник дай.

Гривенник была та сумма, которую обещал дед самому Мишке, и выше её не шло его представление о человеческом счастье. Но долго разговаривать о гостинце не было времени, и такими же гигантскими прыжками Сазонка перебирался к себе и опять садился за работу. Глаза его припухли, лицо стало бледно-жёлтым, как у больного, и веснушки у глаз и на носу казались особенно частыми и тёмными. Только тщательно расчёсанные волосы подымались всё той же весёлой шапкой, и когда хозяин, Гавриил Иванович, смотрел на них, ему непременно представлялся уютный красный кабачок и водка, и он ожесточённо сплёвывал и ругался.

В голове Сазонки было смутно и тяжело, и по целым часам он неуклюже ворочал какую-нибудь одну мысль: о новых сапогах или гармонике. Но чаще всего он думал о Сенисте и о гостинце, который он ему отнесёт. Машинка монотонно и усыпляюще стучала, покрикивал хозяин — и всё одна и та же картина представлялась усталому мозгу Сазонки: как он приходит к Сенисте в больницу и подает ему гостинец, завёрнутый в ситцевый каёмчатый платок. Часто в тяжёлой дреме он забывал, кто такой Сениста, и не мог вспомнить его лица; но каёмчатый платок, который нужно ещё купить, представлялся живо и ясно, и даже казалось, что узелки на нём не совсем крепко завязаны. И всем, хозяину, хозяйке, заказчикам и ребятам, Сазонка говорил, что пойдёт к мальчику непременно на первый день Пасхи.

— Уж так нужно, — твердил он. — Причешусь, и той же минутой к нему. На, милый, получай!

Но, говоря это, он видел другую картину: распахнутые двери красного кабачка и в тёмной глубине их залитую

But, busy with their interesting game, the boys accepted the news coldly and indifferently.

"I should bring him a present. Good idea, I will certainly bring him one," continued Sazonka.

Many responded to the word "present." Mishka Porosyonok, pulling up his pants with one hand—the other was holding the bones in the hem of his shirt—seriously advised:

"Give him a ten-kopeck coin."

Ten kopecks was the sum his grandfather promised him, and it was the pinnacle of Mishka's idea about human happiness. But there was no time to talk about the present, and with the same giant leaps, Sazonka ran back to his place and started working again. His eyes were slightly swollen, his face became yellowish pale, like a sick man's, and the freckles by his eyes and on his nose looked especially dense and dark. Only his well-brushed hair rose with the same jolly shock, and when the master, Gavriil Ivanovich, would look at it, he was always imagining a cozy red tavern and vodka, and he was spitting and cursing in desperation.

Sazonka's head was dizzy and heavy, and for hours, he was clumsily contemplating a pair of new boots or an accordion. But more often Sazonka was thinking about Senista, and the present, which he would bring him. The monotonous tapping of the sewing machine was lulling him to sleep; the master was reprimanding, and Sazonka's tired brain kept imagining the same scenario: how he goes to Senista and gives him the present wrapped in a printed cotton embroidered kerchief. In his heavy daydreaming, he would often forget who Senista was, and he would not able to remember his face, but he could see brightly and vividly the embroidered kerchief, which he still should buy; he even could see that its knots were not tightened enough. And Sazonka told everyone, the master, the customers and the kids that he would surely go to see the boy on the first day of Easter.

"It should be like that," he repeated. "I will brush my hair and the same minute will go to him: 'Here it is, my dear, take it!'"

But saying this, he imagined another picture: the red tavern door wide open, and in its dark depth, the counter wet with

сивухой стойку. И его охватывало горькое сознание своей слабости, с которой он не может бороться, и хотелось кричать громко и настойчиво: «К Сенисте пойду! К Сенисте!»

А голову наполняла серая, колеблющаяся муть, и только каёмчатый платок выделялся из неё. Но не радость в нём была, а суровый укор и грозное предостережение.

III

И на первый день Пасхи и на второй Сазонка был пьян, дрался, был избит и ночевал в участке. И только на четвёртый день удалось ему выбраться к Сенисте.

Улица, залитая солнечным светом, пестрела яркими пятнами кумачовых рубах и весёлым оскалом белых зубов, грызущих подсолнухи; играли вразброд гармоники, стучали чугунные плиты о костяшки, и голосисто орал петух, вызывая на бой соседского петуха. Но Сазонка не глядел по сторонам. Лицо его, с подбитым глазом и рассечённой губой, было мрачно и сосредоточено, и даже волосы не вздымались пышной гривой, а как-то растерянно торчали отдельными космами. Было совестно за пьянство и неисполненное слово, было жаль, что представится он Сенисте не во всей красе — в красной шерстяной рубахе и жилетке, — а пропившийся, паскудный, воняющий перегоревшей водкой. Но чем ближе подходил он к больнице, тем легче ему становилось, и глаза чаще опускались вниз, направо, где бережно висел в руке узелок с гостинцем. И лицо Сенисты виделось теперь совсем живо и ясно с запёкшимися губами и просящим взглядом.

— Милый, да разве? Ах, господи! — говорил Сазонка и крупно надбавлял шагу.

Вот и больница — жёлтое, громадное здание, с чёрными рамами окон, отчего окна походили на тёмные угрюмые глаза. Вот и длинный коридор, и запах лекарств, и неопределённое чувство жути и тоски. Вот и палата и постель Сенисты…

spilled vodka. And he was seized with a bitter understanding of his weakness, which he was not able to defeat, and he wanted to shout loudly and urgently, "I will go to Senista! To Senista!"

And the gray vacillating darkness was filling his head, and only the embroidered kerchief was standing out. No joy was in it, but rather a strict reproach and a terrifying warning.

III

And on the first day of Easter, and on its second day, Sazonka was drunk, had a fight, he was beaten savagely, and spent a night at the police. And only on the fourth day was he able to go see Senista.

The streets were filled with sunshine, and the passersby wearing bright red festive shirts and cheerful grins of white teeth nibbling sunflower seeds were bringing the city to life. Accordions were playing disquietedly, cast iron plates were hitting the bones, and the rooster was yelling loudly, challenging the neighbor's rooster to a fight. But Sazonka was not looking around. His face, with a black eye and a cut lip, was gloomy and concentrated, and even his hair did not rise as a fluffy mane, but somehow was sticking out in disheveled locks in embarrassment. He felt ashamed for his drinking and for not keeping the promise, he felt sorry that he would not show up for Senista in all his beauty—not in a red wool shirt and a vest, but having drunk the last of his wages, filthy and reeking with vodka. But the closer he came to the hospital, the easier he felt, and more often his eyes were looking down to the right, to his hand where he was carefully carrying the bundle with a present. And Senista's face was seen very alive and clear, with parched lips and begging look.

"My dear, aren't we..? Oh, Lord!" Sazonka repeatedly said and quickened his pace.

Here is the hospital—a huge yellow building, with black window frames, which made them look like dark dismal eyes. Here is the long hallway, with the smell of medicine, and uncertain feeling of horror and anguish. Here is the ward and Senista's bed...

Но где же сам Сениста?

— Вам кого? — спросила вошедшая следом сиделка.

— Мальчик тут один лежал. Семён. Семён Ерофеев. Вот на этом месте. — Сазонка указал пальцем на пустую постель.

— Так нужно допрежде спрашивать, а то ломится зря, — грубо сказала сиделка. — И не Семён Ерофеев, а Семён Пустошкин.

— Ерофеев — это по отчеству. Родителя звали Ерофеем, так вот он и выходит Ерофеич, — объяснил Сазонка, медленно и страшно бледнея.

— Помер ваш Ерофеич. А только мы этого не знаем: по отчеству. По-нашему — Семён Пустошкин. Помер, говорю.

— Вот как-с! — благопристойно удивился Сазонка, бледный настолько, что веснушки выступили резко, как чернильные брызги. — Когда же-с?

— Вчера после вечерен.

— А мне можно?.. — запинаясь, попросил Сазонка.

— Отчего нельзя? — равнодушно ответила сиделка. — Спросите, где мертвецкая, вам покажут. Да вы не убивайтесь! Кволый он был, не жилец.

Язык Сазонки расспрашивал дорогу вежливо и обстоятельно, ноги твёрдо несли его в указываемом направлении, но глаза ничего не видели. И видеть они стали только тогда, когда неподвижно и прямо они уставились в мёртвое тело Сенисты. Тогда же ощутился и страшный холод, стоявший в мертвецкой, и всё кругом стало видно: покрытые сырыми пятнами стены, окно, занесённое паутиной; как бы ни светило солнце, небо через это окно всегда казалось серым и холодным, как осенью. Где-то с перерывами беспокойно жужжала муха; падали откуда-то капельки воды; упадёт одна, — кап! — и долго после того в воздухе носится жалобный, звенящий звук.

Сазонка отступил на шаг назад и громко сказал:

— Прощевай, Семён Ерофеич.

Затем опустился на колени, коснулся лбом сырого пола и поднялся.

But where is Senista himself?

"Whom do you need?" asked the nurse who came next.

"One boy laid there. Semyon. Semyon Yerofeev. In that place." Sazonka pointed at the empty bed.

"You must first ask and not force your way here for nothing," she said rudely. "And not Semyon Yerofeev, but Semyon Pustoshkin."

"Yerofeev is his patronymic. His father was Yerofei, so he is Yerofeevich," explained Sazonka, slowly turning horribly pale.

"Your Yerofeevich died. But we do not know this, what his patronymic is. Here it is Semyon Pustoshkin. Died, I say."

"Really, Ma'am?" Sazonka decently expressed his surprise, turning so pale that his freckles showed through as sharp as ink spatters. "When, Ma'am?"

"Yesterday, after the evening service."

"And may I...?" asked Sazonka stumbling.

"Why not?" indifferently replied the nurse. "Ask where the morgue is, and they will show you. Don't be grieving so much! He was weak, a goner."

Sazonka asked the way politely and in detail, his legs were carrying him in the pointed direction, but his eyes did not see anything. And they were able to see only when they got frozen staring at the dead body of Senista. The same moment he felt a terrible cold in the morgue, and everything around became visible: the walls covered in mold, the window covered with the spider web; no matter how bright the sun shone through that window, it always looked gray and cold as if it were in autumn. Somewhere a fly was humming off and on; drops of water were dripping from some place: one fell,—drop! —And long after that, a mournful ringing sound was echoing in the air.

Sazonka stepped back and said loudly, "Farewell, Semyon Yerofeich."

Then he kneeled, touched the wet floor with his forehead, and stood up.

— Прости меня, Семён Ерофеич, — так же раздельно и громко выговорил он, и снова упал на колени, и долго прижимался лбом, пока не стала затекать голова.

Муха перестала жужжать, и было тихо, как бывает только там, где лежит мертвец. И через равные промежутки падали в жестяной таз капельки, падали и плакали — тихо, нежно.

IV

Тотчас за больницей город кончался и начиналось поле, и Сазонка побрёл в поле. Ровное, не нарушаемое ни деревом, ни строением, оно привольно раскидывалось вширь, и самый ветерок казался его свободным и тёплым дыханием. Сазонка сперва шёл по просохшей дороге, потом свернул влево и прямиком по пару и прошлогоднему жнитву направился к реке. Местами земля была ещё сыровата, и там после его прохода оставались следы его ног с тёмными углублениями каблуков.

На берегу Сазонка улёгся в небольшой, покрытой травой ложбинке, где воздух был неподвижен и тёпел, как в парнике, и закрыл глаза. Солнечные лучи проходили сквозь закрытые веки тёплой и красной волной; высоко в воздушной синеве звенел жаворонок, и было приятно дышать и не думать. Полая вода уже сошла, и речка струилась узеньким ручейком, далеко на противоположном низком берегу оставив следы своего буйства: огромные, ноздреватые льдины. Они кучками лежали друг на друге и белыми треугольниками подымались вверх навстречу огненным беспощадным лучам, которые шаг за шагом точили и сверлили их. В полудремоте Сазонка откинул руку — под неё попало что-то твёрдое, обёрнутое материей.

Гостинец.

Быстро приподнявшись, Сазонка вскрикнул:

— Господи! Да что же это?

Он совершенно забыл про узелок и испуганными глазами смотрел на него: ему чудилось, что узелок сам своей волей пришёл сюда и лёг рядом, и страшно было до

"Forgive me, Semyon Yerofeevich," he uttered in the same distinct and loud voice, and again fell to his knees, and pressed his forehead to the floor so long that his head started getting numb.

The fly stopped buzzing, and it was quiet, like it is usually only where the dead lie. And the drops were evenly falling down into the tin bowl, falling down and weeping—quietly and tenderly.

IV

Just behind the hospital, the city ended, and the field started, and Sazonka dragged himself to the field. Not disturbed by either a tree, or a house, the flat field was spreading free, so that even the wind itself seemed to be its free and warm breath. Sazonka was walking on the already dried road, and then he turned left and straight on the fallow land and through the old stubble he headed to the river. Here and there, the ground was still slightly wet, and he left the footprints on it with his heels.

On the bank, Sazonka laid down in the small narrow gully, covered with grass, where the air was still, warm, like in a green house, and closed his eyes. The sunrays were going through his eyelids with a warm red wave, a lark was ringing high in the airy blue sky, and it was pleasant to breathe and not to think. Floodwater had already run off, and the small river was flowing as a narrow stream, having left huge spongy ice floes as witnesses of its rampage far on the other low bank. Their piles towered on top of each other and by white triangles rose up towards the fiery merciless rays, which step by step sharpened and drilled them. In his somnolence, Sazonka threw back his hand, felt under it something hard, and wrapped in fabric.

The present.

Quickly getting up, Sazonka uttered a scream,

"Oh, Lord! What is this?"

He had entirely forgotten about the bundle, and now he was staring at it with his scared eyes: it seemed to him that the bundle itself, by its own will came there and placed itself by

него дотронуться. Сазонка глядел — глядел не отрываясь, — и бурная, клокочущая жалость и неистовый гнев подымались в нём. Он глядел на каёмчатый платок — и видел, как на первый день, и на второй, и на третий Сениста ждал его и оборачивался к двери, а он не приходил. Умер одинокий, забытый — как щенок, выброшенный в помойку. Только бы на день раньше — и потухающими глазами он увидел бы гостинец, и возрадовался бы детским своим сердцем, и без боли, без ужасающей тоски одиночества полетела бы его душа к высокому небу.

Сазонка плакал, впиваясь руками в свои пышные волосы и катаясь по земле. Плакал и, подымая руки к небу, жалко оправдывался:

— Господи! Да разве мы не люди?

И прямо рассечённой губой он упал на землю — и затих в порыве немого горя. Лицо его мягко и нежно щекотала молодая трава; густой, успокаивающий запах подымался от сырой земли, и была в ней могучая сила и страстный призыв к жизни. Как вековечная мать, земля принимала в свои объятия грешного сына и теплом, любовью и надеждой поила его страдающее сердце.

А далеко в городе нестройно гудели весёлые праздничные колокола.

his side, and it was scary to touch it. Sazonka could not tear himself away from looking at it, could not turn his eyes away from it, and stormy, seething grief and furious anger were surging in him.

He was looking at the embroidered kerchief, and could imagine how on the first day, and on the second day and on the third one, Senista was waiting for him, turning to the door, but he was not coming. He died lonely, and forgotten as a puppy thrown into the rubbish pit. Only one day earlier, and with his dimming eyes he would have seen the present, and his child's heart would have rejoiced, and without pain and without terrible anguish of loneliness his soul would have flown away to the high sky,

Sazonka was crying, digging his fingers into his fluffy hair, and rolling on the ground. He was crying and raising his hands to the sky, pathetically justifying himself:

"Oh, God! Are we not humans?"

And he fell down with his lacerated lip on the ground—and quieted down in the burst of silent grieving. New grass softly and tenderly was tickling his face; dense, appeasing odor was rising from the damp ground, and it had mighty power and a passionate call for life. Like the eternal mother, the earth was embracing her sinful son, giving his suffering heart her warmth, her love, and hope.

And far away in the city, the joyful holiday bells were discordantly buzzing.

Skitalets
(Stepan Gavrilovich Petrov)
Икар / Icarus

Илья Ефимович Репин (1844–1930). Голова калмыка. 1871.

I. Repin. *The Head of Kalmyk.* 1871.

SKITALETS
(STEPAN GAVRILOVICH PETROV)
1869–1941

Stepan Gavrilovich Petrov (pen name: Skitalets) was born into a peasant family in the Volga River region and experienced many troubles in his childhood. He had a musical gift, which he inherited from his father, a talented Psaltery player. The boy had to perform with him at provincial fairs and at taverns to earn a living.

He liked literature and started to write verses when he was twelve. He tried to get an education, and after attending the village school he became a student at a teacher's college, but he was expelled for "political disloyalty." In his later years, he was imprisoned several times for revolutionary activity, though after the October Revolution of 1917 he emigrated, living for about ten years in China and returning in 1934.

This writer had to change many jobs. He had worked as a chorister, an actor, and a court clerk. He traveled a great deal around Russia, Ukraine, the Crimea, and probably because of that, he later chose the pen name "Skitalets" ("Wanderer"). Eventually, in late 1890s, in Samara, the big city on the Volga River, he decided to try journalism and he found a job as a topical satirist for a few local newspapers.

When Skitalets met Maxim Gorky, he started treating his own talent more seriously, and in 1900 he published his first successful story. Maxim Gorky helped the young writer publish his first tale, which brought him his first literary fame and the positive responses of famous writers such as Anton Chekhov.

Three years later, Skitalets' first collection of stories and poetry was published. At that time, he was a close member of the literary circle of Maxim Gorky, who befriended him, so that some contemporaries called him an apprentice and a follower of the extremely popular proletarian writer.

Gradually the writer created his own recognizable style. In Skitalets' verses and narratives the reader can notice a lot of warmth and poetic feeling towards Russian nature, for example,

"Night is walking quietly on the starry road..."

"Oh, wonderful and miraculous land of
Summer thunderstorms and winter fairy-tales..."

"The orchards are sleeping,
And the turquoise stars are scattered
Over the black velvet of the sky."

Another quotation is from one of his novels: "The quiet and picturesque city was adorned with churches and monasteries, wrapped around with green front gardens..."

One can find many folklore motifs in his writings (for some time Skitalets collected folklore and dramatized it on stage). His style was so musical that some of his poems were even used as texts for popular romances.

Among Skitalets' literary legacy are memoirs he wrote about famous people whom he was fortunate to meet in his life. In these memoirs the writer amply demonstrated his skill at creating a literary portrait. For example, he described Leo Tolstoy as the "abundant golden light of the festive sun, struggling through the dense green fresh spring leaves, sunlit tenderly his lion-like head and splendid hands. He was all covered from his head to the feet with a thick wide rug, and it seemed to me that I talked only to that unusual magical head. Listening to the story told by that head, I was looking at the majestic face with a big forehead and gray beard, with kind, smart wrinkles by the deep eyes, and I felt that my fear of the Lion disappeared."

Skitalets wrote about the Russian people with a great deal of affection. It is difficult to find a character whom the writer

would seriously dislike. Many narrative pieces by Skitalets show the writer's compassion for the fallen souls and weak people who gave up in their struggle with their destiny and circumstances.

Often, Skitalets' stories describe music and musicians; gifted people with an artistic soul and vision, and eccentric, talented characters among the common people. These odd fellows, like the character of "Icarus," in spite of the bitter reality of surrounding life and the everyday struggle for survival, managed to keep purity of perception and original artistic vision to help them find comfort and enjoyment in art.

СКИТАЛЕЦ

Икар

Деревенский кузнец Назар приехал в город за покупками по хозяйству и по устройству паровика, имея в кармане на эти покупки тридцать рублей.

Он шёл по главной улице, разыскивая магазин с техническими принадлежностями, но магазин всё как-то не попадался ему на глаза.

Наружность у Назара самая непривлекательная: он — сутулый, с пологими плечами, с длинной жилистой шеей и угловатым лицом, с козлиной бородой.

Голова его наклонена, задумчивый взгляд устремился в землю, а походка тяжела и неуклюжа.

Кузнец Назар — странный и «чудной» мужик. Вся деревня смеётся над ним, хотя и считает его «докой» и «хитрецом».

Однодеревенцы отказываются понимать его: он иногда толкует им о том, что можно сделать «вечный двигатель», или вдруг придёт в умиление, смотря на восход или закат солнца, радуется красивому цвету облаков.

А паровик он сделал хотя и хорошо, «умственно» и «хитро», но — «ни к чему», так как гораздо дешевле было бы купить его готовым.

И много было в Назаре такого, что всем казалось непонятным, странным и смешным.

Сооружение паровика стоило ему огромного умственного напряжения; приходилось многое постигать, изобретать, проводить бессонные ночи, но это нравилось ему, и он вложил свою душу в совершенно не нужный ему паровик.

Теперь он почти даром отдает его напрокат.

SKITALETS

Icarus

The village blacksmith, Nazar, came to the city to buy some things for the house and some parts for the boiler; he had thirty rubles on him for those purchases.

He was walking along the main street looking for the hardware store, but somehow still could not find it.

Nazar's appearance was most unattractive: he was stooped, had round-shoulders, with a long sinewy neck, an angular face, and a goatee.

His head was bent, starring down towards the ground with a pensive look, and his gait was heavy and clumsy.

The blacksmith Nazar was a strange and "odd" man. His entire village laughed at him, although they considered him an "expert" and a clever man.

Fellow-villagers gave up trying to understand him; he sometimes told them that it was possible to make a perpetual motion machine, or suddenly he could be moved by looking at the sunset or the sunrise, enjoying beautiful colors of the clouds.

And the boiler he made, although well put together, in a "smart" and "skillful" way, was for no purpose, because it would have been much cheaper to buy it ready-made.

And there was a lot in Nazar that everyone saw as incomprehensible, strange and funny.

It cost him a huge mental effort to design the boiler: he had to learn a lot, invent a lot, spend sleepless nights, but he enjoyed it, and he put his whole soul into making the boiler he did not absolutely need.

Now he hires it out almost for free.

За все эти поступки вся деревня хохочет над ним, и ругательски ругается жена, женщина умная, почтенная, религиозная и хозяйственная.

Вот и теперь Назар, вместо того чтобы попасть в технический магазин да потом идти на базар за покупками по поручению жены, внезапно остановился у огромного окна магазина художественных вещей и фарфоровых изделий.

Его поразила маленькая фарфоровая группа: молодой нагой парень, будто бы ангел с крылами, упал на острый камень около воды; так и видно, что упал он откуда-то с облаков и разбился о камень, и так жалостно и красиво лежит его аккуратное тело, а из-за белых плеч, как паруса, легли изломанные, разбитые крылья.

И ещё две голые девицы подплыли к нему из воды, русалки, должно быть, любопытные, и заглядывают ему в мёртвое пригожее лицо.

И вдруг умиление и слёзы почувствовал Назар, и сам не знает отчего: то ли история чувствительная представлена, то ли в линиях и очертаниях этих фарфоровых тел есть что-то умилительное, тонкое, так бы вот всё и смотрел, и плакал.

Необыкновенное волнение овладело Назаром: ему казалось, что можно вечно стоять здесь и любоваться на эти удивительно красивые тонкие линии, и от этого любования слёзы навёртывались на глаза.

И всё его хозяйство, и паровик, и жена показались ему пустяками в сравнении с тем счастьем, которое должен испытывать обладатель этой вещицы. Почти бессознательно отворил он дверь магазина и остановился у порога, стаскивая шапку.

— Чего тебе? — небрежно крикнул на него барин, стоявший за прилавком, — хозяин, должно быть.

Тогда Назар ткнул корявым пальцем в вещицу и спросил дрожащим голосом, заикаясь:

— Сколько стоит?

Приказчик удивлённо и недоверчиво посмотрел на мужика и ответил:

His entire village laughs at him for all those deeds, and his wife, an intelligent, respectful, religious, and practical woman scolds him awfully.

And now, Nazar, instead of going to the hardware store, and, after that, continuing to the market to make some purchases that his wife had required, suddenly stopped by the huge window of the art gifts and porcelain shop.

He was struck by the small porcelain composition: a young naked lad, looking like a winged angel, who fell down on the sharp rock by the sea. One could see that he had fallen down somewhere from the sky and died in that fall on the rock, with his carefully modeled body lying so beautifully and compassionately, and his broken and crashed wings are seen behind his white shoulders, like sails.

And also two naked girls swam to him out of the water, surely curious mermaids, and were peering into his handsome dead face.

And Nazar suddenly was moved with tenderness and tears, and could not understand why: either because of the sentimental story, or something touching and subtle in the shapes of those porcelain bodies: he felt an urge to just look at it and cry.

Unusual excitement seized Nazar: it seemed to him that it was possible to stand there forever and enjoy looking at those amazingly beautiful delicate lines, and mixed with this admiration he was trying to suppress his tears.

His entire household, the boiler, and his wife seemed to him trifles in comparison with that happiness which an owner of that thing could feel. Almost unconsciously, he opened the door of the store, and stopped by the threshold taking off his hat.

"What do you want?" the gentleman, probably the owner, shouted at him in a casual tone.

Then Nazar pointed with his crooked finger at the statuette and asked with a trembling voice, stammering:

"How much?"

The shop assistant looked at the peasant with surprise and suspicion, and answered:

— Это — «Икар», стоит двадцать пять рублей, ты — от кого?

Назар молча завернул полу кафтана, дрожащими руками вынул деньги и, отдавая, сказал внушительно и проникновенно:

— Получи.

Затем он бережно положил за пазуху тщательно запакованную драгоценность, нахлобучил шапку и удалился из магазина своей тяжёлой походкой, неуклюжий, с наклонённой задумчиво головой, пологими плечами и длинной мужицкой шеей в рубцах и складках.

Назар вернулся домой без покупок, но радостный и улыбающийся своей тихой, детской улыбкой.

Жена удивилась праздничному лицу Назара.

Трое ребятишек обступили его, ожидая гостинцев. Жена стояла в двери чулана и проницательно смотрела ему прямо в лицо.

— Что это, Назар, каким ты именинником приехал нынче? А где у те покупки-то?

Назар молча и загадочно улыбнулся и всё стоял посредине избы, и всё нащупывал что-то за пазухой.

— Покупок я не купил, оставил до другого раза, — медленно, с расстановкой заговорил он и всё улыбался своей хорошей, трогательной улыбкой, которая удивительно преображала его некрасивое лицо.— А вот, жена, погляди-кось, какую вещу я тебе привёз! Двадцать пять рублёв отдал, потому и не купил, все деньги извёл...

Тут он бережно вынул «Икара», дрожащими руками развернул его и любовно поставил на стол.

При взгляде на голые человеческие фигуры почтенная женщина долго не могла вымолвить ни слова, поражённая горем и негодованием. Наконец, она всплеснула руками и неожиданно для Назара вдруг разразилась энергичной и звонкой бранью:

— С ума ты сошёл, старый дурак, греховодник ты этакий, бесстыжие твои глаза!.. Голых баб купил, батюшки мои светы! Да неужто не стыдно тебе глядеть-то на этакую пакость, бесстыдник ты, охальник, озорник бессовестный!

"This is 'Icarus'; it costs twenty-five rubles. Who sent you?"

In silence, Nazar tucked up a flap of his coat, took out the money with shaking hands, and giving it, said in an impressive and heartfelt way,

"Take it."

Then he carefully put the painstakingly wrapped treasure in his bosom, pulled down his hat over his eyes, and left the shop with his heavy gait, clumsily walking with a thoughtfully bent head, round shoulders and his long peasant's neck all in scars and wrinkles.

Nazar came back home without the purchases, but jolly and peacefully smiling like a child.

His wife was surprised by Nazar's happy face.

His three children surrounded him waiting for presents. His wife was standing by the pantry door with a piercing look right at his face.

"What is this, Nazar? What a cheery look you returned with today! Where are your purchases?"

Nazar, smiling mysteriously, did not say a word, and still was standing in the middle of the house, feeling something in his bosom.

"I did not buy anything—I left it for next time," he slowly spoke without haste, and continued smiling with his nice touching grin, which amazingly changed his ugly face. "Come here, wife, look what a thing I brought for you! I paid twenty-five rubles and spent all the money, and that is why I did not buy anything..."

And he carefully took out "Icarus," unwrapped it with trembling hands and put it on the table with a loving glance.

Looking at the naked human figures, the respectable woman was not able to say a word for a long time, struck with grief and anger. Finally she threw up her hands and unexpectedly burst out with energetic and ringing abuse:

"You lost your mind, you old fool, a sinner, shameless eyes!.. Bought naked broads, Lord My Savior! Shame on you to look at this filth, shameless man you are, a mischief-maker, and an impudent man without any scruples! You've wasted twenty-

Да неужто двадцать пять целковых? Батюшки! Ограбил! Разорил! По миру пустил, разбойник… душе-гу-уб! Что мы есть-то теперь будем? Дети-то босиком да без хлеба! Ай, батюшки! Да и что это с тобой попритчилось?

Её укоры мало-помалу перешли в причитания и слёзы. Мысль о двадцати пяти рублях, истраченных так глупо, всё более и более ужасала её.

Она плакала с воем и причитаниями, как плачут по покойникам. Ребятишки, глядя на неё, тоже завыли.

А Назар стоял среди них, как бы пробуждённый от сна, и силился что-то сказать, и на добром лице выражалась острая и внезапная боль.

Смотреть на бесстыдных «голых баб» Назару строго воспрещено. И только по воскресеньям, когда жена с детьми уходит в церковь, Назар отпирает сундук, бережно вынимает оттуда «Икара», садится за стол, держит хрупкую вещицу в своих огромных, корявых пальцах, долго любуясь ею, и детская, прекрасная, трогательная улыбка появляется на его лице.

five rubles, haven't you? My Lord! Robbed! Got broke! Beggared us, a robber, a mu-u-u-rderer...! What are we going to eat now? Your children are barefoot and without a piece of bread! My God! What got into you?"

Little by little, her reproaches turned into lamentations and tears. The thought of twenty-five rubles wasted so stupidly horrified her more and more.

She was crying with howling and lamentations as if she was lamenting over a deceased. Looking at her, the kids also started weeping.

And Nazar was standing in the middle as if he was awakened, tried to say something and his kind face expressed sharp and sudden pain.

Nazar is strictly prohibited to look at the shameless "naked broads." And only on Sundays, when his wife and children leave for church, Nazar opens the chest, carefully takes out the "Icarus," sits by the table, holds the fragile treasure in his huge crooked fingers, admiring it for a long time, and a childlike and wonderfully touching smile appears on his face.

Valery Yakovlevich Bryusov

Мраморная головка
(Рассказ бродяги) /
Marble Head
(Story of a Hobo)

Илья Ефимович Репин (1844–1930). Портрет Е.Д. Баташевой. 1891.
[Музей в Абрамцеве]

I. Repin. *The Portrait of E. Batasheva*. 1891.
[Abramtsevo Museum, Russia]

VALERY YAKOVLEVICH BRYUSOV

1873–1924

Valery Bryusov is one of the most prominent poets of the Russian "Silver Age" of literature. He was born in Moscow to a merchant's family, a grandson of I. Bakulin, a Russian writer of fables. Only three generations separated Valery Bryusov from serfdom: even his last name originated from the name of his grandfather's master, the estate owner Bryus.

Bryusov's maternal grandfather, Alexander Bakunin, was a minor writer; the father of the poet was interested in literature, had a huge library at home, and wrote poetry. He was fond of revolutionary ideas and of philosophical materialism, and, as a result, he tried to raise his son as an atheist, protecting the boy from exposure to any kind of religious literature. It brought its fruits, so that Valery once was even expelled from one private school for atheistic propaganda. It is very likely that the home atmosphere of leftist revolutionary ideas later influenced Bryusov, when soon after the October Revolution of 1917, he joined the Communist Party and actively collaborated with the Soviet regime—in this new Socialist society the poet saw the beginning of a new transformed culture, different from the bourgeois one and seemingly better.

Bryusov received a good basic education from high-quality schools. In Bryusov's teenage years, his favorite readings were scientific articles about mathematics, as well as adventure fiction by Jules Verne and Thomas Mayne Reid. Later, being a student in the Historical-Philological Department of

Moscow's University, he became fond of history, art, languages, philosophy, literature, and theater. Bryusov began to write poetry and fiction rather early in his life; as a student he published a self-made literary magazine. Three French symbolists especially strongly influenced the young poet: Charles Baudelaire, Paul Verlaine, and Stéphane Mallarmé.

Bryusov created his best verses at the turn of the century, when he became one of the leading poets of the Symbolist movement. His poetry was filled with historical and mythological motifs, urban landscapes, and advanced liberal revolutionary social ideas of the times. He was known for his brave experimentation in verse and skillful stylization, from classical poetry to exotic and contemporary Russian folklore genres.

With the great popularity of his poetry, not many readers are aware that Bryusov also was a gifted translator, a journalist, an editor, an art history professor, a literary critic, and a theoretician. He wrote historical novels, early Russian narrative in the science fiction genre, and drama. Among his literary pieces are a number of short stories.

The brief novella "The Marble Head" is one of the most popular among his short fiction. It is possible that in the fate of the main character the writer described his father, who went broke because of gambling debts and drinking. Bryusov's life was not ascetic at all. Following his character traits, he had numerous love affairs, without any real emotional attachment to his lovers, and he often used opium and cocaine.

Among Bryusov's best-known love affairs, there were two, both with much younger women. These stories finished tragically for the women, who were deeply and emotionally involved with him, whose feelings towards Bryusov were profound and serious but were never reciprocated. All of these stories developed according to the same recurring script in the poet's life: first, a passionate love affair, then the poet's growing coolness and indifference, and, later, the suicide of the women, who were not able to overcome the separation and bitter parting. That happened first to Nina Petrovskaya, and then many years later to a young poet, Nadezhda Lvova.

Women usually inspired Bryusov to write wonderful poetry. However, in real life, there were other innocent victims of that *homme fatal*, whom the contemporaries compared with Mephistopheles and a wizard because of his devilish personal aura, style of life, and excellent writing.

Before committing suicide, Nadazhda Lvova wrote to her beloved, "I do not have any strength... to tell you endlessly that I love you, and that you will be happy with me, that... I want to be with you... Give me your hand, be with me, if you come in time, come to me. And you must take my love and my life." The tragedy of all such love affairs finishing badly for those who were attracted to Bryusov's orbit was explained by the poet Vladislav Khodasevich, who wrote about Valery Bryusov: "He did not love people, because, first of all, he did not respect them... He never loved any of them... He really admired love itself. But he did not notice his lovers. He loved only literature, exclusively. And he loved himself also only for the sake of literature."

The best evidence of the poet's real feelings can be found in his verses (although, one knows how deceptive it is to try to guess what is going on in someone's soul, especially if one is a prominent poet living a life of inspiration). In 1899, Bryusov wrote the verses that can be called *"The Ode to a Woman."* They begin:

"You are a woman, a Book among the books,
You are a scroll rolled up and sealed;
In its content, there are a lot of thoughts and words,
And in its sheets each moment is insane.

You are a woman; you are a witches' drink!
It burns you with the fire in the throat;
But when one drinks that flame, one doesn't cry,
One madly praises suffering under torture."

And it finishes with "We pray to you since the Creation of the World!"

However, in 1902, Bryusov wrote:
"I was waiting for love,
But I did not taste it
In its bottomless fullness—
I gave away my heart to coldness,
I betrayed my dream!"

In the story "Marble Head," Bryusov wrote in the classical Russian fiction style of narrative, quite realistic and traditional in its compassion and forgiveness for fallen souls. Its mood and passion for a "fallen human being" recalls the bitter monologue-confession by Marmeladov in Dostoevsky's *Crime and Punishment*. However, what makes it so interesting and unusual is that he also added a light note of sentimentality, with a bright hint of mystery and puzzles, which leaves the question posed at the end without an answer. Was that a real story or only the play of the imagination of a poor crazy old man? You can judge for yourself, dear reader.

ВАЛЕРИЙ ЯКОВЛЕВИЧ БРЮСОВ

Мраморная головка
(Рассказ бродяги)

Его судили за кражу и приговорили на год в тюрьму. Меня поразило и то, как этот старик держал себя на суде, и самая обстановка преступления. Я добился свидания с осуждённым. Сначала он дичился меня, отмалчивался, наконец, рассказал мне свою жизнь.

— Вы правы,— начал он, — я видал лучшие дни, не всегда был уличным горемыкой, не всегда засыпал в ночлежных домах. Я получил образование, я — техник. У меня в юности были кое-какие деньжонки, я жил шумно: каждый день на вечере, на балу, и всё кончалось попойкой. Это время я помню хорошо, до мелочей помню. Но есть в моих воспоминаниях пробел, и, чтобы заполнить его, я готов отдать весь остаток моих дряхлых дней: это — всё, что относится к Нине.

Её звали Ниной, милостивый государь, да, Ниной, я убеждён в этом. Она была замужем за мелким чиновником на железной дороге. Они бедствовали. Но как она умела в этой жалкой обстановке быть изящной и как-то особенно утончённой! Она сама стряпала, но её руки были как выточенные. Из своих дешёвых платьев она создавала чудесный бред. Да и всё повседневное, соприкасаясь с ней, становилось фантастическим. Я сам, встречаясь с ней, делался иным, лучшим, стряхивал с себя, как дождь, всю житейскую пошлость.

Бог простит ей грех, что она любила меня. Кругом было всё так грубо, что она не могла не полюбить меня, молодого,

VALERY YAKOVLEVICH BRYUSOV

Marble Head
(Story of a Hobo)

He was tried for larceny and sentenced to a year of imprisonment. I was struck by the old man's behavior in court, and the content of the crime itself. I obtained permission for a visit to see the convict. At first, he was shy, and not responsive. Finally, he told me his life story.

"You are right," he started, "I saw better days, I was not always a poor street vagrant, and I did not always spend nights in a flophouse. I got an education—I am an engineer. In my young years, I had some money, and I led a rowdy life: every day I was at parties, at balls, and everything finished with drinking bouts. I remember that time well, and remember even the smallest details. But in my memories, there is one blank, and, to fill it in, I am ready to pay with the rest of my decrepit days: this is the time associated with Nina.

Her name was Nina, sir, yes, Nina, I am sure. She was married to a minor official at the railway. They were struggling. However, how well she managed to stay elegant and especially refined in that pathetic atmosphere! She cooked by herself, but her hands looked perfectly formed. She could make fantastic dream-like dresses from her cheap clothes. And even anything casual she touched became miraculous. I, myself, while meeting her, became different, better; shook off all my everyday coarseness like rain water.

God will forgive her the sin of loving me. Everything around was so vulgar, and she could not help falling in love with me,

77

красивого, знавшего столько стихов наизусть. Но где я с ней познакомился и как — этого я уже не могу восстановить в своей памяти. Вырываются из мрака отдельные картины. Вот мы в театре. Она, счастливая, весёлая (ей это выпадало так редко!), впивает каждое слово пьесы, улыбается мне... Её улыбку я помню. Потом вот мы вдвоем где-то. Она наклонила голову и говорит мне: «Я знаю, что ты — моё счастье ненадолго; пусть, — всё-таки я жила». Эти слова я помню. Но что было тотчас после, да и правда ли, что всё это было с Ниной? Не знаю.

Конечно, я первый бросил её. Мне казалось это так естественно. Все мои товарищи поступали так же: заводили интригу с замужней женщиной и, по прошествии некоторого времени, бросали её. Я только поступил, как все, и мне даже на ум не приходило, что мой поступок дурен. Украсть деньги, не заплатить долг, сделать донос — это дурно, но бросить любовницу — только в порядке вещей. Передо мной была блестящая будущность, и я не мог связывать себя какой-то романтической любовью. Мне было больно, очень больно, но я пересилил себя и даже видел подвиг в том, что решился перенести эту боль.

Я слышал, что Нина после того уехала с мужем на юг и вскоре умерла. Но так как воспоминания о Нине всё же были мне мучительны, я избегал тогда всяких вестей о ней. Я старался ничего не знать про неё и не думать о ней. У меня не осталось её портрета, её письма я ей возвратил, общих знакомых у нас не было — и вот постепенно образ Нины стёрся в моей душе. Понимаете? — я понемногу пришёл к тому, что забыл Нину, забыл совершенно, её лицо, её имя, всю нашу любовь. Стало так, как если бы её совершенно не существовало в моей жизни... Ах, есть что-то постыдное для человека в этой способности забывать!

Шли годы. Уж не буду вам рассказывать, как я «делал карьеру». Без Нины, конечно, я мечтал только о внешнем успехе, о деньгах. Одно время я почти достиг своей цели, мог тратить тысячи, живал по заграницам, женился, имел детей. Потом всё пошло на убыль; дела, которые я затеивал, не удавались; жена умерла; побившись с детьми, я их рассовал

a young, handsome man, knowing so much poetry by heart. But where I met her and how, I already am not able to recall from memory. Only separate episodes come to light out from the darkness. Here we are at the theater. She is happy, jolly (it happened to her so rarely!), she is absorbing each word of the play, smiling to me... I remember her smile. Then we are somewhere together. She is bending her head saying to me, 'I know that you are my short-lived happiness, let it be so, but I will have nevertheless lived.' I remember those words. But what was right after that, and was it with Nina? I do not know.

Certainly, it was I who left her. I thought that it was so natural. All my friends did the same—started an affair with a married woman, and after a while left her. I only did like everyone, and it never even occurred to me that what I did was ugly. To steal money, not pay debts, to inform on someone—it is ugly, but to leave a lover—it is in the order of things. Magnificent prospects waited for me, and I could not be bound in some romantic affair. It was painful to me, very painful, but I overcame it, and even saw the endurance of that pain as something heroic.

I heard that Nina left with her husband for the South, and she died soon after. However, the memories about Nina were painful for me, and at that time, I tried to avoid any news about her. I tried not to learn anything about her and not to think about her. I did not have her portrait, I had returned her letters, we did not have any common acquaintances, and gradually Nina's image erased itself from my heart. Do you understand? Little by little, I came to the state when I forgot Nina, forgot entirely, her face, her name, and our love. It became as if she had never existed in my life... Oh, there is something shameful for a human with this ability to forget!

Time passed. I am not going to tell you how I 'made my career'. Without Nina, I, of course, only dreamed about cheap success, about money. In time, I almost reached my goal; I was able to spend thousands, live abroad; I got married and had children. Then everything began to decline: the business that I started failed, my wife died; after struggling with the children, I

по родственникам и теперь, прости мне Господи, даже не знаю, живы ли мои мальчишки. Разумеется, я пил и играл... Основал было я одну контору — не удалось, загубил на ней последние деньги и силы. Попытался поправить дела игрой и чуть не попал в тюрьму — да и не совсем без основания... Знакомые от меня отвернулись, и началось моё падение.

Понемногу дошёл я до того, чем вы меня ныне видите. Я, так сказать, «выбыл» из интеллигентного общества и опустился на дно. На какое место мог я претендовать, одетый плохо, почти всегда пьяный? Последние годы служил я месяцами, когда не пил, на заводах рабочим. А когда пил, — попадал на Хитров рынок и в ночлежки. Озлобился я на людей страшно и всё мечтал, что вдруг судьба переменится и я буду опять богат. Наследства какого-то несуществующего ждал или чего-то подобного. Своих новых товарищей за то и презирал, что у них этой надежды не было.

Так вот однажды, продрогший и голодный, брожу я по какому-то двору, уж сам не знаю зачем, случай привёл. Вдруг повар кричит мне: «Эй, любезный, ты не слесарь ли?» «Слесарь», — отвечаю. Позвали меня замок в письменном столе исправить. Попал я в роскошный кабинет, везде позолота, картины. Поработал я, сделал что надо, и выносит мне барыня рубль. Я беру деньги и вдруг вижу, на белой колонке, мраморную головку. Сначала обмер, сам не зная почему, всматриваюсь и верить не могу: Нина!

Говорю вам, милостивый государь, что Нину я забыл совсем и тут-то именно впервые это и понял: понял, что забыл её. Вдруг выплыл предо мной её образ, и целая вселенная чувств, мечтаний, мыслей, которая погребена была в моей душе, словно какая-то Атлантида, — пробудилась, воскресла, ожила... Смотрю я на мраморный бюст, сам дрожу и спрашиваю: «Позвольте узнать, сударыня, что это за головка?» — «А это, — отвечает она, — очень дорогая вещь, пятьсот лет назад сделана, в XV веке». Имя художника назвала, я не разобрал, сказала, что муж вывез

placed them with relatives and now, God forgive me, I even do not know if my boys are still alive. Certainly, I drank and gambled... I founded one firm, but failed and lost all my money and energy. I tried to mend my finances with gambling, and almost got into prison—and not without a reason... My acquaintances turned away from me, and my degradation started.

Little by little, I came to the condition where you see me now. I, so to speak, 'dropped out' of the educated circle and went down to the scum of society. What job could I ask for—badly dressed, and almost always drunk? Lately, I worked on a monthly basis as a worker in plants—when I did not drink. And when I drank, I found myself at Khitrov Market and in flophouses. I became horribly embittered at people, and all the time I dreamed that suddenly my fate would change and I would be rich again. As if I were waiting for some non-existent inheritance or something of the sort. I despised my new acquaintances for not having even such a hope.

So, once, cold and hungry, I was wandering around somebody's yard, even not realizing for what reason, simply some chance brought me there. When suddenly, the cook called out to me: 'Hey, my good man, are you a locksmith, by chance?' 'A locksmith,' I answered. They called me in to repair the lock in the desk. I found myself in a luxurious study: there were gilding and paintings everywhere. I worked some, did what was asked of me, and the lady brought me a ruble. As I was taking the money, suddenly I saw the marble head on a white, column-shaped pedestal. At first, I became numb, not knowing why, then gazed and could not believe my eyes: 'Nina!'

I am telling you, sir, that I absolutely forgot Nina, and at that moment I realized for the first time that I had forgotten her. All of a sudden, her image cropped up, and the whole world of feelings, dreams, thoughts buried in my soul, like in some Atlantis – was awakened, recalled to my memory and revived... I was looking at the marble bust, shivering and said, 'Could I ask you, Ma'am, whose head this is?' 'This is,' she answered, 'a very expensive thing, made five hundred years ago, in the 15th Century'. She named the artist, but I did not recognize him, and

эту головку из Италии и что чрез то целая дипломатическая переписка возникла между итальянским и русским кабинетами. «А что, — спрашивает меня барыня, — или вам понравилось? Какой у вас, однако, современный вкус! Ведь уши, — говорит, — не на месте, нос неправилен...» — и пошла! и пошла!

Выбежал я оттуда как в чаду. Это не сходство было, а просто портрет, даже больше — какое-то воссоздание жизни в мраморе. Скажите мне, каким чудом художник в XV столетии мог сделать те самые маленькие, криво посаженные уши, которые я так знал, те самые чуть-чуть раскосые глаза, неправильный нос и длинный наклонённый лоб, из чего неожиданно получалось самое прекрасное, самое пленительное женское лицо? Каким чудом две одинаковые женщины могли жить — одна в XV веке, другая в наши дни? А что та, с которой делалась головка, была именно одинакова, тождественна с Ниной, не только лицом, но и характером, и душой, я не мог сомневаться.

Этот день изменил всю мою жизнь. Я понял и всю низость своего поведения в прошлом, и всю глубину своего падения. Я понял Нину как ангела, посланного мне судьбой, которого я не признал. Вернуть прошлое невозможно. Но я с жадностью стал собирать воспоминания о Нине, как подбирают черепки от разбившейся драгоценной вазы. Как мало их было! Сколько я ни старался, я не мог составить ничего целого. Всё были осколки, обломки. Но как ликовал я, когда мне удавалось обрести в своей душе что-нибудь новое. Задумавшись и вспоминая, я проводил целые часы; надо мной смеялись, а я был счастлив. Я стар, мне поздно начинать жизнь сызнова, но я ещё могу очистить свою душу от пошлых дум, от злобы на людей и от ропота на Создателя. В воспоминаниях о Нине я находил это очищение.

Страстно мне хотелось посмотреть на статую ещё раз. Я бродил целые вечера около дома, где она стояла, стараясь увидеть мраморную головку, но она была далеко от окон. Я простаивал ночи перед домом. Я узнал всех

she said that her husband had brought that head from Italy, and it even caused a diplomatic correspondence between the Russian and Italian Cabinets. 'I wonder,' the lady asked me, 'if you really like it? What a modern taste you have, though!' 'Look,' she said, 'the ears are not in their place, the nose is not of a good shape...' and so on! And so forth!

I ran out from there, dazed. It was not a similarity, but a portrait, even more—a recreation of Nina in marble. Tell me, by what miracle, the artist of the 15th Century could make those small awry set ears that I knew so well, those slightly slanting eyes, irregular nose, and the long inclined forehead? From all of that together, unexpectedly, came out the most wonderful, the most charming face of a woman. By what miracle could two similar women live: one in the 15th century, and the other nowadays? And I did not have any doubt that the woman—the model that inspired the artist, was exactly the same, she was identical to Nina, not only by her face, but also by her character and her heart.

That day changed my whole life. I realized both the meanness in my past and the depth of my degradation. I understood that Nina was an angel that my fate had sent to me, but I did not recognize it. It was impossible to revive the past. But with eagerness, I began to gather my memories of Nina, as though they were the pieces of a broken precious vase. How few I had!

In spite of all my efforts, I was not able to put together any parts into a whole. There were only fragments. But how much I rejoiced, when I managed to uncover something new in my memory. I was spending hours plunged deep in my thoughts and reminiscing. People laughed at me, but I was happy. I am old, and it is too late to begin all over again, but I still can clear my soul of past thoughts, bitterness toward people and reproaches directed at our Lord. I found all the cleansing in my memories of Nina.

I desperately wanted to look at that statue again. For many evenings, I had been strolling by that house, trying to see the marble head, but it was too far from the window. I stayed in front of the house for nights on end. I learned about all the

живущих в нём, расположение комнат, завёл знакомство с прислугой. Летом владельцы уехали на дачу. И я уже не мог более бороться со своим желанием. Мне казалось, что, взглянув ещё раз на мраморную Нину, я сразу вспомню всё, до конца. Это было бы для меня последним блаженством. И я решился на то, за что меня судили. Вы знаете, что мне не удалось. Меня схватили ещё в передней. На суде выяснилось, что я был в комнатах под видом слесаря, что меня не раз замечали подле дома... Я был нищий, я взломал замки... Впрочем, история кончена, милостивый государь!

— Но мы подадим апелляцию, — сказал я, — вас оправдают.

— К чему? — возразил старик. — Никого моё осуждение не опечалит и не обесчестит, а не всё ли равно, где я буду думать о Нине — в ночлежном доме или в тюрьме?

Я не нашёлся, что ответить, но старик вдруг поднял на меня свои странные выцветшие глаза и продолжал:

— Одно меня смущает. Что, если Нины никогда не было, а мой бедный ум, ослабев от алкоголя, выдумал всю историю этой любви, когда я смотрел на мраморную головку?

people living there, the layout of the rooms, I got to know the servants. One summer, the owners left for their country house. And I could not resist my desire anymore. It seemed to me that if I looked at the marble Nina one more time, I would remember everything, to the end. It would have been for me the last perfect bliss. And I decided to do exactly what I was on trial for today. You know that I failed in my design. I was caught while still in the hall. At the court, they found out that I had been in the room as a locksmith and that I was seen near the house many times... I was a pauper, I broke in... Anyway the story is finished, sir!"

"But we will appeal," I said, "and you will be acquitted."

"What for?" the old man asked. "Nobody will be upset or disgraced by my conviction, and is there really any difference where I will be thinking about Nina: in a flophouse or in prison?"

I did not find the right words for the occasion, but the old man suddenly cast a glance at me with his strange faded eyes and continued:

"Only one thing disturbs me. What if Nina had never existed, and my poor mind, weakened with alcohol, had invented the whole story of this love, while I was looking at that marble head?"

Dmitry Narkisovich Mamin-Sibiryak

Трататон / Trataton

Илья Ефимович Репин (1844–1930). Нищий с сумой. 1879.

I. Repin. *The Beggar with a Bag.* 1879.

DMITRY NARKISOVICH MAMIN-SIBIRYAK

1852–1912

This well-known writer is famous mainly for his novels about Siberia and the Urals, as well as for his children's fairy tales.

Mamin-Sibiryak (the pseudonym of the last name Mamin) was born in the Urals, the son of a priest. After school, he studied at a seminary; then he entered the Veterinary Department of St. Petersburg's Medical-Surgical Academy; and later on he was a student of jurisprudence at St. Petersburg University. His first fiction dates from his university years.

Unfortunately, Mamin-Sibiryak could not graduate due to a lack of money and illness (tuberculosis). He had to return to the Urals to support his family, which was in financial trouble after his father's death. He needed to move to a big city, and tried to find a job in Nizhny Tagil, an industrial center. However, Mamin-Sibiryak had to leave town, afraid of being persecuted for the newspaper articles he sent to St. Petersburg and Moscow criticizing the administration of the local metal works for illegal actions against workers.

Later, he described that area (called "the Urals' Switzerland") in many stories and essays with a great deal of affection. Once he wrote: "My dear green mountains! [...] When I am sad, I fly in my thoughts to my native green mountains, and it seems to me that the sky is higher and clearer there, and the people are so kind, that I myself become better." And this is true: with special love he wrote about the people he observed: peasants, hunters, barge haulers, gold prospectors, members of the reli-

gious group of Old Believers, ethnic minorities, former state convicts, and workers.

Then Mamin-Sibiryak moved to Yekaterinburg to try to earn his living. He started working there, and continued to write. He traveled extensively around the Urals, and even participated in ethnographical and archeological expeditions to study the region better.

First flirtations with literary fame occurred in the 1880s after the publication of a series of traveler's essays, *From the Urals to Moscow*. However, Mamin-Sibiryak's all-Russian popularity came to him after the novel *The Privalov's Millions*, which created his reputation as a gifted writer of fiction. His realistic narrative, often dramatic and naturalistic, gave his contemporaries a reason to call him the "Russian Émile Zola." As in his French contemporary's novels, there is gloominess and dramatic realistic detail in the works of Mamin-Sibiryak.

In the history of Russian literature, Mamin-Sibiryak is chiefly remembered as the creator of beautiful narratives about Siberia and the Urals. His name is so tightly connected to the region, that the Union of the Russian Writers established a literary award in his name for the best fiction written about the Urals.

The writer also traveled a lot in Siberia and was published there in local newspapers and ethnographical research collections. It was significant that in 1882 Mamin chose his pen name "Sibiryak" ('The Siberian'), in spite of his "roots" in the Urals. He was fascinated with the history of Siberia and published many historical essays about that area, as well as articles about the contemporary economic and social situation there.

In 1891, he and his family moved to St. Petersburg. There, he created his best collections of stories for children, *Alyonushka's Fairy-Tales* (1894–1896). Mamin-Sibiryak wrote them for his little daughter, Alyonushka. It is remarkable that his wonderful fairy tales are still a part of the school curriculum in Russia. It is also interesting that some of his characters are childlike by nature; both naive and wise in their simplicity, and mighty, yet kind-hearted, giants.

Mamin-Sibiryak was very skillful in depicting nature. The landscapes in his narrative could be compared to canvases by famous Russian painters of realistic style, such as Ivan Shishkin and Isaak Levitan. Nature plays an important role in his fiction. In an allegorical way, it is another character in the plot, with its feelings, its own mood and "face." It always creates an important background for the plot, and is often personified.

The story "Trataton" is one of the writer's late narratives that he wrote after traveling around Finland. In it, one can see two realities, which the storyteller inhabits. The first one is his country-house life near St. Petersburg, and the second one is the Siberia that he knows and misses, and which he "meets" again impersonated by a lumberjack Trataton—an original, eccentric personality. He looks like a mighty epic hero from Russian folklore, and from those far lands where the narrator used to travel and he grew to love. Trataton appears as though he were coming from a fairy-tale: he works in the forest and talks to trees as if they were living creatures. He really likes to talk, and it was probably due to his talkative nature that he got the nickname Trataton (the old residents of the Siberian Tobolsk area called the settlers from Southern Russia "Tratatons," for their habit of talking a lot, since "to chat" in the local language is "to tratatonit"). In this story, like in many others, the writer even shows the local Siberian dialect and manner of speech. The language of Trataton is filled with those local specific features to such a degree that the story itself could be viewed as a reliable linguistic artifact.

Mamin-Sibiryak is impressed by the original distinctive, optimistic, and self-confident character of the man. Trataton relates some episodes from his life in Siberia, showing his independent ways, a slightly cynical sense of humor, and a lot of common sense combined with a rebellious nature and strong sense of justice. One of his traits is the pride of being a Siberian, sometimes, to the degree of being arrogant towards both the Russians and local Finns. However, the writer admires Trataton for all his goodness in spite of some shortcomings.

ДМИТРИЙ НАРКИСОВИЧ
МАМИН-СИБИРЯК

Трататон

I

Нынешнее лето мне привелось просидеть в настоящем чухонском дачном болоте. Почему и как я попал туда, — трудно сказать. Вероятно, и большинство дачников тоже не в состоянии привести более или менее разумных причин своего летнего пребывания в том или другом дачном уголке, о котором обыкновенно мечтают в течение длинной и кислой петербургской зимы. Одним словом, выражаясь языком полицейских протоколов о пожарах и самоубийствах, «причины остались неизвестны».

Итак, мне пришлось всё лето, как кулику, просидеть среди благословенного чухонского болота. Рядом были ещё две дачки, где «отсиживали лето» такие же горемыки. А всё-таки лето... Кругом чахлая болотная сосна, гнилая, изъеденная лишаями, корявая берёза, какая-то обтрёпанная, жалкая болотная ель, напрасно вытягивавшая свою вершину к скупому северному небу и как-то безнадёжно топорщившая по сторонам ветви, напоминавшие лохмотья из зелёной хвои. Вид непривлекательный... И такое замаскированное чахлой растительностью болото разлеглось до самого Ледовитого океана, унылое, безнадёжное, без воспоминаний о счастливом прошлом и без надежды на лучшее будущее. Вообще вся Финляндия напоминает старинную выцветшую акварель, а тысячи озёр смотрят на вас слезящимися старушечьими глазами... Всё как-то архаично, серьёзно, как выражение лица больного ребёнка, и вместе полно той

DMITRY NARKISOVICH
MAMIN-SIBIRYAK

Trataton

I

I happened to spend this summer in a real Finnish country marsh. Why and how I found myself there—it is difficult to tell. Probably, most of the country cottage folks also cannot give any more or less reasonable explanation as to why their summer rest is spent in this and no other countryside place, which they usually dream about during the long and sour Petersburg winter. Briefly speaking, and using the language of police reports of fires and suicides, the "reasons remain unknown."

So, I had to spend the whole summer as a surfbird amongst the blessed Finnish marshes. Nearby, there were two more small summerhouses where some unfortunate people like me were "imprisoned for summer." But it is summer, after all... All around there are poor marsh pines eaten by lichen, gnarled birch trees, strangely worn out pathetic marsh fir-trees, vainly pulling their heads towards the stingy northern sky, somehow hopelessly bristling their branches, reminiscent of rags of green needles. An unattractive view it is... And this marsh, disguised by poor greenery, is spread as far as the Arctic Ocean. It is cheerless, hopeless, bereft of both the memory of a happy past, and of a hope for a better future. In general, all of Finland is reminiscent of an old faded watercolor, and its thousand lakes look at you with their old woman's watering eyes... Everything is somehow archaic, serious, like a sick child's face, and at the same time, every-

строгой наивности, которая наполняет каждое движение взрослого сильного человека.

А спросите финляндца, — он не променяет это корявое, скупо освещённое болото ни на какой благословенный уголок в целом мире. Святая любовь к родине проявляется здесь, может быть, в самой убедительной и яркой форме... И я понимаю этого угрюмого «пасынка природы», который с такой трогательной нежностью относится к своему родному святому углу. Прибавьте к этому, что в лесу ржавый мох вместо травы и, главное, нет тех безыменных лесных птичек, которые своим беззаботным щебетаньем, тревожным писком и незамысловатыми песенками оживляют леса средней России. И скупое солнце, которое отпускает здесь свою животворящую теплоту в микроскопических, аптекарских дозах, и короткое лето, и суровая зима с её саженными снегами, иссушающим холодом, вьюгами и метелями, — всё сошлось здесь в одну семью. Но эту обиженную Богом природу согревает любовь тех, кто пользуется более чем скромными её благами. Да, иногда некрасивых женщин любят больше, чем записных красавиц. Если хотите, есть какая-то высшая справедливость, которая нивелирует и корректирует пробелы и недочёты естественного порядка вещей, точно старается пополнить ошибки и несправедливость собственного творчества.

Тянулись скучные и однообразные летние дни. Конечно, природа — вещь хорошая и сама по себе интересная, но лучшей и самой интересной частью этой природы является всё-таки человек. Мои соседи вели обычный всем петербургским дачникам образ жизни, то есть мужчины утром уезжали в Петербург на службу, а вечером возвращались. Дамы вели жизнь затворниц и в своих дачных стенах продолжали свои неустанные женские дела. Мимо дачи утром торопливо шли на вокзал «дачные мужья», проезжали туда же чухонские «вейки», а потом проходили разносчики с разным съедобным товаром — и больше ничего. В течение двух

thing is filled with some serious naïveté that fills every movement of a vigorous adult male.

Try asking any Finn: he will never exchange those gnarled
poorly lit marshes for any blessed part in the whole world.
Sacred love for the motherland manifests itself here, probably,
in the most convincing and brightest form... And I understand
this gloomy "Step-son of Nature," who feels such touching
tenderness toward his native home. Add to this picture the
rusty moss instead of grass in the forest, and what is the most
important, there are none of those nameless wild birds, making the woods of central Russia so alive with their light-
hearted twittering, and their warning cheeping and simple
songs. And here the stingy sun, which releases its life-giving
warmth in microscopic drug store doses, and short summers,
and severe winters with their foot-deep snows, blistering dry
cold, snowstorms and blizzards—everything came together
here as one family. But this God-forsaken land is warmed by
the love of those who use its more than modest gifts. Yes,
sometimes plain women are loved more than stunning beau-
ties. You can put it like this: there is some supreme justice,
which smoothes over and corrects gaps and deficiencies in the
natural order of things, as though it were trying to correct and
erase mistakes and injustice of its own creation.

Boring and monotonous summer days were creeping on. Of
course, nature is good and interesting even of itself, but a
human being, by all means, is the best and the most interesting
part of this nature. My neighbors were following a usual rou-
tine typical for all St. Petersburg's summerhouse dwellers: the
men were leaving for work in the morning, and were returning
in the evening. The ladies were leading hermits' lives, and
within the walls of their houses they continued with their
usual female preoccupations. In the morning, "country cottage husbands" were hurriedly passing by my house rushing
towards the railway station, Finnish carts were also heading
there, and then the street vendors were walking past, carrying
their eatable goods,—and that was all. Within two weeks,

недель невольно выучишь каждое дачное лицо и вперёд знаешь, когда и кто пойдёт мимо. Вообще никаких впечатлений.

Раз утром я проснулся довольно рано и услышал доносившиеся из леса мерные удары топора. Это уже было целым событием в нашей болотной жизни. Невольно являлись вопросы: кто рубит и зачем рубит? Какой смелый пионер забрался в эту чухонскую трущобу? Не дожидаясь утреннего чая, я отправился через дорогу в лес и ещё издали увидел двигавшееся в сетке деревьев красное пятно, то есть красную кумачную рубаху таинственного незнакомца, нарушавшего мёртвый покой нашего лягушатника. Подхожу ближе и вижу высокого, широкого в кости, бородатого русского мужика, который с каким-то ожесточением хлещет топором по чахлой, искривлённой берёзе.

— Бог помочь...

— Милости просим...

Таинственный незнакомец смотрел на меня через очки, связанные верёвочкой. Вероятно, он счёл нужным из вежливости улыбаться, и эта добродушная улыбка как-то особенно шла к его богатырской фигуре, — ведь все слишком сильные физически люди отличаются добродушием. Кроме того, от могучей фигуры незнакомца так и пахну́ло чем-то давно знакомым и родным, точно мы только недавно расстались. Низкорослые, сморщенные и с какими-то чахлыми бородёнками чухонцы рядом с этим богатырём казались какими-то медицинскими препаратами, какие сохраняются на поучение благородного потомства в банках со спиртом по разным специальным музеям.

— Расейский будешь? — спросил я.

— Считай подальше, барин.

— Из Сибири?

— Около того... Про Тобольскую губернию слыхал?

— И слыхал, и живал...

— Ну, так она самая, матушка... да. Одним словом: пространство. А только желторотые сибиряки это — опять особь статья, а у меня отец, значит, был Московской губернии...

whether you like it or not, you will learn by heart each local face, and even could guess in advance who would go past and when. No new impressions at all.

One morning I awoke rather early and heard measured strikes of an axe in the forest. That by itself was an event in our country life on the marshes. Involuntarily there appeared some questions: who fells and what for? What brave adventurer came to this Finnish thicket? Not waiting for my morning tea, I went to the forest across the road, and from afar, I noticed a red spot moving behind the net of branches, the red cotton shirt of a mysterious stranger who disturbed a deathly silence of our frog's pond. I came closer and saw a tall, broad-boned bearded Russian peasant who with frantic zeal was thrashing with his axe a wilted bent birch tree.

"May God help you..."

"Welcome..."

The mysterious stranger was looking at me through his glasses tied with a string. Probably, he decided to smile because of politeness, and the kind smile was especially becoming to his giant figure—it is known that all physically strong people are notoriously good-natured. Moreover, I felt a puff of something very familiar and dear in the mighty figure of the stranger, as if we had only recently parted. In comparison with this epic hero, the Finns, short, shriveled, with their thin tiny beards, looked like medical freaks preserved in special museums for the education of future generations.

"Are you Russian?" I asked.

"Count a little further, mister."

"From Siberia?"

"Close... Did you hear about Tobolskaya Guberniya?"

"Both heard of it and lived there..."

"That's our mother right there... yes. In a word—it's a space. And Siberian callows, they belong to a quite another category, and my father, I mean, came from Moskovskaya Guberniya... You know, from the former

Значит, из прежних дворовых... да... За какие качества попал он в эту самую немшоную Сибирь, — старик-то нам не сказывал. Известное дело, не своей волей. Ну, а я вот опять в Расею выворотился, то есть не в самую Расею, а к чухне попал.

— Далеконько...

— А уж, видно, так Бог велел... Всё от Бога. Значит, сперва-то я овдовел, ну, ребята раньше вымерли, а тут племянница из Питера пишет: «Так и так, дядя, приезжай... Де́ла найдётся». Ну, и разное такое протчее. Ну, я продал избёнку (неважная была), хлам разный ...

Сибирский богатырь почесал в затылке и прибавил уже другим тоном:

— А вот топор до сих пор жаль... Сам-то давал за него сорок копеек, а продал на базаре за пятачок. Хороший был топор, не чета здешним, чухонским. Здесь только одно звание, что топор, а взять в руки нечего...

Богатырь показал свой топор, презрительно взмахнул им в воздухе и прибавил:

— Вон какая бабья орудия... Разве такие топоры-то бывают? Ты им ударишь по дереву, а он отскакивает да ещё звонит, как игрушка. Вот как жаль своего-то, тобольского топора... Не топор был, а угодник. Верно говорю... Слово-то одно: топор, а вещь-то даже совсем кожей наоборот выходит... Да и то сказать: чухонец малоёмный народ, значит, бессильный, ну где же ему управиться с настоящей-то орудией? Одно уже к одному: по бабе веретено, а по мужику — топор.

Между разговором сибирский богатырь продолжал свою работу. В каждом движении чувствовалось то рабочее уменье, когда напрасно не расходуется ни малейшего усилия, и невольно кажется, что топор как-то сам собой точно липнет в дерево, а столетние пни сами собой с каким-то стариковским покряхтыванием выдираются из земли. Сибиряк и разговаривал с ними, как с живыми существами.

— Ну, ну, чего ещё держишься-то? Ишь ведь, как ухватился за землю корневищем, точно руками... Другой

house serfs... yes... For what qualities he had found himself in that redneck Siberia, the old man never told us. It is clear, not by his will. And here I am returning to Russia, I mean, not to Russia itself, but to the Finns."

"Quite far..."

"I think it was God's will, really... Everything is by His will. Well, first, I lost my wife, well, my children had died earlier, and that time my niece wrote from Piter: 'Such and such. Come to me, uncle... You will find a job'. Well, and so on. So I sold my hut (it was not very good), along with some other useless trinkets..."

The Siberian giant scratched his head and added in a different tone:

"Though I still miss my axe... I myself had bought it for forty kopecks, but sold it for a nickel in the market. It was a good axe, not a local Finnish kind... Here they only call this an axe, but there it's nothing to hold in hand..."

Hercules showed his axe, contemptuously waved with it and added:

"Here it is a woman's tool... Can such an axe exist? I strike with it on the tree, but it rebounds off the tree, and even clinks, like a toy. I miss my own axe from Tobolsk... It was not an axe, but a saint. I speak the truth. This one is only called an axe, but this thing is something opposite to it. I can say that Finns are feeble people, I mean, weak, so how can they manage to deal with a real tool? It only proves that the right spindle is for the right woman, and the right axe is for the right man."

While telling that, the strapping Siberian fellow continued his work. In each of his movements one could feel the working skill, where not a bit of energy is wasted, and one gets an impression that the axe sticks to the tree by itself, and hundred year old stumps are pulling out of the ground by themselves groaning like old timers. The Siberian even talked to them as if they were live beings:

"Come on, come on, why are you still holding? Look how it grasped the ground with its roots, as if with hands... Another

пень, который помоложе и не успел ещё подгнить, сидит в земле, точно зуб во рту. Одним словом сказать: пререда.

— Ведь это тяжёлая работа корчевать пни?

— А работа от человека... Одному — всё тяжело да трудно, а другому — всё легко. Всё от карахтера и от сноровки... Заставь-ка меня обедню служить, так я бы вот как устал с непривычки.

— А тебя как зовут?

— Прежде-то Иваном Тихонычем величали, а по фамилии — Середонин. Отец-то у меня писался Мокроносовым, а как я вышел Середонин — не могу знать. Ну, Середонин так Середонин... От слова-то не убудет и не прибудет... Другие фамилии попадаются прямо обидные... У нас был приказчик на барже Дураков... Он и у преосвященного хлопотал, чтобы выдали ему другую фамилию... Ну, ничего не вышло... Да она, другая фамилия-то, и к лицу иногда подойдёт... Наш-то Дураков действительно малым делом дурашлив был. Оно и вышло, что по шерсти волку и кличка... Носи да не потеряй...

Попался какой-то узловатый корень, который никак не желал вылезать из земли, несмотря на все усилия обрубить его топором или выворотить ломом. Середонин остановился и только покрутил головой.

— Это, барин, дурак навязался... да... Ни взад ни вперёд, а место напрасно занимает. И люди такие бывают... Значит, в голове-то, в черепушке, пустым-пусто, а словами вот как привяжется. Не дай Бог с таким-то пустым человеком связываться... Не отцепишься от него.

— А ты плавал на барже? — спросил я.

— А то как же? — удивился Середонин, точно каждый человек должен плавать на барже. — Можно сказать, всю Обь-матушку на барже-то без малого произошёл... Ох! и велика только наша матушка Обь... В другом месте разольётся, так и берегов не видать. Расейским-то рекам далеко до Оби... Недаром остяки её святой считают и даже молятся. Известно, нехристи... Каждый пень ему бог. Пряменько сказать: омморошный народ... А вот что

stump, a little younger, and not even slightly rotten yet, is sitting in the ground like a tooth in the mouth... In one word, it is nature."

"This is difficult work to stub up stumps, isn't it?"

"It depends on the man... For one man everything is difficult and heavy, for another man everything is easy. Everything depends on character and skills. Make me officiate at divine service, I would get deadly tired, not being used to it."

"What is your name?"

"Before people called me Ivan Tikhonovich, and my last name is Seredonin. My father's last name was Mokronosov, and how I got 'Seredonin'—I do not know. So what: let it be Seredonin... Nothing can be good or diminishing from a word... Other last names can be really offensive... On our barge there was a clerk Durakov... He even tried to persuade the Bishop to allow him to get another last name... Well, everything was in vain... It happens that some last names can sometimes match the character... Our Durakov was really a little stupid. So it happens that a wolf is called Gray from its fur... Wear it and don't lose it..."

Then some knotted root stuck out, and it did not want to be pulled out of the ground, in spite of all the attempts to lop off or drag it out with a crowbar. Seredonin stopped and only shook his head:

"This one, mister, is a stubborn dummy... well... At a standstill, and only occupies the space for nothing. And there are some people like that... So, there is nothing in the head, absolutely empty skull, but he can impose with his words on you so... God forbid dealing with such dummy... You will not be able to break free off him."

"Did you sail on a barge?" I asked.

"Of course!" Seredonin was surprised, as if every man should sail a barge. "I can say that I went along the whole River Ob, our mother... Oh, such a big river, our mother Ob... In some places, it can overflow its banks, so that one cannot see them. Russian rivers cannot be compared with Ob... For a reason the Ostyaks consider it divine and even pray to it. It is known, that they are pagans... Each stump is a god for them. To tell the truth, they are weird people... But as to vodka, they understand everything

касаемо водки, так это вот как отлично даже понимает. Хлеба не умеет есть, а водку лакает даже очень превосходно. Можно сказать прямѣнько, что из-за этого своего лакомства и пропадает... Купцы-то спаивают остяка и всё у него отбирают, да и самого по пути в кабалу возьмут. Не выкупиться ему, остяку-то... Ну, он с горя мухомор настаивает и пьёт, пока не одуреет окончательно.

II

Таким образом завязалось дачное знакомство. Мой сибиряк «Трататон» питался всухомятку разной дрянью, запивая свою еду болотной водицей, и был как-то по-детски рад, когда я начал ему посылать чего-нибудь горяченького: супу, варёной говядины, горячей картошки «в мундире», горячего чаю в медном охотничьем чайнике и т. д.

— Первое это дело — горяченького хлебнуть, — благодарил Трататон. — Великая в ём сила, значит, в горячем... Так по всем жилкам и прокатится, а главное — в животе тепло. Это — первое дело, чтобы живот был тёплый. Оно хоть и есть поговорка, что «держи голову в холоде, брюхо — в голоде, а ноги — в тепле», только это — неправильно. Плепорции настоящей нет... Да.

Старик любил употреблять разные мудрёные слова и, видимо, гордился этим исключительным даром, как бывалый человек. Про себя в прошлом он отзывался таинственной фразой: «Бывали рога в торгу...»

— У нас в Тобольской-то губернии народ совсем отличный от расейских, — объяснял он. — С бору да с сосенки набрались, ну, и всякий по-своему живёт... Первое дело: господ нет, значит, помещиков, а всякий промышляет в свою голову. Что наработал, то и получил...

— А чиновники?

— Чиновник-то? Ну, это прежде чиновник был велик в перьях, а теперь его даже незаметно... Даже становых нет, а заседатели. Писаря́ больше орудуют... Тоже вот и земство ещё не налажено. Кто ежели с умом, так вот как жить

excellently. They don't know how to eat bread, but lap vodka quite superbly. To say it straightforward, they come to a bad end because of this delicacy... Merchants make them drunkards and fleece them, and on the way, they got into bondage to the merchants. There is no way to pay off the debts... And the Ostyak, because of his misfortune, makes a potion of fly-agaric mushrooms and drinks this until he gets high."

II

Thus, our country friendship had started. My Siberian "Trataton" lived on snacks and washed them down with marsh water, and showed child-like joy when I began to send to him some hot meals: soups, boiled beef, hot potatoes boiled in their skins, hot tea in a hunter's copper pot, and other treats.

"This is the first thing—to have a drop of something hot," Trataton would thank me. "A hot meal has great power, you know... It rolls in all your veins, and the main thing—that it is warm in the stomach. This is the main thing, to keep one's belly warm. Though there is a saying, 'Keep your head cold, your belly hungry, and your feet warm', but it is wrong. There is no real proportion... Yes."

The old man liked to use different outlandish words, and obviously, as an experienced man, he was proud of this exclusive gift. Telling about his past, he used a mysterious statement: "I used to fight for my own hand..."

"People in our Tobolskaya Guberniya are absolutely different from Russians," he explained. "They 'got together a scratch lot,' well, so everyone lives in his own way... The most important thing is, there are no landlords, there is no master, and everyone has his own business. What one earns, one gets..."

"And what about the officials?"

"And what about the officials? It was in the old times when an official was a big bird in feathers, but he is not noticeable anymore... Even now, there are no local police superintendents, but only assessors. Clerks are at work more... Also *zemstvo* has not been established yet... If one has a head, one can survive... Our mother Siberia is huge, everything is in plenty, well, so

можно... Велика матушка Сибирь, всего через край, ну, значит, расейской тесноты и не знают. Ещё столько народу нагнать — всем ме́ста хватит... Вольных местов неочерпаемо...

Последнее мнение о «неочерпаемом» множестве свободной земли в Сибири идёт совершенно вразрез с исследованиями разных казённых комиссий, которые в Сибири свободной земли нигде не нашли...

О своей реке Оби старик говорил с какой-то особенной нежностью, как говорят о близком, родном человеке.

— Другой такой реки нигде не сыщешь, — убеждённо говорил он при всяком удобном случае. — Только лиха беда, что в устье-то её льды запирают чуть не на целый год... По-настоящему-то ей и цены нет, а пропадает, можно сказать, совершенно здря. Так, мало-мало рыбой промышляют по пескам... Песками называют там мелкие места, куда рыба икру выходит метать... Ну и рыба на этих песках... И какая рыба: осетёр, нельма, стерлядь, моксун... Первый сорт рыба. Глядел я волжскую рыбу, — ничего не стоит. Жиру в ней нет настоящего... А наша обская стерлядь жирная, и жир у неё жёлтый, как воск. Которые есть настоящие господа, так прямо её живую едят... Лучку покрошишь, перчиком её вспрыснешь, уксуском обольёшь, лучше закуски не бывает. Она и на вилке-то ещё шевелится... Да. Смеются надо мной, когда здесь рассказываю, а потому, что настоящего скусу не понимают... Ведь икру-то сырую едят, — то же самое и выходит. Так мы этой рыбы целую баржу набьём, тыщи три пудов надо считать... Рыбка-то укладывается вот всё одно, как поленница дров. Ну, а приедем в Тобольск, там уж её и разберут по сословиям... Богатеющее дело, ежели купец с умом...

Трататон остановился, почесал в затылке и с улыбкой прибавил:

— А мы Дуракова-то, нашего приказчика, вот как тогда уважили... Больно лют был ругаться, и чуть что — сейчас в зубы. Карахтерный мужичонка оказался... Ну, мы его малым делом и поучили. Обвязали верёвкой да в воду и

people do not know the Russian lack of space. If one brings the same number of people, there will be space for as many. There, free space is inexhaustible..."

This opinion about "inexhaustible" land in Siberia totally contradicts the reports of different government commissions, which have not found any free land anywhere...

The old man would talk about the Ob River with special tenderness, like people would say things about a close, dear friend.

"You will never find such a river anywhere," he was repeating convincingly at any convenient moment. "Only it is a trouble that in its mouth ice locks it up almost for a year... It is really priceless, but it is wasted, I can say, for absolutely nothing. They only fish a little around the sandbanks... People call 'sands' some shallow places, where fish come for spawning... What fish there are on these sands! And what wonderful fish they are: sturgeon, inconnu, sterlet, muksun... The best of the best. I saw the Volga fish – it is not worth anything. It does not have real fat... But our Ob sterlet is fat, and its fat is yellow like wax. Some real connoisseurs even eat it alive... Chop some onion on it, sprinkle it with some pepper, pour on vinegar, and it cannot be a better appetizer. It even moves on your fork... Well. They laugh at me when I tell about this here, and the reason is that they do not understand what is really delicious... People eat caviar raw, don't they? So, it is the same. We used to stuff our barge with this fish, to a count of more than a hundred thousand pounds... The fish is piled one on one, like a firewood stake. Well, when we arrive in Tobolsk, they sort it out according to its kind... It is the most profitable business, if the merchant is smart..."

Trataton stopped, scratched his head, and added with a smile:

"And once we 'showed our respect' to Durakov, our clerk at that time... He cursed so fiercely, and if something was wrong, the same time he punched people in the face. He appeared to be a real bad character... So we taught him a little lesson. Tied him up with a rope and threw him in the water. So he had to swim behind the barge for about three miles, sturgeon-like."

бросили. Он за баржой-то у нас верстов с пять осетром плыл.

Пауза. Трататон с покрякиваньем рубит глубоко заползший в землю смолистый корень.

— Ну, а потом-то, что же Дураков-то?

— А ничего... Нам же ведро водки выставил, чтобы молчали. Совестно тоже... Один паренёк из наших было проболтался, так мы его своим средствием поучили... Растянули раба Божия да лычагами и вздули. Оно и вышло, что ешь пирог с грибами, а язык держи за зубами... Когда умнее будет, нам же спасибо скажет. Попадья Федосья Ивановна вот как смеялась, когда я ей рассказал.

— Какая попадья?

— А которой я дом с мензелином строил.

— Ты и домá умеешь строить?

— А то как же?.. Не на улице попадье-то жить. Ну, покучилась (попросила), я ей и приспособил хороминку. Она-то минюрнинькая (маленькая) такая, Федосья-то Ивановна, ну, я и дом такой наладил. Потом она мне вот какое угощенье устроила... Пирогов это со всякой всячиной напекла, а, как на грех, я в те поры (тогда) водки трёкнулся... Ну, попадейка меня угощает, а я съем три пирожка — и конец тому делу. Не могу больше, хоть расколи брюхо надвое. Очень даже обиделась Федосья Ивановна и даже гордостью попрекнула... Известно, женским делом сердце-то тут и есть. Тоже вот и племянница у меня: порох порохом. Никакого терпения не имеет... Всё ей сейчас вынь да положь, всё с срыву.

Проезжавшие мимо моей дачи чухонцы-извозчики имели скромную привычку к вечеру каждый день напиваться «вдребезги». Они останавливались около Трататона и заводили какой-нибудь разговор. Старик относился к ним свысока и любил пошутить. Разговоры велись приблизительно в таком роде:

— Озеро-то у вас есть? — спрашивал Трататон.

— Озеро-то? Нет озеро-то...

— Ну, значит, река есть?

— Нет река-то... Одна-то вода стоит, другая вода-то бежит...

Pause. Growling, Trataton is chopping the resinous root crawling deeply into the ground.

"And then, what did he do afterwards, that Durakov?"

"He did nothing... He even paid us with a bucket of vodka for our silence. He felt ashamed... One of our guys began to chat about that, so we taught him according to our ways... We stretched him on the ground and lashed him. As they say, 'Keep your breath to cool your porridge'... When he becomes more intelligent, he will thank us. The priest's wife, Fedosiya Ivanovna laughed so much when I told her that story."

"What priest's wife?"

"That one, for whom I built a house with a mezzanine."

"Can you build houses too?"

"You bet!.. The priest's wife could not live on the street. Well, she asked me, and I built her a small house. She is so miniature, Fedosiya Ivanovna, so I arranged the same kind of house for her. After that, she offered me such a meal... She baked pies with different fillings, but that time, as bad luck would have it, I had tanked up too much vodka... Well, she was serving me food, but I ate three pies and that was it. I was not able to squeeze any more, even if I had split my belly in half. Fedosiya Ivanovna got very much offended; she even reproached me with too much pride... It is known that women behave as their heart tells them. And my niece is the same way, like gunpowder. She does not have any patience... She wants everything here and now, right away."

The Finns-draymen passing my country house had a modest habit to get deadly drunk by the evening every day. They stopped by Trataton and started chatting. The old man treated them with arrogance and liked to make fun of them. The conversation was approximately conducted like this:

"Do you have a lake?" Trataton asked.

"Lake? No lake..."

"So you might have a river?"

"No, no river... Some water stays still, some water runs..."

— Вот-вот, это самое... Договорились, слава Богу. Значит, рыба есть?

— Рипа-то нет...

— И щуки нет?

— Чука-то нет...

— Ну, может, окуни там али ерши?

— Нет ерши-то...

— Ах вы, ежовые головы! Ничего-то у вас нет... Раков, может, ловите?

— Раки-то? Нет раки-то...

— А куда же господа с удочками ходят? Каждый день мимо меня идут...

— А наша-то рипа ловить...

Трататон только качал головой, а потом объяснил мне:

— Это самое чухно — мудрёное... В том роде, как наши остяки на Оби. Как говорится: ни из кузова, ни в кузов, как козьи рога. Пива с ними не сваришь... А только чухно куда похитрее остяков будет... Вон у них лошади какие... Меньше ста целковых и цены нет. Известное дело, господами кормятся... Повернулся один раз перед барином-то, ну, сейчас и получай двугривенный в зубы. Вот он, чухно, и сыт, и пьян, и нос в табаке... А всё-таки живёт справно, потому ему везде прибыль, — и с барина, и с земли, и с дороги.

С чухонцами словоохотливый сибиряк как-то не мог разговориться и отводил душу с бойким разносчиком Иваном Богданычем, который на своей тверской голове носил чуть не целый фруктовый магазин. Можно было только удивляться удивительной выносливости тверской шеи.

— Тяжёлая твоя работа, Иван Богданыч, — жалел Трататон. — Поди, вот как шея-то болит...

— Мы люди привычные... — уклончиво отвечал разносчик. — Сначала-то бывает даже очень трудно, а потом ничего... Шея-то точно вывихнута... Ягода-то ещё ничего, а вот арбузы донимают...

— Уж это известно... Тяжёлый он, этот самый арбуз.

— Господа очень уважают, ну и потрафляешь. Наше уж дело такое... Прежде-то я живой рыбой в Питере торговал.

"Well, well, it's what I mean... Thank God, we have agreed on something. So there is some fish?"

"No fish..."

"Don't you have pikes?"

"No pikes..."

"Maybe there are carps or ruffs by chance?"

"No ruffs..."

"Oh you, dumbheads! You don't have anything... Maybe you catch crawfish at least?"

"Crawfish? No crawfish..."

"Then where do the gentlemen go with their fishing lines? They go past me everyday..."

"You know, they go fishing our fish..."

Trataton only shook his head, and later he explained to me:

"These Finns are intricate... In the same way, they are like our Ostyaks on the Ob River. As they say, 'not out of the basket, not into the basket, like with goat's horns'. You will not get anywhere with them.... But these Finns are much cleverer than the Ostyaks... Look at their horses... Not less than one hundred rubles each. It is known that they earn money from the country cottage tenants... They show up in front of a gentleman, and get 20 kopecks on the spot. And so the Finns live in clover... And they live decently, because they get income from everything: from a city gentleman, and from the land, and from the road."

The talkative Siberian was not able to talk to the Finns too much, and he unloaded his heart with the smart street vendor Ivan Borganych, who carried on his Tver city's head the tray with almost the whole fruit store. One could only get astonished with such resiliency of this Tver's neck.

"You have a difficult job, Ivan Borganych," Trataton pitied him. "Your neck must hurt so much..."

"We people got used to this..," the vendor answered evasively. "At the beginning, it could be very difficult, but later it is not so bad... The neck is surely dislocated... It is quite tolerable with berries, but watermelons kill me..."

"Yes, everyone knows this... They are heavy, watermelons."

"Gentlemen like them very much, so I should please them.

Ну, это ещё, пожалуй, похуже будет... Шайка-то деревянная, тяжёлая...

— А что же до́ма-то? Не у чего жить?

— То-то вот и есть, что не у чего... Нас три брата... Ну, один управляется дома, большак, а мы кто чем промышляем. Надо кормиться.

— Вот-вот... Брюхо-то не зеркало и молча просит, как неправедный судия. Так старинные-то люди сказывали... А зимой-то куда?

— Тоже вразнос торгую в Питере... Из-за хлеба на квас...

— Так, так... Только и квас ваш питерский разный бывает: один — как вода, а другой — пожиже воды. Я вот тоже на чужой стороне околачиваюсь...

— Неужто у вас земли в Сибири мало стало?

— Да как тебе сказать-то? Кому много, а кому и нет ничего. По рукам она, матушка-землица, разобрана... Вот каждое лето сколько этих переселенцев к нам в Сибирь валит... Поищут, походят да назад оглобли поворотят...

О земле Трататон говорил с какой-то особенной нежностью.

— Конечно, всё от земли, — рассуждал он. — Теперь, к примеру, случись неурожай... Первым делом всякий красный товар станет, некому его покупать... И всё такое прочее. Попу́ и тому тяжело приходится... В недород и то, — кому охота жениться... Вот он, поп-то, голодный и распевает в пустой церкви. Тоже вот война эта самая сколько веку унесла... У меня, значит, здесь племянница в горничных живёт... Да... Так у ней на войне-то, сказывает, трёх женихов убили... Прежде-то женским делом скрывалась, значит, что касаемо женихов... Ну, а теперь всё одно. Так, придёт это, поскулит, поплачет бабьим делом, а взять не с чего...

— Уж это что говорить... Война-то во все стороны бьёт.

— И ещё как бьёт-то!.. Племяннице-то вот как обидно на японца... Поищи-ка теперь четвёртого-то жениха...

This is our business... Before I used to sell live fish in Piter... Well, that, I think, was more difficult... The washtub is wooden, heavy..."

"And what do you have at home? Can you earn your living there?"

"It is true, I cannot earn my living there... There are three of us brothers... So, one manages the house, the elder, and we, the other two of us, we make a living however we can. We need to sustain ourselves."

"Quite so... Our belly is not a mirror, and asks us in silence, like an unjust judge. The old timers used to say that... And where do you go in winter?"

"I also peddle in Piter... But it is barely enough to live from hand to mouth..."

"Well, well... Only daily bread in your Piter can also be different: some is bad, other is even worse. I am also hanging around in a foreign land..."

"Don't you have enough land in Siberia?"

"What can I say? Some people have a lot, and some don't have any. Our land, our Mother Earth, is all taken... See, every summer so many settlers throng to us, to Siberia... First they look around, walk around, and then go back where they came from..."

Trataton talked about land with particular tenderness.

"Certainly, everything is from the land," he speculated. "Now, for example, a year of poor crops comes... First, all luxury goods won't be sold, nobody can buy them... And everything the same kind... Even a priest suffers then... Who wants to marry in bad harvest... Here the priest, hungry, chants in an empty church. Also, this war has taken so many lives... My niece lives here, works as a maid... Yes... She tells that her three fiancés have been killed in war... At first, she, like all women, did not want to tell anything, as to her fiancés... But now she does not care anymore... So, she comes here, whines, cries in her womenfolk's manner, but cannot do anything..."

"What can you say?... The war hits from all directions."

"You bet!.. My niece is so angry with the Japanese... Just go

Не мышь, не поймаешь. Со стороны жаль смотреть, как бабочка убивается. Дело-то ещё не старое, пожить хочется, как другие прочие, а тут свет тебе клином...

III

Наступала осень, и солнце, по картинному выражению Трататона, «начало задумываться».

— Светит-то светит, а силы в ём настоящей нету, — объяснял он. — Всё одно, как старый человек. Мудрёно сотворено у Господа. Только вот мы-то ничего не видим... Нас-то, как слепых щенков, надо прямо рылом в молоко тыкать... Главное: понятия в нас настоящего нет, значит, что и к чему принадлежит. У Бога-то везде порядок, а вот у нас в черепушке (в голове) труха насыпана, особенно ежели который человек возгордится. Самое это последнее в человеке дело: гордость... да. У нас так-то в Тобольске один купец возгордился. Нет его лучше, — и конец тому делу. Ну, гордился он, гордился, а лавка-то с товаром и сгорела. Вперёд не гордись... Такой же случай с чиновником был... Этот уж совсем превознёсся от гордости и руки никому не подавал... А тут ревизия, ну, его и по шапке. Ступай, милый, на все четыре стороны! Оно уж завсегда так бывает.

Старик любил пофилософствовать, причём постоянно иллюстрировал свои мысли живыми примерами. Как у человека бывалого, недостатка в материалах у него не было, хотя выводы и заключения на основании этих материалов получались иногда совсем оригинальные. Долбит-долбит Трататон какой-нибудь упрямый пень, остановится перевести дух и проговорит свою любимую фразу:

— Главное дело: по правде надо жить... да. Ежели бы теперь все человеки сговорились промежду себя: «Братцы, давайте жить по сущей, истинной правде...» Ведь это всё одно, что получили бы агромадный капитал. Ей-богу... Дела-то, конечно, у всех разные, а правда-то матушка для всех одна... Уж это верно!..

and find now a fourth fiancé... It is not a mouse to catch. From an outsider's viewpoint, it is so sad to see how she grieves. She is still not old, and she wants to live like others, and here it is—every avenue comes up a dead end..."

III

The autumn was coming, and according to Trataton's poetic expression, the sun "began to plunge into a reverie."

"It certainly shines, but does not have a real power anymore," he explained. "Like an old man. It is hard to understand Our Lord's creation. Only we are not able to see everything... We, like blind puppies, should have milk thrust under our noses... The main thing is that we do not have any true understanding, what belongs to what. God keeps everything in order, but what we have in our stupid head is trash, especially if one becomes conceited about something. Pride is the worst thing in a man... oh, yes... Once in Tobolsk, one merchant became very proud. He is the best and that's it. So, he nurtured his pride, grew it, and one day his store and all its goods burned down. Don't get a swelled head ever... The same happened to one official... That man got entirely stuck-up in his pride, so that he even did not shake hands with anyone... At that moment the inspection came, and he was up to his neck with it. Go, my dear wherever you choose! It always happens like that."

The old man liked philosophizing, and constantly illustrated his thoughts with real-life examples. As an experienced man, he never was short of material for that, though his conclusions and deductions on the basis of that material sometimes came out very original. Trataton hews, hews some stubborn stump, then stops to catch his breath and says:

"The main thing is that a man should live according to truth... yes. If now all people agreed among themselves: 'Brothers, let's live according the very gospel truth.' This would be the same as getting a huge fortune. Really and truly...

Мысль об этой всеобщей правде засела в голове Трататона гвоздём, как живой результат собственного жизненного опыта.

— Вот в Питере понастроены пятиэтажные дома… А ведь хозяин-то не будет жить во всех пяти этажах. Так? Значит, всё дело для корысти сделано… Она, эта самая корысть, съедает живого человека, как ржавчина. И всё-то человеку мало, и всё-то он завидует, и всё-то ему кажется в чужом рту кусок велик. Жаль со стороны глядеть, как жадный-то человек беспокоится целую жисть. А только он одного не подумает: умрёт, и всё останется… У меня вот, кроме своих двух рук, ничего нет, а я не ропщу. Слава Богу, и жисть прожил, и свой хлеб ел… Маленький кусок хлеба, а всё-таки он свой…

Да, наступала осень. К станции со всех сторон потянулись воза с мебелью и разным домашним скарбом. Начался перелёт всякой дачной птицы на зимовку…

Мне как-то было особенно жутко расставаться с Трататоном. Ведь в другой раз не встретимся… Он проводил меня до станции и проговорил на прощанье с грустью в голосе:

— Гладкой дороги, барин…

— Спасибо, Трататон.

Everyone, of course, has his own interest, but the mother truth is the same for everybody... This is the real truth!.."

This idea about this universal truth became firmly fixed in Trataton's head, as a living result of his life experience.

"See here, in Petersburg they built five-story houses... But an owner is not going to live on all five floors, is he? So, all of that was done for love of gain... This greediness eats a man alive like rust. And all the time, everything is not enough for a man, and all the time he is envious, and all the time he sees that the grass is greener on his neighbors' lawn. It is pitiful to see how a greedy man worries his whole life. And he forgets only one thing: he will die, but everything will stay here... For instance, I do not have anything except my two hands, but I do not complain. Thank God, I have lived my life and eaten my own bread... A small piece of bread, but still my own..."

Yes, the autumn was coming. The wagons, loaded with furniture and different household goods, were going to the railway station from all directions. It was the time for all "country house birds" to fly towards their winter quarters...

I felt especially sorry to part with Trataton. After all, we will not see each other again... He saw me off to the station and said sadly at parting:

"Good journey, my lord..."

"Thank you, Trataton."

Lydia Dmitrievna Zinovieva-Annibal

Электричество / Electricity

Илья Ефимович Репин (1844–1930). Портрет Е.Г. Мамонтовой. 1879.

I. Repin. *The Portrait of E.G. Mamontova.* 1879.

LYDIA DMITRIEVNA
ZINOVIEVA-ANNIBAL

1866–1907

Lydia Zinovieva-Annibal was a gifted poet, a talented writer, an original playwright, and a literary critic, not to mention her important role in the literary world of the 1900s. She was a well-known hostess of a literary salon, influential in that "Silver Age" time known for its abundance of talents in literature, visual and musical arts. The writer was a "literary lioness," an energetic uniting nucleus of the prominent artistic circle "Tower," which was holding its meetings in her apartment. There were famous receptions arranged by Lydia and her husband—a poet, literary critic and theoretician of Russian Symbolism, Vyacheslav Ivanov. The members of that literary circle called her Diotima in honor of Plato's "Diotima" from his *Symposium*. She played the role of inspirer for those who were starting out in the literary world, and created an atmosphere of "gifted femininity" (according to the philosopher Nikolai Berdyaev).

This woman is probably the most scandalous female artistic personality of the "Silver Age," the period which already was rich in exotic characters. During the Soviet times, she was stricken from the list of writers "worthy of mention" from the point of view of the Communist censorship. Rare notes in reference materials about Zinovieva-Annibal would often characterize her as "a typical representative of the corrupting nobility, enjoying digging in psychopathology, choosing hysterical char-

acters for her fiction, extreme egocentrism, ugly individualism, mysticism and eroticism."

Her name was returned to the readership only during Perestroika, when her poetry and fiction were published again and became available to the reading audience. Finally, her literary legacy was appreciated at its true value. The readers had an opportunity to decide for themselves who Zinovieva-Annibal was: the first female to write openly and describe lesbian love affairs. She was a gifted writer of narrative, who was the first to write about the interactions between people and animals with compassion for the stinging pain endured by the animals in the cruel human world, and with empathy for the suffering of the "lesser creatures."

The biography of Zinovieva-Annibal actually could become the basis of a novel. Born into a noble family, she had Swedish and Serbian blood in her veins. However, the subject of her special pride was her consanguinity with the Russian national poet Alexander Pushkin. Through these relations the poet was a descendant of Pushkin's grandfather, Abram Gannibal (Annibal), who was (according to the popular version) a son of an Ethiopian prince, and Peter the Great's godson. This kinship was a matter of pride for Lydia, and the reason that she decided to accept that pen name, adding the last name of that prominent man to her maiden name, Zinovieva.

However, the path to literary fame was, for Lydia, rather long and not at all smooth. From her childhood, she differed from the girls of her age. She was talented, energetic, independent, self-confident and eccentric, and she was noted for her rebellious nature. This was why Lydia was expelled from school for disobedience. When her parents hired a tutor for her, she fell in love with him and also fell under the spell of the socialist ideas she learned from him. As a result of that affair, she ran away from home and married her tutor; she had three children with him. Then she became disillusioned with this marriage, took the children and left her husband and Russia. While Lydia was abroad, in 1895, she met her future second husband, Vyacheslav Ivanov, a poet, a critic and a scholar. It was love at

first sight; she was happily married to Ivanov to the end of her life. Lydia died at the age of forty of scarlet fever while taking care of sick children in the village. After her death, the poet Alexander Blok said, "What she could give to Russian literature, we cannot even imagine."

Lydia began to publish fiction in 1889, and from her very first stories, her fiction was imbued with compassion for poor people. Though she wrote beautiful poetry and dramas, real fame was brought to her by her narrative pieces in 1907, when the tale "Thirty-three Abominations" and the collection of stories *Tragic Menagerie* were published.

One of Lydia's best short stories is "Electricity." In comparison with the other writings, it does not have any real plot, resembling rather a sketch of an impressionist painting, like a stream of consciousness framed by a travel episode. This story is written as a realization of her idea of distancing a narrator from the described reality. She had a dream to create a different type of realism, which can impress a reader with its "careful sluggishness." This can be clearly seen in Zinovieva-Annibal's poetry, which she liked to mix in with her narratives:

"A darkened hot-red shield was sinking,

But could not drown,

Glowing in golden heaven streams..." (from the sonnet "White Night")

This fluctuation of reality, the instability of life, was a challenge for Zinovieva-Annibal, who desperately wanted to catch that exact moment of life in its fluidity and flickering changes. In "Electricity" she succeeds in catching that moment of a live reality by showing how the soul of the storyteller is "dissolving" into the air of the surrounding impressions. The writer shows how the soul is mentally "separated" from the physical body, flowing into the events the storyteller was observing. While reading this story, one can truly experience this magical "incorporeal flight" that Zinovieva-Annibal describes. She interweaves her narrative into the rhythm of the refined "lace" of poetry, blending them and creating her unusual style. It is not poetry, nor is it fiction, but an inseparable alloy of both.

ЛИДИЯ ДМИТРИЕВНА
ЗИНОВЬЕВА-АННИБАЛ

Электричество

На этот раз я решила обедать и пить утренний кофе в столовом вагоне.

Решила потому, что не имела в себе позыва снова ощутить то тягучее, глухое, знобящее истомление в совсем пустом теле, доставлявшее раньше какое-то тихое и очень изысканное сладострастие моим нервам, душе — молчание и полёт.

Душа молчала, словно мукою немного умирённая, словно несла и на своих запылённых крыльях частицу мутной и скорбной, в вирном вихре мчащейся земной жизни, причащалась ей тоской смертельной.

Дело в том, что я не сильна и устаю от неподвижного движения тряской, гулкой и безучастной быстроты...

И ещё в том, что я похожа на электрическую рыбу — её показывают в роскошных научных аквариумах; если к ней прикоснуться рукой — так чётко, сухо, как маленький разряд, ударит по ручным мускулам электрический ток. Мне говорили, что эти рыбы умирают в изнеможении, выпустив свою силу.

Каждый нерв моего тела — маленькая электрическая рыбка, и всё, что глядит, — а глядят на меня и люди и вещи, — прикасается ко мне, и всем я отдаю чёткими, сухими разрядиками свои токи до изнеможения — до смерти...

И это — не любовь, а электричество.

LYDIA DMITRIEVNA
ZINOVIEVA-ANNIBAL

Electricity

That time I decided to have lunch and drink my morning coffee in the dining car.

I decided to do that, because I did not have any urge to feel again that slow, indistinct, chilling languor in my entirely exhausted body—the languor, which used to give some quiet and very refined enjoyment to my nerves, and silence and a flight—to my soul.

My soul kept silent, as if the torment had subdued it a little, and as if my soul were carrying on its powdery wings a particle of turbid and sorrowful earthy life, which was rushing along in a turbulent vortex, and my soul followed it with its deadly anguish.

The thing is, I am not strong and I get tired of the motionless movement of a constantly shaking, resounding and indifferent speed...

And moreover, I resemble an electric fish,—it is demonstrated in luxurious research aquariums—if one touches the fish—then, so clear and so accurate, a small discharge, the electrical current will strike one's hand muscles. I was told that such fish die of exhaustion after having released all their power.

Each nerve of my body—like a tiny electric fish, and everything that looks at me—both people and things are looking at me—everything touches me, and I give away my power with clear and accurate discharges to exhaustion—to death...

And this is not love, just electricity.

И вот, когда дрожью я пронизывала гладко уносящиеся, плоские и прибранные поля, — ударялась о голые, размеренные стены безмятежных красно-кирпичных домиков, —

расчёсывалась сквозь ровные проборы саженых прозрачных лесков, —

трепеталась по доброкровным, широким лицам на строгих станциях, синим глазам и ртам, возглашающим и чрезмерно взволнованным, и по широким спинам высокоплечих лошадей в лёгких упряжках, — и переливалась, сочувствуя и не проникая, в души странных и тайных людей, что так близко теснились, рядом и напротив меня, — что вместе со мною, неподвижные в быстром лёте, мимо гладко убегающих предметов и пёстро-горланистых остановок, мчали свои участи радостей, пыток и разлук;

опустошаясь, отчуждаясь, изнемогало моё тело; тусклое, в слабых, остреньких ознобах умирало; а душа из большой тишины чрезмерного сочувствия вызволялась, получая тот крылатый, бестелесый полёт, который и есть начало и конец всякой жизни.

На этот раз, отправляясь в дальний путь, я не чувствовала позыва к муке знакомого полёта. Мои нервы все сжались одним нетерпеливым устремлением — вместе с поездом действенно преодолеть все эти пустые и слишком тесные пространства чужой, плоской и крикливой страны.

Домой нужно было, где — большое и страстное, и никому Завтра не обещано…

Поэтому, чтобы разбить сосредоточенность своих переливаний в попутные предметы, — я решила обедать и пить утренний кофе в столовом вагоне.

Против меня, за моим прикреплённым к стене столиком у зеркального окна, села прямая немка, высокая, полная, в дамской шляпе с сиренями, с сумочкой через плечи, пухлыми, крупными, белыми руками, приятно-мягким,

And when I was trembling, piercing the fields smoothly rushing along, flat and harvested—when I was striking against bare, monotonous walls of serene red-brick small houses,—

when I was brushing through straight partings of planted transparent small forests,—

when I was quivering at healthy wide faces at burdensome stations, the blue eyes and the mouths, exclaiming something and extremely agitated, on the wide backs of tall horses in light harness,—then I was flowing, sympathizing, but not percolating into the souls of those strange and mysterious people, who were clustering by my side and in front of me so closely; those people, who, like me, were frozen in their rapid flight, were passing the things, smoothly running away, and motley-noisy stations; those people were rushing, carrying with them their destinies of joy, torments, and separations;

and my body was draining, alienating itself, growing exhausted; it was getting dull and was dying in weak and sharp chills; and my soul was becoming free from the endless calm of overwhelming compassion and was gaining that winged incorporeal flight, which is really the beginning and the end of any life.

This time, leaving on a long journey, I did not feel the urge for the torment of this familiar flight. All my nerves were clenched by one impatient desire—to come forcefully, together with the train, through all the empty and too condensed space of this non-native, flat and loud country.

I wanted to return home, where everything was large and passionate, and Tomorrow was not promised to anyone...

That is why, to gain a distraction from my otherwise uninterrupted transposition into the objects passing along in succession, I decided to have lunch and drink my morning coffee in the dining car.

A German woman sat down at my small table, attached to the wall by the mirror-like window, just in front of me. She was, upright, tall, portly, in a bonnet decorated with lilacs, with a small purse hanging around her neck, with big plump, white hands, and

стареющим лицом и пустыми, совсем синими глазами. Она спросила чашку чаю и вгрызлась решительно и степенно крупными, белыми зубами в молочный хлебец через его хрусткую, золотистую корочку.

Мы долго сидели так, молча, я — потребляя свою порцию кофею, она — чаю.

Потом, вдруг, она подняла на меня свои синие пустые глаза, и я увидела, что они слегка косят. Это тотчас отметило её в моём восприятии: я отдала ей лёгкий, чуткий разрядик своего тока...

Она сказала строгим, ровным, густым голосом, приятным моему слуху и человека достойным:

— Я еду домой. Пробыла лето в Испании, в Пиренеях.

Я спросила, волнуясь:

— Вам было хорошо в горах?

— Да, там красиво и дико. Я отдохнула. Зимой я утомилась.

Не выручал удобный столовый вагон, приятный подносик с тёплым кофеем — моё тихое, трепетное волнение росло.

Какое дело мне до немки? А вот она говорит — слышу голос строгий и чужой и вижу немного тревожный взгляд синих косых глаз...

Она говорит:

— Вы вот кофе пьёте. А я его по утрам пить не могу. Только после обеда. Если бы хотя одну чашку выпила — на весь день была бы больна. Он на меня плохо действует... Прощайте! Доброго пути! Скоро моя станция.

Она плавно встала и, положив деньги на свой подносик, где остался металлический чайник с приподнятой крышкой и сливочник с недопитым молоком, прямая, прошла узким ходом между столиками и скрылась за раскатными дверьми ресторана.

Я ещё осталась сидеть. Меня бросало плавно из стороны в сторону, почти как на море. Плавно колыхалась вода в полуотпитом сифоне на соседнем столике.

a pleasantly mild aging face, with empty, bright blue eyes. She asked for a cup of tea, and resolutely and solemnly sank her big white teeth into the milk bread, through its crispy golden crust.

We were sitting like that for a long while, in silence: I—consuming my cup of coffee, and she—her tea.

Then, suddenly, she lifted up her empty blue eyes at me, and I noticed that she had a slightly lazy eye. Right away, this detail marked her in my perception: I gave her a light, sensitive tiny discharge of my current...

She said, with her reserved, steady deep voice, pleasant to my ear, and worthy of a human being:

"I am going home. I spent my summer in Spain, in the Pyrenees."

Excited, I asked:

"Was it good for you in the mountains?"

"Yes, it is beautiful and wild there. I rested. I had gotten tired during the winter."

The comfortable dining car, the pleasant tray with warm coffee did not help, because my quiet, anxious nervousness was growing.

Why do I care about this German woman? But when she is talking, I hear her reserved voice of a stranger, and I see the slightly worried look of her slightly disoriented blue eyes...

She says, "I see, you are drinking coffee. But I cannot drink it in the mornings. Only after lunch. If I drank even a cup—I would be sick the rest of the day. It does not make me feel good... Good-bye! Have a nice trip! We are approaching my station."

She stood up gracefully and, having left the money on her little tray, where remained a metal kettle with a slightly opened lid and a creamer with milk she did not finish. And she, upright, walked along the narrow aisle between the tables and disappeared behind the restaurant's sliding doors.

I remained sitting. I was swayed smoothly from side to side, almost as though I was on the high seas. The water was smoothly heaving in a half-empty carafe on the next table.

Я думала о немке. Потом решила забыть, чтобы не думать о человеке, которого никогда не встретишь и который состарится и умрёт без твоего ведома.

Но к чему же я узнала, что она не может пить кофею по утрам? Это было тепло, так животно, матерински, сестрински тепло — знать о ней, что она пьёт чай по утрам, а если кофей, то весь день после него больна.

Верно, это от сердца. У немки, верно, нездоровое сердце.

Но какое мне дело?

I was thinking about that German woman. Then I decided to forget her, in order not to think about a person whom one would never meet again, and who would get old and die without one's knowledge.

But why did I learn that she could not drink coffee in the mornings? That knowledge was warm, so much in the flesh, so motherly, so sisterly warm—to learn about her that she drank tea in the morning, but if she had coffee, she would be sick the rest of the day.

Probably, it was because of her heart. Perhaps, the German woman had a bad heart.

But why should I care?

Aleksandr Ivanovich Kuprin
По-семейному / Like a Family

Борис Кустодиев (1878–1927). Купчиха за чаем. 1918.

Boris Kustodiev. *Merchant's Wife at Tea*. 1918.

ALEKSANDR IVANOVICH KUPRIN

1870–1938

Aleksandr Kuprin is still one of the most popular writers in Russia, a representative of mature Russian Realism, the author of numerous stories and tales, written in a wide range of styles, from essay-type sketches to romantic love stories.

After the death of his father, Kuprin grew up in bitter poverty and the humiliation of being raised in a boarding school for poor children and struggling day to day to survive. Later, this would become one of the main motifs of his fiction. Kuprin finished army college and became an officer. However, he started dreaming about writing and not pursuing a military career.

A few years later, Kuprin retired from the military and moved to Kiev. He had a small suitcase and four rubles in his pocket, without any friends to support him, without knowledge of any profession or working skills. There, he had to live in cheap rented apartments, struggling, not having any serious permanent job to earn a living. Kuprin tried journalism, as well as many different temporary jobs, such as an actor, a fisherman, a real estate manager, a land surveyor, an organizer of circus performances, a dentist, a loader, and there were rumors that he even tried to join a monastery. Describing one of his characters, Kuprin actually meant to tell about his own fate, showing that man's very diverse life with many ups and downs. Regardless of all this, he did not lose his "kindness or his clarity of spirit under fate's whipping."

His intensive journalism work as a reporter for Kiev's newspapers helped the future writer. Kuprin gathered experience and impressions about Russian life of all social levels. There is plenty of "gloom and doom" in many of his strata. They reflected, like a mirror, the dark sides of Russian life, especially the lowest levels of his contemporary society—the bottom of life, called by Maxim Gorky "the lower depth." For example, Kuprin was the first to write the bitter truth about whorehouses—their dwellers and their clients. His tale "Pit" was severely criticized for its "naturalism," although it was filled with compassion towards women and condemnation toward the society for allowing such appalling exploitation of human beings.

That was a very productive Kiev period of his life (he started writing articles, essays, and short stories). He described that time in many narrative pieces. One of them is "Like a Family." In this story, Kuprin again touched upon the image of a Russian woman, who, in spite of her oppressed and humiliating condition, did not lose her spiritual innocence—kindness, compassion, and deep religious feeling. In all Kuprin's stories, a woman is a special being who always has an inexhaustible source of love and is able to keep purity and high spirit, courage, and mercy to others, and find forgiveness under any condition. In these qualities, Kuprin saw the real dignity of a female character. In the story "Like a Family," he created the image of a poor woman who, in spite of being at the bottom of society, kept her dignity and still tried to support others, comforting them with kind words. That character was so attractive to the writer that he created two versions of this story. The first one, in 1887, was called "Natashka" and was essentially a rough draft, the basis for the later second version developed in 1910.

Kuprin retold the same story under the title "Like a Family," with some changes and adding several details. He made it warmer, sunnier, and more optimistic. Kuprin also enriched the plot, making it brighter and livelier. He emphasized the idea of the unity of all people, forgiveness, and mercy on such miraculous days as Easter for Christians.

АЛЕКСАНДР ИВАНОВИЧ КУПРИН

По-семейному

Было это... право, теперь мне кажется порой, что это было триста лет тому назад: так много событий, лиц, городов, удач, неуспехов, радостей и горя легло между нынешним и тогдашним временем. Я жил тогда в Киеве, в самом начале Подола, под Александровской горкой, в номерах «Днепровская гавань», содержимых бывшим пароходным поваром, уволенным за пьянство, и его женою Анной Петровной — сущей гиеной по коварству, жадности и злобе.

Нас, постоянных жильцов, было шестеро, все — люди одинокие. В первом номере обитал самый старинный постоялец. Когда-то он был купцом, имел ортопедический и корсетный магазин, потом втянулся в карточную игру и проиграл всё свое предприятие; служил одно время приказчиком, но страсть к игре совершенно выбила его из колеи. Теперь он жил бог знает каким нелепым и кошмарным образом. Днём спал, а поздно вечером уходил в какие-то тайные игорные притончики, которых множество на берегу Днепра, около большого речного порта. Был он — как все игроки не по расчёту, а по страсти — широким, вежливым и фатальным человеком.

В номере третьем жил инженер Бутковский. Если верить ему, то он окончил лесной, горный, путейский и технологический институты, не считая заграничной высшей школы. И правда, в смысле всевозможных знаний он был похож на фаршированную колбасу или на чемодан, куда, собираясь в путь, напихали всякого тряпья сверх меры,

ALEKSANDR IVANOVICH KUPRIN

Like a Family

It happened... really, now it seems to me sometimes that it happened three hundred years ago: so many events, faces, cities, fortunes made, failures, joys and sorrows have taken place now and in those older days. At that time, I lived in Kiev, at the very beginning of Podol, down by hilly Alexandrovskaya street, in the rented apartments "Dneprovskaya Harbor," owned by the former boat cook fired for drinking, and his wife, Anna Petrovna, a real hyena considering her perfidy, greediness and meanness.

There were six of us, permanent tenants, and all were single people. The oldest tenant lived in the first apartment. He used to be a merchant, had a store selling orthopedic supplies and corsets before he was sucked into gambling and lost his business. For some time he worked as a shop manager, but his passion for gambling entirely knocked him out of normal life. Now he was getting by only God knows how. He slept during the day, and, then, late at night he left for some secret gambling dens: there are a lot of them on the Dnieper riverbank by the big river port. He was, like all gamblers, not by calculation, but by pure passion, a generous, polite, and fatalistic man.

The engineer, Butkovsky, lived in apartment three. If one is to believe him, he graduated from the Forest, Mining, Railway Communications, and Technological Colleges, not to mention some foreign higher educational institution. And truly, considering the knowledge of various facts, he was like a stuffed sausage, or a suitcase, packed for the road, into which one squeezed

придавили верхнюю крышку животом и с трудом заперли чемодан на ключ, но если откроешь, то всё лезет наружу. Он свободно и даже без просьбы говорил о лоции, об авиации, ботанике, статистике, дендрологии, политике, об ископаемых бронтозаврах, астрономии, фортификации, септаккордах и доминантах, о птицеводстве, огородничестве, облесении оврагов и городской канализации. Он запивал раз в месяц на три дня, когда говорил исключительно по-французски и по-французски же писал в это время коротенькие записочки о деньгах своим бывшим коллегам-инженерам. Потом дней пять он отлёживался под синим английским клетчатым пледом и потел. Больше он ничего не делал, если не считать писем в редакцию, которые он писал всюду и по всяким поводам: по случаю осушения болот Полесья, открытия новой звезды, артезианских колодцев и т. д. Если у него бывали деньги, он их рассовывал в разные книги, стоявшие у него на этажерке, и потом находил их, как сюрпризы. И, помню, часто он говорил (он картавил):

— Дгуг мой. Возьмите, пгошу вас, с полки Элизе Геклю, том четвёгтый. Там между двухсотой и тгёхсотой стганицами должны быть пять гублей, котогые я вам должен.

Собою же он был совсем лыс, с белой бородой и седыми бакенбардами веером.

В восьмом номере жил я. В седьмом — студент с толстым безусым лицом, заика и паинька (теперь он *прокурор с большой известностью*). В шестом — немец Карл, шоссейный техник, жирный остзеец, трясущийся пивопийца. А пятый номер нанимала проститутка Зоя, которую хозяйка уважала больше, чем нас всех остальных, вместе взятых. Во-первых, она платила за номер дороже, чем мы, во-вторых, — платила всегда вперёд, а в-третьих, — от неё не было никакого шума, так как к себе она водила — и то лишь изредка — только гостей солидных, пожилых и тихих, а больше ночевала на стороне, в чужих гостиницах.

Надо сказать, что все мы были и знакомы и как будто бы незнакомы. Одолжались друг у друга заваркой чая, иголкой, ниткой, кипятком, газетой, чернилами, конвертами и бумагой.

different clothes over and above the top, pressed the cover closed with one's belly, and with a lot of difficulty locked the suitcase, but when opened, everything would fall out. He freely, and without even being asked, could talk about sailing directions, aviation, botany, statistics, dendrology, politics, brontosauruses, astronomy, fortifications, seventh-chords and dominants, about raising poultry, vegetable growing, the forestation of ravines and a city's sewage. He had fits of hard drinking once a month for three days, then he spoke entirely in French, and in that time he wrote short messages in French, asking his former colleague-engineers for money. Then for five days, he would lie under a blue English checkered blanket and sweated. He did nothing else, except for writing letters to newspapers. He wrote everywhere on any occasion: the drying of the marches of the Polesie, the discovery of a new star, artesian wells, and so on. If he had money, by any chance, he shoved it into different books standing on his bookshelves to discover it later as a surprise. And I remember, he used to say (he burred):

"My fiend, could I ask you to take off the shelf *Élisée Eeclus*, volume four? There, between pages two hundedth and thee hundedth there should be five lubles I owe you."

He was entirely bald, with a white beard and gray fan-shaped sideburns.

I lived in apartment eight. In number seven—a student with a fat face without a mustache, a stutterer, and "a good boy" (now he is *a well-known prosecutor*). In apartment six lived a German, Karl, a road engineer, a fat Baltic German, a shaking beer-drunkard. And in number five there lived a prostitute, Zoya, whom the hostess respected the most among all of us together. First, she paid for the room more than we did, second, she always paid in advance, and third, she never was a source of noise, because she rather rarely brought clients, only respectable, old and quiet ones, and mostly she spent nights somewhere else, in different hotels.

I should say that we all were acquainted and unacquainted at the same time. We borrowed from each other tea, a needle, a thread, hot water, a newspaper, ink, envelopes, and paper.

Всех номеров было в нашем прибежище девять. Остальные три занимались на ночь или на время случайными парочками. Мы не сердились. Мы ко всему привыкли.

Наступила быстрая южная весна. Прошёл лед по Днепру: река разлилась так мощно, что до самого горизонта затопила левый, низменный черниговский берег. Стояли тёплые тёмные ночи, и перепадали короткие, но обильные дожди. Вчера деревья едва зеленовато серели от почек, а наутро проснулся — и видишь, как они вдруг заблестели нежными, яркими первыми листиками.

Тут подошла и Пасха с её прекрасной, радостной, Великой Ночью. Мне некуда было пойти разговеться, и я просто в одиночестве бродил по городу, заходил в церкви, смотрел на крестные ходы, иллюминацию, слушал звон и пение, любовался милыми детскими и женскими лицами, освещёнными снизу тёплыми огнями свечек. Была у меня в душе какая-то упоительная грусть — сладкая, лёгкая и тихая, точно я жалел без боли об утраченной чистоте и ясности моего детства.

Когда я вернулся в номера, меня встретил наш курносый коридорный Васька, шустрый и лукавый мальчуган. Мы похристосовались. Улыбаясь до ушей и обнаруживая все свои зубы и дёсны, Васька сказал мне:

— Барышня с пятого номера велела, чтобы вы зашли до её.

Я немного удивился. Мы с этой барышней совсем не были знакомы.

— Она и записку вам прислала, — продолжал Васька. — Вон на столе лежит.

Я взял разграфлённый листок, вырванный из записной книжки, и под печатной рубрикой «Приход» прочитал следующее:

«Глубокожамый № 8.

Если вам свободно и не по Брезгуете очень прошу вас зати ко мне У номер разговеца свячёной пасхой.

Извесная вам Зоя Крамаренкова».

Я постучал к инженеру, чтобы посоветоваться с ним. Он

In total, there were nine apartments in our shelter. The other three were rented by night or by hourly transient couples. We did not get irritated. We got used to everything.

The fast southern spring came. Ice floated down the Dnieper: the river flooded so powerfully that it covered the left lower Chernigov bank to the horizon line. There were warm dark nights, and short, but abundant showers fell. Yesterday the trees hardly showed up greenish from the gray butts, and when one woke up this morning, one could see how they suddenly shined with tender, bright, first leaves.

Then Easter came with its wonderful, jolly Holy Night. I did not have anywhere to go for a holiday lunch on the Lent break, and I simply was wandering alone around the city. I stepped into churches, watched church processions, illuminations, listened to bells and singing, admired lovely children's and women's faces lightened from below with warm candle lights. I felt in my soul some ravishing sadness: sweet, light and peaceful, as if I felt sorry without pain about the lost purity and brightness of my childhood.

When I came back to the apartments, there was our snub-nosed floor bellboy, Vaska, a smart and sly boy. We exchanged a traditional Easter triple kiss. Grinning from ear to ear and showing all his teeth and gums, Vaska said to me, "The lady from the number five asked you to come to her."

I was a little surprised. I was not acquainted with the lady at all.

"She even sent you a note," Vaska continued. "There it is, on the table."

I took a ruled page torn out of a notebook, and under the printed title "Income" read the following:

"Dear # 8,

"If you has free time and if you are no sqeemish I ask you to plis come to me to my room to have bleset pasha.

Knawn by you, Zoya Kramarenkova."

I knocked at engineer's door to ask for his advice. He was standing in front of the mirror and with persistence, with all

стоял перед зеркалом и с упорством всеми десятью пальцами приводил в порядок свои жёсткие, запущенные седины. На нём был лоснившийся сюртук, видавший виды, и белый галстук вокруг заношенного, порыжевшего с краю воротничка.

Оказывается, он тоже получил пригласительную записку. Мы пошли вместе.

Зоя встретила нас на пороге, извиняясь и краснея. У неё было самое заурядное, самое типичное лицо русской проститутки: мягкие, добрые, безвольные губы, нос немного картофелем и безбровые серые глаза навыкате — «лупетки». Но её улыбка — нынешняя, домашняя, безыскусственная улыбка, такая застенчивая, тихая и женственная — вдруг на мгновение делала лицо Зои прелестным.

У неё уже сидели игрок и шоссейный Карл. Таким образом, за исключением студента, здесь собрались все постоянные обитатели номеров «Днепровская гавань».

Комната у неё была именно такая, какой я себе её представлял. На комоде пустые бомбоньерки, налепные картинки, жирная пудра и щипцы для волос. На стенах линялые фотографии безусых и курчавых фармацевтов, гордых актёров в профиль и грозных прапорщиков с обнажёнными саблями. На кровати гора подушек под тюлевой накидкой, но на столе, покрытом бумагой, вырезанной, как кружево, красовались пасхи, кулич, яйца, нога ветчины и две бутылки какого-то таинственного вина.

Мы похристосовались с ней щека об щеку, целомудренно и манерно, и сели закусывать. Надо сказать, что все мы в этот час представляли собою странное и редкое зрелище: четверо мужчин, в конец изжёванных и изглоданных неудачной жизнью, четверо старых кляч, которым в общей сложности было во всяком случае больше двухсот лет, и пятая — наша хозяйка — уже немолодая русская проститутка, то есть самое несчастное, самое глупое и наивное, самое безвольное существо на всей нашей планете.

his ten fingers, he was putting order to his coarse neglected gray hair. He was wearing a shiny old jacket from time immemorial, and a white tie around the worn reddish-edged collar.

It turned out that he also had received the written invitation. We went together.

Zoya met us by the door, blurting out apologies and blushing. She had the most common, the most typical face of a Russian prostitute: soft, kind, weak-willed lips, a slightly potato-like nose and bulging gray eyes without eyebrows. But at that moment, her smile, homey and natural, so shy, quiet, and feminine, suddenly, for an instant, made Zoya's face charming.

Both the gambler and the road specialist, Karl, already were there. Thus, except for the student, all dwellers of the "Dneprovskaya Harbor" house came here together.

Her room was exactly as I had imagined. On the chest of drawers, there were empty bonbon boxes, glued pictures, oily face powder and curling irons. On the walls there were faded photos of young pharmacy employees without mustaches and with curly hair; proud actors in profile and brave warrant officers with naked sabers. There was a pile of pillows on the bed under the tulle cover, but on the table covered with lace-like cut paper, there were paskhas, a kulich, eggs, a leg of ham, and two bottles of some strange wine standing in a beautiful arrangement.

We chastely and affectedly exchanged triple kisses, cheek-to-cheek, and sat down to eat. I should say that all of us at that moment presented a strange and rare view. There were four men, chewed up and gnawed utterly to shreds by their unlucky destinies, four old horses, whose total age summed up could be more than two hundred years, and the fifth, our hostess, already not a young Russian prostitute, that is to say the unhappiest, the stupidest, the most naïve, and the most weak-willed creature on our Earth.

But how clumsily nice, shy and hospitable, friendly and simply sensitive she was!

Но как она была неуклюже мила, как застенчиво гостеприимна, как дружески и деликатно проста!

— Получайте, — ласково говорила она, протягивая кому-нибудь из нас тарелку, — получайте и кушайте, пожалуйста. Номер шестой, вы, я знаю, больше пиво пьёте. Мне Вася рассказывал. Так достаньте около вас под столом. А вам, господа, я налью вина. Это очень хорошее вино. Тенериф. У меня есть один знакомый пароходчик, так он его постоянно пьёт.

Мы четверо знали всё в жизни и, конечно, знали, на какие деньги был устроен весь этот пасхальный стол вместе с пивом и «тенерифом». Но это знание, однако, совсем не коробило и не угнетало нас.

Зоя рассказывала о своих ночных впечатлениях. В Братстве, где она отстояла заутреню, была страшная теснота, но Зое удалось занять хорошее место. Чудесно пел академический хор, а Евангелие читали сами студенты, и читали поочерёдно на всех языках, какие только есть на свете: по-французски, по-немецки, по-гречески, и даже на арабском языке. А когда святили на дворе пасхи и куличи, то сделалась такая толкотня, что богомольцы перепутали свои припасы и перессорились.

Потом Зоя задумалась, развздыхалась и стала мечтательно вспоминать Великую Неделю у себя в деревне.

— Такие мы цветочки собирали, называются «сон», синенькие такие, они первые из земли выходят. Мы делали из них отвар и красили яйца. Чудесный выходил синий цвет.

А чтобы жёлтый был цвет, так мы луком яйца обёртывали, шелухой, — и в кипяток. А то ещё разноцветными тряпочками красили. А потом целую неделю ходили по селу и били яйцо об яйцо. Сначала носиком, потом ж..кой, кто перебьёт другого, тот забирает себе. Один парнишка достал где-то в городе каменное яйцо — так он всех перекокал. Но когда дознались, в чём дело, то у него все яйца отняли, а самого поколотили.

И целую Святую Неделю у нас качели. Одни — большие посередь села: это общественные. А то ещё отдельно у каждых ворот маленькие качели — дощечка и пара верёвок. Так всю

"Take it," she was saying gently, handing a plate to one of us. "Take it and please eat." "You, number six, I know you like beer more. Vasya told me. So, take a bottle from under the table, it is near you. And I will pour some wine for you, gentlemen. This is very good wine. 'Tenerife'. I know one steamboat owner, and he always drinks it."

All four of us knew everything about life, and certainly, we were aware, with what money this Easter table was arranged, together with beer and "Tenerife" wine. However, this knowledge did not bother us or make us depressed.

Zoya was telling us about her Easter night impressions. In the Ecclesiastic Academy, where she attended the morning service, there was an awful crowd, but she managed to find a good spot. The Academy choir sang wonderfully, the students themselves read the New Testament, and read it, taking turns, in all languages of the World: in French, German, Greek, and even in Arabic. And when in the yard, pashas and kuliches were blessed, there was such a crush, that the pilgrims mixed up their possessions and quarreled.

Then Zoya pondered over something; she began sighing and started pensively to recollect the Holy Week celebration in her village.

"We were picking small flowers, called 'dream', blue ones when they were only poking through the ground. We boiled them and painted eggs. The blue color turned out wonderfully.

And to get the yellow, we wrapped the eggs in onion peels, and then put everything in boiling water. And also, we painted with multi-colored fabric shreds. And then we walked around the village and hit an egg against another egg. First, with its point, then with its butt, and who broke the other's egg, got that egg. One guy brought a stone egg somewhere from the city, beat us and he got all the eggs. But when people learned the reason, they took all the eggs from him, and beat him.

And during the whole Holy Week we had had the swings. One was large—in the middle of the village for the whole public. And also by each gate there was a separate small swing—a plank and a

неделю качаются все — мальчишки и девчонки, и все поют: Христос воскресе. Хорошо у нас!

Мы слушали её молча. Жизнь так долго и ожесточённо колотила нас по головам, что, казалось, навеки выбила из нас всякие воспоминания о детстве, о семье, о матери, о прежних пасхах.

Между тем коленкоровая занавеска на окне холодно поголубела от рассвета, потом стала темнеть и переходить в жёлтый тон и вдруг незаметно стала розовой от отражённого солнца.

— Вы не боитесь, господа, я открою окно? — сказала Зоя.

Она подняла занавеску и распахнула раму. Вслед за нею и мы все подошли к окну.

Было такое светлое, чистое праздничное утро, как будто кто-то за ночь взял и вымыл заботливыми руками и бережно расставил по местам и это голубое небо, и пушистые белые облака на нём, и высокие старые тополи, трепетавшие молодой, клейкой, благоухающей листвой. Днепр расстилался под нами на необозримое пространство — синий и страшный у берегов, спокойный и серебряный вдали. На всех городских колокольнях звонили.

И вдруг все мы невольно обернулись. Инженер плакал. Ухватившись руками за косяк оконной рамы и прижавшись к нему лбом, он качал головой и весь вздрагивал от рыданий. Бог весть, что делалось в его старческой, опустошённой и израненной душе неудачника. Я знал его прежнюю жизнь только слегка, по случайным намёкам: тяжёлая женитьба на распутной бабёнке, растрата казённых денег, стрельба из револьвера в любовника жены, тоска по детям, ушедшим к матери...

Зоя жалостно ахнула, обняла инженера и положила его седую, с красной бугристой плешью голову себе на грудь и стала тихо гладить его плечи и щёки.

— Ах, миленький, ах вы, мой бедненький, — говорила она певуче. — Сама ведь я знаю, как трудно вам жить. Все вы, как пёсики заброшенные... старенькие... одинокие. Ну, ничего,

couple of strings. And like that the whole week everyone swung—boys and girls, and all sang, 'Christ has risen!' It is so good there!"

We were listening to her in silence. Life had been pushing us around for so long and so hard, that it seemed that it knocked out of us any memories of childhood, of our families, mothers, previous Easters.

Meanwhile, calico curtains on the window became light, cold bluish from the sunrise, and then darkened and started to turn yellow, and suddenly became pink from the reflected rays of the sun.

"Do you mind if I open the window, gentlemen?" asked Zoya.

She raised the curtain and threw the window frame open. We all followed her to the window.

The holiday morning was so bright and clean, as if during the night someone washed all of it with caring hands and carefully put back everything in its place—the blue sky, and fluffy white clouds in it, and tall old poplars, trembling with their young sticky and fragrant leaves. The Dnieper was spreading in front of us to the boundless space—blue and scary by the banks, and calm and silver in the distance. All the city bell towers were ringing.

And suddenly we all involuntarily turned around. The engineer was crying. Grabbing the window jamb, and pressing his forehead against it, he was shaking his head and flinching from sobbing. God only knows what was going on in his old, exhausted and wounded soul of a loser. I knew about his previous life only a little, from occasional hints: a painful marriage to a spoiled woman, embezzlement of government money, shooting at his wife's lover with a revolver, missing his children who left him for their mother...

Zoya compassionately gasped, hugged the engineer and pressed his gray head, with red knobby bald patches, to her heart, and began quietly patting his shoulders and cheeks.

"Oh, my dear, oh my poor one," she was saying melodiously. "I know myself how difficult it is for you to live. All of you are like neglected doggies... old... lonely... Well, it is

ничего... потерпите, голубчики мои... Бог даст, всё пройдёт, и дела поправятся, и всё пойдёт по-хорошему... Ах вы, родненький мой...

С трудом инженеру удалось справиться. Веки у него набрякли, белки́ покраснели, а распухший нос стал почти синим.

— Чёгт! Негвы пгоклятые! Чёгт! — говорил он сердито, отворачиваясь к стене.

И по его голосу я слышал, что у него в горле, во рту и в носу ещё стоят едкие невылившиеся слёзы.

Через пять минут мы стали прощаться и все почтительно поцеловали руку у Зои. Мы с инженером вышли последними, и как раз у самых дверей Зоиного номера на нас наскочил возвращавшийся из гостей студент.

— Ага! — воскликнул он, улыбаясь и многозначительно вздёрнув брови. — Вы в-вон откуда? Гм... раззз-говелись, значит?

В тоне его голоса мы услышали определённую гнусность. Но инженер великолепно и медленно смерил его взглядом от сапог до верха фуражки и после длинной паузы сказал через плечо тоном непередаваемого презрения:

— Сссуслик!

nothing; it is all right... be patient, my darlings... God willing, everything will pass, and things will be well again, and everything will go in a good way... Oh, my dear..."

The engineer managed to pull himself together with difficulty. His eyelids were swollen; his eyes red, and his swollen nose almost blue.

"Damn it! Damned nerves! Damn it!" he said angrily, turning away to the wall.

And from the sound of his voice I felt that, in his throat, mouth and nose, there were still scalding tears that did not pour out.

Five minutes later, we started saying good-bye, and everyone respectfully kissed Zoya's hand. The engineer and I left last, and just by Zoya's door, the student, coming back home after his visits, ran into us.

"Aha!" he exclaimed, smiling and raising his eyebrows with meaning. "I see w-where you c-came from? Hmm... broke your aa-bstinence, didn't you?"

We felt certain dirt in his tone. However, the engineer magnificently and slowly eyed him from his boots to his hat, and after a long pause turned from him and said with a tone of inexpressible contempt,

"Ssskunk!"

Vladimir Alekseevich Gilyarovsky
Беглый / The Fugitive

Н. А. Ярошенко (1846–1898). Заключенный. 1878.
[Государственная Третьяковская галерея. Москва]

N. Yaroshenko. *The Prisoner*. 1878.
[The State Tretyakov Gallery. Moscow]

VLADIMIR ALEKSEEVICH GILYAROVSKY

1855–1935

In the history of Russian literature, this author is probably the most exotic figure among the writers of the late nineteenth century and early twentieth century. The memoirs about Gilyarovsky are numerous and exciting. They describe a very bright personality: a talented and energetic journalist and a gifted writer who turned his life into an adventure novel, while at the same time trying to incorporate into its content the moral rules of the New Testament.

Gilyarovsky was born in the Russian North, near Vologda, into the family of a real estate manager. Maybe the unusual genealogy of the family (his ancestors were Cossacks) can explain that in his childhood he was notorious for his rebellious nature, and for his disrespect for the authorities. For example, he wrote epigrams about his teachers. However, the teenager paid attention only to those things to which he felt an inclination; for example, he translated French poetry and practiced circus arts such as acrobatics and trick horse riding. During his adolescence he became acquainted with revolutionaries/political convicts (the Vologda region was one of those places where the Tsar's government sent those who were disagreeing with the Monarchy). Those political exiles were the first to introduce him to leftist literature.

In 1871, Gilyarovsky ran away from home without money and documents. Due to his outstanding physical stature, he worked all over Russia as a barge hauler on the Volga, a stevedore, a stoker, a factory worker, a firefighter, a fisherman, an

actor, a horse-hearder, and a circus horse rider. When the Russo-Turkish War started in 1877, he joined the army as a volunteer and showed himself to be such a brave soldier that he was rewarded for courage with medals. All that time, Gilyarovsky was thinking about his career in literature.

Gilyarovsky had encountered fame for the first time while working as a successful and prolific journalist in Moscow, when in 1881 he started writing for newspapers. His contemporaries called him the "King of Reporters." Gilyarovsky wrote about accidents, about poor people, about the bad conditions of factory workers. Literally speaking, he was permanently on the front line. For example, in May 1896, on the Day of Coronation of Nicholas II, Gilyarovsky survived only by a miracle during the deadly, bloody crush of the crowds gathered on Moscow's Khodynskoye Field (that day about 1,500 people died). He became famous as a discloser of the dangerous dark world of Moscow's criminal "lower depths" and the life of the poorest of the poor in the city's slums. Gilyarovsky's writings are filled with compassion, and their main theme is the spiritual value of every human being.

Contemporaries wrote about his bearlike strength and the childlike tenderness of his soul. Anton Chekhov called "Uncle Gilyai" (Gilyarovsky's nickname) a man "with a pure heart" and characterized him thus: "No one could describe you: you are breaking out of all the canons." People admired Gilyarovsky's bright personality, great sense of humor, wit, constant practical jokes, eccentric behavior, incredible personal kindness, and readiness to help the needy with his last kopeck. He used to say,

"Don't be afraid to bother me,
When you are in need,
If you want to eat."

This attracted many people to him: from the poorest workers to the most famous writers, such as Leo Tolstoy, Maxim Gorky, Aleksandr Kuprin, Leonid Andreev, Valery Bryusov, and many others.

In addition to literature, Gilyarovsky was involved in differ-

ent activities and original projects. For instance, he was a man of extraordinary physical strength. His friends remembered that he could bend coins with his hands, unbend a horseshoe, and make a knot out of a poker. He became one of the founders of the Russian Gymnastic Society. And because of his physical appearance, he was a model for artists—Ilya Repin's "The Cossacks are Writing the Letter to the Turkish Sultan"—and sculptors.

The story "The Fugitive" was published in the collection *Negatives* in 1900. The author wrote an epigraph mentioning that the book would present the "bitter suffering of people."

In this story, Gilyarovsky described a familiar character: a fugitive escaping from a political prison. It is quite possible that one of the revolutionaries whom young Gilyarovsky befriended in Vologa told him about this escape. The narrative is filled with compassion for the poor man striving for freedom and with admiration for his courage.

Here one can see some of the favorite themes of the writer, such as the portrayal of close ties between a man and nature. It was the influence of Gilyarovsky's poetic vision of the Russian landscape. One of his poems, entitled "Night Thunderstorm," starts as follows:

"The sun set. The dead of night will soon
Cover the forest with its black veil.
Lightning is flashing through the terrifying clouds,
And it is throwing the fiery arrows in front of me..."

In general, the romantic motifs of thunderstorm, abyss, dark forests, clouds, and ocean waves are among Gilyarovsky's favorite themes. He especially loved spring, with its "golden beauty." This love of spring may have been the reason that the writer chose the beginning of the season as the background for "The Fugitive."

In 1887, the writer was preparing the collection of his stories for publication, but the police confiscated and burnt it due to the censor's prohibition. In response to Gilyarovsky's protests, he was accused of depicting only a dark side of reality in his fiction, constantly blaming the regime. He was also told that no

one should write such truth. No wonder that even now, Gilyarovsky is frequently quoted:
"In Russia there are only two disasters:
Down below—the power of darkness,
And on top—many different kinds of power."

ВЛАДИМИР АЛЕКСЕЕВИЧ ГИЛЯРОВСКИЙ

Беглый

Стояла весна. Кое-где в глубоких оврагах вековечной тайги белелся снег, осыпанный пожелтелыми хвоями, а на скатах оврагов, меж зеленевшей травы кое-где выскакивали из-под серого хвороста голубоватые подснежники. Верхушки мелких сосенок пустили новые ростки, светло-зелёные, с серыми шишечками на концах, заблистали бриллиантовые слёзки на стволах ели, сосны и кедра. Молодая берёзка зазеленила концы своих коричневых почек, а на окраинах и вся покрылась изумрудным убором, рельефно отделяясь от тёмной стены старых елей и сосен и ещё черневшихся лиственниц.

По утрам окраины тайги оживали: тысячи птиц кричали без умолку на разные голоса. Самый воздух, согретый яркими лучами солнца, был полон весеннего аромата сосны и берёзовой почки, полон расцветающей жизни, полон могучей силы.

Никогда не бывает так прекрасна тайга, как весной! И чем дальше человеческое жильё, чем тайга глуше, тем она прекраснее, величественнее и тише.

В самой глуши никто не нарушит её тихой жизни, никто не мешает её концерту, её гармонии.

Каждая птичка поёт сама по себе, дятел сердито стучит в дерево, ловя червячков, проделавших удивительные ходы в древесине, плачет кукушка, ветер гудит, стонут от него косматые головы седых великанов.

Всякий звук сам по себе, а дирижер — сама тайга — все

VLADIMIR ALEKSEEVICH GILYAROVSKY

The Fugitive

It was spring. In the deep ravines of the eternal taiga some snow was still lying here and there, sprinkled with yellowish pine needles, and light bluish snowdrops were furtively showing their white tops from under gray brushwood on the slopes of the ravines and among green grass. The tops of young pines shot new sprouts, light green, with gray small cones at their ends; diamond tears shined on the fir trees, pines and cedar trunks. Young birches showed the tops of their brown buds, and on their edges they were all covered with an emerald robe, impressively separated against the background of the dark wall of old fir trees, pines, and larches—still black leafless stains on the background of greenery.

In the mornings, the taiga edges came to life: thousands of birds shrilled incessantly, with different voices. Even the air itself, warmed with the bright rays of the sun, was saturated with the spring aroma of pines and birch buds, full of blooming life, filled with mighty power.

The taiga is never as beautiful as in the spring! And the farther one goes from human dwellings, the denser, the more wonderful, majestic, and quiet it becomes.

In the deep wilderness, nobody will bother its peaceful quiet life; no one will disturb its performance, its harmony.

Each bird sings its own melody; a woodpecker angrily knocks the tree, catching worms having dug amazing tunnels in the wood, the cuckoo cries, and the wind howls making the shaggy heads of gray-haired giants groan.

Each sound is different, and the taiga, like a conductor,

эти раздельные звуки сливает в одно, и выходит концерт поразительный.

Человек заслушается этого весеннего, дикого и очаровательного таёжного концерта, так заслушается, что всю жизнь тайга будет ему мерещиться и живо будет вставать в памяти.

И тем живее встаёт она, чем безотраднее ему. И скажет тот человек, если он болен лежит или заброшен в душный каземат, скажет одно:

— Послушать бы тайгу денёк, как кукушка кукует, как дятел долбит, как ветер гудит по вершинам, послушать бы ещё раз, а там хоть и умереть!

И манит тайга человека бывалого, неудержимо манит из душной тюрьмы на вольный простор.

Рискует старый бродяга попасть под плети, под меткую пулю часового, а всё-таки рвётся хоть денек послушать кукушку в тайге, поплакать с ней, как и он, бездомной, и умереть, отощав с голоду, или опять вернуться в тюрьму, обновлённым таёжной волей, до следующей весны, до следующих надежд на побег.

Бывалого бродягу зовёт кукушка, а молодого удальца тянет родина далёкая, дойти до которой редким приходится.

Раза два удалец попробует побороть неизмеримое расстояние тайги, раза два опять неволей вернётся в каземат, а на третий он и родину, пожалуй, готов забыть, а всё-таки неудержимо бежит поплакать с кукушкой о далёкой родине.

И вытягивает весна удалых добрых молодцев из-за решёток железных, из-за каменных стен, из-за острых штыков. И не страшны им в ту пору стены, не грозна смерть — они сами не помнят себя, очарованные притягательною силой благоухающей вольной тайги.

— Воля! Вот она, воля-то, где! А-ох!.. Не надышишься просто! И сосной, и берёзкой пахнет... А там...

Он вздохнул и задумался.

unites all these separate sounds in one, and the concert turns out striking.

A man will listen to this magic wild spring concert of the taiga, and he will get so carried away that the taiga will forever remain with him, and it will constantly come alive as his most vivid memory.

And the more alive the taiga is in his memory, the gloomier he becomes. And if he is sick or imprisoned in a stuffy cell, he will say only one thing:

"I wish I could listen to the taiga only one day, how a cuckoo cries, how the woodpecker knocks, how the wind howls in the tree-tops: I wish I could listen to this one more time, and then I can die!"

And the taiga beckons the worldly-wise man; it beckons him irrepressibly away from the suffocating prison toward freedom.

An old fugitive risks lashings, to be shot by the well-aimed bullet of a guard, but in spite of this, he struggles to break free in order to listen to a cuckoo song in the taiga and to cry with it, with the bird homeless like him, and then die of starvation, or come back to prison, revived with the taiga freedom, until the next spring, until a new hope of escape.

The cuckoo bird calls for the experienced fugitive, and a young daring lad hears the call of the far-away native land, the motherland, which only few people are able to reach.

A couple of times a brave man will try to conquer the endless space of the taiga, a couple of times he will have to come back to his prison cell, and for the third time, he is even ready to forget his motherland, but nothing will ever stop him from fleeing to cry together with a cuckoo bird about his distant homeland.

And the spring pulls the brave men out from behind the iron bars, from behind the stone walls, away from the line of sharp bayonets. And at that time, they are not afraid of walls, they are not terrified of death—they are obsessed, charmed by the magnetic power of fragrant free taiga.

"Freedom! Here it is, freedom, here! Ooh!.. Such a joy to breathe! This smell of pine and birch trees... And there..."

He sighed and got lost in his thoughts.

Это был плотный тридцатилетний человек, в арестантском халате и шапке без козырька.

— А-ах! Хорошо! — вздохнул он ещё раз. — А чего стоило добраться сюда. Да! Даже страшно. Впрочем, чего страшного — пуля, смерть, и только.

Страшно там, в этих подземельях, где, того и гляди, тебя задавят землёй, как червя в норе, в темноте. Сгинешь и свету божьего не увидишь! Пуля что! Чик и шабаш! А там всю жизнь под землёй, без надежды на солнышко взглянуть! Всю жизнь...

Он задумался.

— А солнышко-то, солнышко!

Бродяга прикрыл глаза сверху, как козырьком, рукой и посмотрел на запад.

А оттуда сквозь чащу дерев прорывались режущие, ярко-красные лучи заходящего солнца. Они играли и бегали на стволах деревьев, соскакивали с них и блестящими «зайками» прыгали дальше на следующих стволах, на чуть зазеленевшейся траве, на сети сучьев.

Лучи всё ярче и ярче горели, и наконец меж стволами начал скользить самый диск солнца, переливавшийся, как расплавленный металл, брызгавший сиянием ослепительных лучей.

Бродяга, стоявший на берегу лесного оврага, жмурился, а всё продолжал смотреть на солнце, опускавшееся за верхушки леса.

Чем ниже опускалось солнце, тем темнее и темнее становилась пропасть оврага.

Всё выше и выше бежали золотые «зайки» по старым великанам, блеснули на их шапках, прошли розовой полоской по беловатым облакам и исчезли.

Как-то сразу почернели овраг и лес, будто задёрнулись от света чёрной занавесью. Сразу холодно стало.

Бродяга вздрогнул, нащупал спички в кармане и стал опускаться на дно оврага, захватывая по пути сухой валежник.

Снизу тянуло холодом. Там ещё белелся снег. Бродяга

He was a solidly built man of thirty, in a prisoner's robe and wearing a peakless hat.

"Ooh! So good!" He sighed again. "And what it took to get here. Yes! It is even terrifying to think of. Though, what is it to be afraid – a bullet, death, that's it."

It is back there where it is horrible, in those underground caves, where one would expect at any moment to be buried alive, as a worm in a hole, in darkness. And one would disappear and would never see God's world again! What is a bullet? Snap, and the end! And be there, all of life, underground, without any hope to see the sun! The whole life..."

He sank into his thoughts.

"And this sun, this sun!"

The fugitive covered his eyes with his hand as with a visor and looked to the west.

And from that side, through the thick of the forest, sharp bright-red rays of the sunset were breaking through. They were playing and running on the trunks of the trees, jumping off them, and those sunbeam-shining spots were jumping further on other trunks, on the freshly greenish grass, on the net of branches.

The rays were sparkling brighter and brighter, and finally, the sun's disc itself began to slide between the trunks, gleaming like melted metal, and sprinkling with the radiance of blinding rays.

The fugitive, standing on the edge of the forest ravine, was squinting, but kept looking at the sun sinking behind the tree-tops.

The lower the sun was going down, the darker and darker the abyss of the ravine looked.

The golden spots of light were running up higher and higher along the trunks of the old giants, then they flashed on their heads, gave a pink lining to the white clouds and disappeared.

Somehow all at once the forest and the ravine turned black, as if they were blocked from the light by a black curtain. Soon it became cold.

The fugitive shivered, groped for the matches in his pocket and began to descend into the ravine, picking up dry branches on his way.

Cold was coming up from down below. White snow was still

взглянул на дно и переменил свое намерение. Он опять поднялся наверх, выбрал чистую полянку, натаскал хворосту, вынул спичку, погрел её сначала за ухом и зажёг.

Чуть заметными, беловатыми полосками побежал огонь по сухому валежнику, зачернелся дым, а потом полосы огня, по мере того как темнело небо, краснели; клубы дыма исчезали в темноте, сверкая по временам мчавшимися кверху звёздочками искр, или прорезывались кровавыми языками пламени, когда бродяга шевелил костёр или бросал свежий валежник.

Он вынул из мешка хлеб, воткнул кусок на палочку и стал жарить над угольями. Хлеб дымился, трещал и слегка обгорел.

Бродяга аппетитно понюхал, снял шапку, положил её на колена, перекрестился и стал есть.

Свежий ветерок подул из-за оврага и гулко зашумел вершинами.

— Наш, рассейский ветерок, с заката. Ишь, тёплый какой!

Он подкинул ещё валежнику в костёр, нахлобучил шапку до ушей, устроил постель из еловых ветвей и хворосту и лёг, плотно закутавшись в широкий арестантский халат.

— Дом, а не халат... Спасибо смотрителю, будто знал, что понадобится, — новый дал! — улыбнулся он.

И представилось ему, как перетрусил носатый смотритель, придиравшийся за каждую мелочь к арестантам и дрожавший, как осиновый лист, перед начальством. Вспомнился ему и последний побег из деревянной полусгнившей тюрьмы.

Ночь была такая же тёмная; окно его секретной камеры с заржавленной решёткой выходило в поле, за которым синела бесконечная тайга. Под окном торчали острые концы бревенчатого частокола, заменявшего тюремную стену, и за частоколом постоянно двигалась взад и вперёд полоска штыка, — днём синяя и ночью светлая, от красноватого отблеска закоптелого, грязного фонаря.

lying there. The man looked down, and changed his mind. He climbed up again, chose a clearing, gathered dried branches, took out a match, warmed it up first behind his ear, and lit it up.

Hardly noticeable, whitish flames ran on dry wood, black smoke appeared, and then—while the sky was getting dark, ribbons of flame were turning red; puffs of smoke were disappearing into the darkness, glittering now and then, star-like sparks were racing up, or were cutting through the bloody tongues of flames, when the fugitive was stirring the campfire or was throwing more branches in it.

He took out some bread from his sack, stuck a piece on a twig and began to toast it over live coals. The bread was smoking, crackling and got slightly black.

The fugitive smelled it with contentment, took off his hat, put it on his lap, crossed himself, and started eating.

A fresh breeze blew from behind the ravine and boomed in the treetops.

"It's our Russian breeze there, from the sunset side. See, so warm!"

He threw more branches into the fire, pulled his hat down over his ears, made a bed of fir branches and brushwood, and laid down, wrapped himself tightly in a loose prisoner's robe.

"It is not a robe, it is a house...Thank the guard: as if he had known that I would need it—he gave me a new one," the fugitive smiled.

And he imagined how the big-nosed guard became scared, the man who found fault with prisoners for trifles and shook like a leaf in front of his superiors. And the fugitive also recalled his escape from the wooden, half-rotten prison.

That night was as dark as this one; the window of his solitary cell with rusty bars looked out onto the field, behind which the endless bluish taiga could be seen. Under the window, sharp ends of wooden paling, the prison wall, were sticking out, and behind the paling, a stripe of a bayonet was moving: blue in the daylight and shiny at night from the reddish reflection of the sooty, dirty lantern.

Он долгое время смотрел на тайгу, на частокол, на штык, мелькавший то вправо, то влево от окна.

По этому штыку можно было знать, где часовой, близко или далеко.

Тогда ночь была тёмная, туманная, фонарь мигал красноватою точкой среди густого весеннего тумана, как тлеет керосиновая лампа в бане.

Он выставил полугнилую раму, скрутил из белья верёвку, связал этой верёвкой два прута решётки, всунул в верёвку полено, принесённое из коридора под халатом ещё накануне, и начал его повёртывать. Верёвка скручивалась. Вольный, свежий ветер прорывался в тесную, душную камеру и освежал, ободрял его, уставшего до поту. Верёвка скручивалась, связанные ею прутья сжимались.

С другой стороны он также связал два прута и скрутил верёвку.

Образовалось отверстие, голова в него проходила свободно.

Вспомнил он, как хлопали по грязи кеньги часового, удалялся влево отблеск штыка, вспомнил он смелый прыжок, крики, выстрелы, шум сзади, свист пули около уха.

Но вспомнилось всё это как-то неясно, будто давно это случилось, а не три дня назад.

А ветер всё гудел вершинами...

Бродяга сквозь полусон прислушивался к этому шуму, напоминавшему ему ночи — далеко, далеко отсюда...

Яркий огонь близкого костра грел ему лоб, и сквозь закрытые веки бродяга видел, или, лучше сказать, чувствовал, сначала красное, а потом фиолетовое зарево, глазам было больно, но он напрасно напрягал усилия открыть их. При каждой тщетной попытке поднять веки зарево только принимало более яркую окраску и ещё крепче сковывало глаза и усталые члены.

Он был как бы в забытьи, голова горела, мозг сжимался, грудь давило, и всевозможные картины, одна другой фантастичнее, мелькали в его воображении...

Он забыл в этот миг всё, всё...

He stared long at the taiga, the paling, and the bayonet flashing right and left.

By that bayonet it was easy to guess where the sentry was: far away or close by.

That night was dark, foggy; the lantern was flashing as a reddish dot in the dense spring mist, like a glimmering kerosene lamp in a steamy sauna.

He removed a half-rotten frame, twisted a rope using the bed sheet, and tied up two bars with the rope, placed in it a wooden log, which he stole from the corridor the day before and hid under his robe, and began to rotate it. The rope was twisted. The fresh air of freedom started blowing into the small stuffy cell and refreshed him, cheered him up, he was exhausted and perspiring. The rope was twisted, and the tied up bars were bending.

He also bound together two bars with the rope on the other side.

An opening was made, and his head could go through it easily.

The man also remembered how the sentry's fir shoes were flapping on the mud, the gleam of the bayonet was moving to the left; he remembered his brave jump, shouts, shots, noise behind, bullet whistling by his ear.

But that recollection was somehow vague, as if it had happened long ago, not just three days before.

And the wind was booming in the treetops...

Through his nap, the fugitive was listening to that noise, which reminded him of the nights—somewhere far, far from this place...

The bright flame of campfire was warming his forehead, and through closed eyelids, the man saw, or rather, felt, first a red, then a purple glow. His eyes hurt, but in vain, he desperately tried to open them. At each failed attempt to open his eyes, the glow became brighter and stronger, fettering his eyes and his tired body.

He felt as if he were unconscious, his head was feverish, his brain was drained, and different visions, one more fantastic than the other, were flashing in his imagination.

And at that moment, he forgot everything, everything...

Aleksandr Grin
(Aleksandr Stepanovich Grinevsky)

Подаренная жизнь / Life Granted

Илья Ефимович Репин (1844–1930). Невский проспект. 1887.
[Государственный Русский музей. Санкт-Петербург]

I. Repin. *Nevsky Avenue.* 1887.
[The State Russian Museum. St. Petersburg]

ALEKSANDR GRIN
(ALEKSANDR STEPANOVICH GRINEVSKY)

1880–1932

Aleksandr Grin represents Romantic Realism in Russian literature, though he always considered himself a Symbolist. His stories are filled with symbols and subtle psychological analysis, very often intertwined with adventures in exotic countries. Grin liked to place his characters in some foreign fantastic reality, and some of his contemporaries even began to spread rumors that the writer had stolen manuscripts from a British sailor when he was imprisoned.

The other facets of Grin's stories are about the Russian reality of his time. They are often melancholic, dramatic, and written in the style of classical Realism. However, even in those stories, he likes to "open the door" to another dimension, another reality. There is always an unexpected turn of events changing the life of Grin's characters. We witness such changes in his story "Fandango," when, in the middle of freezing and starving Petrograd in post-revolutionary years, a storyteller buys an amazing picture. It depicts an empty room in an unknown southern city. Then, a moment comes when he is able to go through the frame and find himself inside another reality.

Because of this permanent presence of other fantastic worlds in the writer's fiction, there is even a special term coined for Grin's invented world—"Grinlandiya" (The Land of Grin). But wherever the plot takes place—in Africa or in

St. Petersburg—the character always has a chance to change his path in life.

From his childhood, Grin dreamed about travel and adventure, and when he was sixteen, he left home, for some time living the life of a hobo and an unskilled laborer. He tried many professions, such as sailor, fisherman, logger, and gold prospector. During that time, Grin gained a lot of life experience, living together with degraded people and observing the scum of society. But even during this time of hardship, when he was destitute, without a penny and completely alone, sometimes on the verge of starvation, he carried with him a beautiful china cup that he believed to be endowed with magical powers—and which he viewed in times of desperation. It raised his spirit, reminding him of other, better worlds. He wrote about it in his autobiography.

Almost dying of starvation, Grin joined the army and became a common soldier. He deserted and became involved in revolutionary activity, was arrested for revolutionary propaganda, and after the October Revolution he served in the Red Army. He started writing his first stories in the 1900s, and his pen name, Grin, appeared in 1907. Even though he started his literary career with realistic narratives, the reader could still see sparkles of sunny romanticism, which provided refreshing contrast with the cold boredom of everyday reality.

After the revolution, Grin became the author of numerous stories and a few novels, loved by his contemporaries; he is still extremely popular in modern Russia. However, in the Soviet times, there had been almost ten years during which Grin was blamed for "Bourgeois Cosmopolitism" and his books were not published. Later he was "rehabilitated." Nowadays, there are four literary museums dedicated to Aleksandr Grin, as well as many screen adaptations of his writings, and a literary prize, established in 2000, for romantic fiction.

The story "Life Granted" was published in 1915. It is a psychological sketch showing Grin's interest in the "life-death" theme, the value of human life, and the idea of "evil." He was

inspired by the circle of Russian terrorists during his active collaboration with them in pre-revolutionary times. That could explain the characteristics given to Grin's narrative by some literary critics writing about the gloominess of the content combined with the sharpness of the storytelling.

"Life Granted" reflects the writer's favorite theme of a mighty force of beauty and its power over the human soul, which he showed in his narrative. Grin was convinced that the beauty of the world in its different manifestations could be a turning point. It could be a song in the "Airy Ship," or music in the "Black Diamond," or a painting in the "Water Color," or a ship with scarlet sails in his most popular novel of the same name. Grin believed that the beauty around us could change the life of a man to give him a chance for a new beginning. It happened in the story "Life Granted." Its title has a double meaning: life was granted and life was changed.

АЛЕКСАНДР ГРИН

Подаренная жизнь

I

Коркин был человек средней физической силы, тщедушного сложения; его здоровый глаз, по контрасту с выбитым, закрывшимся, смотрел с удвоенным напряжением; он брился, напоминая этим трактирного официанта. В общем, худощавое кривое его лицо не производило страшного впечатления. «Джонка», бурое пальто и шарф были его бессменной одеждой. Он никогда не смеялся, а говорил голосом тонким и тихим.

В субботу вечером Коркин сидел в трактире и пил чай, обдумывая, где бы заночевать. Его искала полиция. Хлопнула, дохнув морозным паром, дверь; вошёл испитой мальчишка, лет четырнадцати. Он осмотрелся, увидел Коркина и, подмигнув, направился к нему.

— Тебя, слышь, хотят тут, дело тебе есть, — сказал он, подсаживаясь. — Фраер спрашивал.

— Чего это?

— Какой-то барин, — сказал хулиган, — я с ним снюхался на вокзале. Надо ему кого-то «пришить». Мастера ищет.

— Он где?

— Поедем в «Ливерпуль». Он там в кабинете засел, пьёт и бегает. Кулачонко сжал, по столу треснул, зубами скрипнул. Псих.

— Пойдём, — сказал Коркин. Он встал, закрыл шарфом нижнюю часть лица, «джонку» сдвинул к бровям, торопливо докурил папироску и вышел с хулиганом на улицу.

ALEKSANDR GRIN

Life Granted

I

Korkin was a man of average physical strength and of a skinny constitution. His healthy eye, in contrast to the one knocked out and closed, looked out with doubled intensity; he was shaven like a tavern waiter. In general, his lean and one-eyed face did not make a frightful impression. The "Junk boat"-shaped hat, a brown coat, and a scarf were his permanent outfit. He never laughed, and always spoke with quiet falsetto.

One Saturday evening, Korkin was sitting in the tavern and drinking tea, thinking where to spend the night. The police were looking for him. The door slammed open, breathing in frosty fog, and a haggard teen, about fourteen, came in. He looked around, saw Korkin, winked to him, and proceeded in his direction.

"You listen, you are a wanted fugitive, there is some business for you to do," he said, sitting down close by.—One dude asked..."

"What is it?"

"Some nobleman,"—the hoodlum said,—"I met him at the station. He needs someone to be done in. He is looking for a 'specialist'."

"Where is he?"

"Let's go to 'Liverpool'. The guy is stuck in the room, drinking and pacing around. He clenched his tiny fist, hit the table, and gritted his teeth. Psycho."

"Let's go," said Korkin. He stood up; covered the lower part of his face with his scarf, pulled down the "Junk" hat to his eyebrows, hastily finished the cigarette, and went outside with the hoodlum.

171

II

По выцветшему, насквозь пропахшему кисло-унылым запахом кабинету «Ливерпуля» расхаживал, нервно потирая руки, человек лет тридцати. На нём был короткий, в талию, серый полушубок, белый барашек на рукавах и воротнике придавал полушубку вид фатовской, дамский. Шапка, тоже белая, сидела на бородатой, жеманно откинутой голове очень кокетливо. Мрачное лицо с выдающейся нижней челюстью, обведённой густой, подстриженной клинышком, тёмной бородой; впалые, беспокойные глаза, закрученные торчком усы и нечто танцующее во всех движениях от скользящей, конькобежной походки до выворачивания наотлёт локтей, — давали общее впечатление холёного, истеричного самца.

Коркин, постучав, вошёл. Неизвестный нервически заморгал.

— По делу звали, — сказал Коркин, смотря на бутылки.

— Да, да, по делу, — заговорил шёпотом неизвестный. — Вы — т о т с а м ы й ?

— Тот самый.

— Вы... пьёте?

По тому, как он резко сказал «вы», Коркин видел, что барин презирает его.

— Пьёте, — нахально ответил Коркин; он сел, налил и выпил.

Барин некоторое время молчал, воздушно поглаживая бороду пальцами.

— Обтяпайте мне одно дело, — хмуро сказал он.

— Говорите... зачем звали.

— Мне нужно, чтобы одного человека не было. За это получите вы тысячу рублей, а задатком теперь триста.

Левая щека его задёргалась, глаза вспухли.

Коркин выпил вторую порцию и съязвил:

— Самому-то вам... слаб?... или как?..

— Что? Что? — встрепенулся барин.

— Сами... трусите?..

II

The "Liverpool" room was half dark, reeking through and through of something gloomy and sour. A man around thirty was pacing back and forth nervously rubbing his hands. The gentleman was in a short grey sheepskin coat fitted around the waist, and with white fur trimming on the collar and sleeves gave that coat some foppish, female look. His hat, also white, was sitting very coquettishly on his bearded head thrown back in a mincing manner. His gloomy face with a jutted out jaw outlined with a dense, wedge-shaped dark beard, sunken anxious eyes, twirled mustache, and something dancing in all his movements—from his sliding, skating gait to his elbows turned inside out—made a general impression of well-groomed hysterical male.

Korkin knocked and came in. The man nervously blinked.

"You called about that business," said Korkin looking at the bottles.

"Yes, yes, about business,"—the man whispered.—Are you *that man?*"

"Exactly that man."

"Do you... drink?"

From that harsh manner of pronouncing you, Korkin understood that the nobleman despised him.

"...You... drink,"—repeated Korkin impudently. He sat down, took a glass, and drank.

The gentleman kept silent for a while, lightly patting his beard.

"Handle some business for me,"—he said somberly.

"Speak... why you have called me."

"I want one man to disappear. You will get one thousand rubles for this, and three hundred as a down payment right now."

His left cheek began to twitch, and his eyes bulged out.

Korkin drank the second glass and said sarcastically:

"And what about you... too weak ...or—what?"

"What? What?" The nobleman winced.

"Are you... too cowardly to do this by yourself?"

Барин устремился к окну и, постояв там вполоборота, кинул:

— Болван!

— Сам болван, — спокойно ответил Коркин.

Барин как бы не расслышал этого. Присев к столу, он объяснил Коркину, что желает смерти студента Покровского; дал его адрес, описал наружность и уплатил триста рублей.

— В три дня будет готов Покровский, — сухо сказал Коркин. — По газетам узнаете.

Они условились, где встретиться для доплаты, и расстались.

III

Весь следующий день Коркин напрасно подстерегал жертву. Студент не входил и не выходил.

К семи часам вечера Коркин устал и проголодался. Размыслив, решил он отложить дело до завтра. Кинув последний раз взгляд на чёрную арку ворот, Коркин направился в трактир. За едой он заметил, что ему как-то не по себе: ныли суставы, вздрагивалось, хотелось тянуться. Пища казалась лишённой запаха. Однако Коркину не пришло в голову, что он простужен.

Преступник с отвращением доел щи. Сидя потом за чаем, он испытывал неопределённую тревогу. Бродили беспокойные мысли, раздражал яркий свет ламп. Коркин хотел уснуть, забыв о полиции, железной гирьке, приготовленной для Покровского, и всём на свете. Но притон, где он ночевал, открывался в одиннадцать.

У Коркина оставалось два свободных часа. Он решил провести их в кинематографе. На него напало странное легкомыслие, полное презрение к сыщикам и тупое безразличие ко всему.

Он зашёл в какой-то из «Биоскопов». При кинематографе этом существовал так называемый «Анатомический музей», произвольное собрание восковых моделей частей человеческого тела. Коркин зашёл и сюда.

The man ran to the window and, standing there half-turned, blurted out:

"Dummy!"

"It is you who is a dummy," Korkin said calmly.

The gentleman did not reply, as if he did not hear that. Sitting down at the table, he explained to Korkin that he wanted the death of the student Pokrovsky, gave his address, described his appearance, and paid three hundred rubles.

"In three days Pokrovsky will be done in," said dryly Korkin. "You will learn from newspapers."

They agreed where to meet for the payment of the rest of the money and parted.

III

The entire following day, Korkin was on the watch for the catch. The student did not come in, or come out.

By seven in the evening Korkin was tired and hungry. Thinking a little, he decided to put off the business until tomorrow. After a last glance at the dark arch of the gate, Korkin headed for the tavern. While eating, he noticed that he was not quite well: his joints ached; he could not stop wincing, and he even tried stretching. The meal seemed to be without aroma. However, the idea that he had caught a cold did not cross his mind.

The fugitive finished his cabbage soup with disgust. Then, sitting and drinking tea, he felt a strange sense of anxiety. Uneasy thoughts were bothering him; the bright light of the lamps disturbed him. Korkin wanted to fall asleep and forget about the police, about an iron weight prepared for Pokrovsky, and about everything in this world. However, the shelter where he stayed was opened only from eleven.

Korkin had two hours to kill. He decided to spend the time in the movie theater. He suddenly became unusually careless, felt contempt for the police, and senselessly indifferent to everything.

He came to one of the "Bioskops." At that movie theater, there was a so-called "Anatomical Museum": a random collection of wax copies of parts of the human body. Korkin stopped by that place, too.

С порога Коркин осмотрел комнату. За стёклами виднелось нечто красное, голубое, розовое и синее, и в каждом таком непривычных очертаний предмете был намёк на тело самого Коркина.

Вдруг он испытал необъяснимую тягость, сильное сердцебиение — потому ли, что встретился с объектом своего «дела» в его, так сказать, непривычном, бесстрастно интимном виде, или же потому, что на модели, изображающие сердце, легкие, печень, мозг, глаза и т. п., смотрели вместе с ним незнакомые люди, далёкие от подозрения, что такие же, только живые механизмы уничтожались им, Коркиным, — он не знал. Его резкое, новое ощущение походило на то, как если бы, находясь в большом обществе, он увидел себя совершенно нагим, раздетым таинственно и мгновенно.

Коркин подошёл ближе к ящикам; заключённое в них магически притягивало его. Прежде других бросилась ему в глаза надпись: «Кровеносная система дыхательных путей». Он увидел нечто похожее на дерево без листьев, серого цвета, с бесчисленными мелкими разветвлениями. Это казалось очень хрупким, изысканным. Затем Коркин долго смотрел на красного человека без кожи; сотни овальных мускулов вплетались один в другой, тесно обливая костяк упругими очертаниями; они выглядели сухо и гордо; по красной мускулатуре струились тысячи синих жил.

Рядом с этим ящиком блестел большой чёрный глаз; за его ресницами и роговой оболочкой виднелись некие, непонятные Коркину, похожие на маленький станок, части, и он, тупо смотря на них, вспомнил свой выбитый глаз, за которым, следовательно, был сокрушён такой же таинственный станок, как тот, которые он видел.

Коркин осмотрел тщательно всё: мозг, напоминающий ядро грецкого ореха; разрез головы по линии профиля, где было видно множество отделений, пустот и перегородок; лёгкие, похожие на два больших розовых лопуха, и ещё много чего, оставившего в нём чувство жуткой оторопелости. Всё это казалось ему запретным, случайно и преступно

Standing at the threshold, he looked around. Behind the glass something red, light blue, pink and dark blue could be seen, and in each of these uncommonly shaped things there was a message sent to the body of Korkin himself.

Suddenly he felt an unexplained heaviness, a strong palpitation. He did not know whether it was because he had met with the object of his "business" in its uncommon and impassive intimate view, or because the items depicting heart, lungs, liver, brain, eyes and other parts were observed also by other unknown people, and who were far from suspecting, that similar, but alive mechanisms were destroyed by him, by Korkin himself. His new glaring feeling was similar to a moment when, surrounded by the crowd, he would have found himself absolutely naked, mysteriously stripped of his clothes, in a blink of an eye.

Korkin approached the boxes: their content attracted him in a magical way. First, the inscription struck his eyes, "Blood circulatory system of the respiratory tract." He saw something reminding him of a tree without leaves, of a gray color, with countless tiny branches. It looked very fragile and refined. Then, Korkin stared long at a red man without the skin: hundreds of oval muscles were plaited one into another tightly covering the skeleton with their resilient shapes. They looked cold and haughty; thousands of blue veins were streaming along the red muscles.

Next to the box, a large black eye was shining: behind was its eyelashes and cornea, some tiny parts similar to a small machine tool were seen. Staring at them, he remembered his knocked-out eye, and behind it, consequently, had been destroyed the same mysterious tool, exactly like the one he had just seen.

Korkin looked at everything very thoroughly: the brain reminding him of a walnut kernel; a head section on a profile line, where one could see numerous parts, hollow elements and partitions. Lungs reminded him of two big pink burdock leaves, and many other things that left him in horrible confusion. Everything seemed forbidden to him and accidentally and hos-

подсмотренным. В целомудренной восковой вырази-
тельности моделей пряталась пугающая тайна.

Коркин направился к выходу. Проходя мимо старика-
извозчика, стоявшего рядом с бабой в платке, он услышал,
как извозчик сказал:

— Всё, как есть, показано, Вавиловна. Работа Божья...
хитрая... и-их — хитрая заводь! Всё это... мы, значит,
вовнутри, вот... да-а!

Суеверный страх проник в Коркина — страх мужика,
давно приглушённый городом. В среде, где все явления
жизни и природы: рост трав, хлеба, смерть и болезнь,
несчастье и радость — неизменно связываются с Богом и его
волей, — никогда не исчезает такое суеверное отношение
к малопонятному. Коркин шёл по улице, с трудом одолевая
страх. Наконец страх прошёл, оставив усталость и
раздражение.

Коркин хотел уже направиться к ночлегу, но вспомнил
о студенте Покровском. Его непреодолимо потянуло увидеть
этого человека, хотя бы мельком, не зная даже, удастся ли
убить его сегодня; он испытывал томительное желание
прикоснуться к решению, к концу «дела»; войти в круг
знакомого, тяжкого возбуждения.

Он подошёл к т е м воротам и, подождав немного, вдруг
столкнулся лицом к лицу с вышедшим из-под ворот на
улицу высоким, прихрамывающим молодым человеком.

— Он, — сличив приметы, сказал Коркин и потянулся,
как собака, сзади студента. Вокруг не видно было прохожих.
«Амба! — подумал Коркин, — ударю его». Дрожа от
озноба, вынул он гирьку, но тут, останавливая решение,
показалось Коркину, что у студента, если забежать вперёд,
окажутся закрывающие всё лицо огромные глаза
с таинственными станками. Он увидел также, что тело
студента под пальто лишено кожи, что мускулы и
сухожилья, сплетаясь в ритмических сокращениях, живут
строгой, сложной жизнью, видят Коркина и повелительно
отстраняют его.

tilely observed. Some frightening secret was hiding in those innocent impressions of the wax exhibits.

Korkin went to the exit. Walking past an old cabman standing by a woman in a shawl, he overheard the man saying:

"Everything is shown as it is, Vavilovna. God's work ... skillful ... oh... skillful mechanism! All of us, this, I mean, inside, here we are... ye-e-s!"

Superstitious fear struck Korkin, the fear of a farmer, long ago deadened by city life. Superstitions from the village, where all phenomena of life and nature—the growth of herbs and crops, death and sickness, troubles and happiness—are always related to God and His will—such a superstitious attitude about things difficult to understand never disappears. Finally, the fear went away, leaving feelings of tiredness and irritation.

Korkin already wanted to go to the shelter, but remembered the student Pokrovsky. He got an irresistible impulse to see that man, even catch a glimpse of him, not being sure if he would manage to kill him today. Korkin felt an insuperable desire to approach the final decision, to make one more step to end the "business," and get back into the familiar heavy anxiety.

He went to *those gates*, and after a short wait, he suddenly ran into the tall limping young man who came out of the gate.

"It is he,"—said Korkin, remembering the description and stretched himself like a dog, walking behind the student. There were no passersby around. "That's it," Korkin thought, "I will strike him." Shivering from chills, he took out the weight, but at that moment, stopping the decision, it appeared to Korkin that if he ran in front of the student, he would see, covering the whole face, these enormous eyes with those mysterious mechanisms. He would also see that the body of the student under his coat did not have a skin, and that the muscles and the tendons, intertwining in rhythmical contractions, lived their haughty complicated life, and were able to see Korkin and were forcefully moving him away.

Чувствуя, что рука не поднимается, что страшно и глухо вокруг, Коркин прошёл мимо студента, кинув сквозь зубы:

— Даром живёте.

— Что такое? — быстро спросил студент, отшатываясь.

— Даром живёте! — повторил Коркин и, зная уже, с тупой покорностью совершившемуся, что студент никогда не будет убит им, — свернул в переулок.

Feeling that he could not raise his hand, and that it was terrifying and lonely all around, Korkin went past the student, spitting:

"Have your life."

"What did you say?"—asked the student, quickly jumping back.

"Have your life," repeated Korkin, and with a blank resignation to what had just happened, and already realizing that the student would never be killed by him, turned into the side street.

Yevgeny Ivanovich Zamyatin
Дракон / Dragon

Владимир Маяковский (1893–1930).
Плакат из серии «Окна РОСТа». 1920.

Vladimir Mayakovsky.
A poster from the series "ROST Windows." 1920.

YEVGENY IVANOVICH ZAMYATIN

1884–1937

Zamyatin, the original and talented writer and gifted play-wright, was born into the family of a priest and spent his childhood in a quiet provincial town, Lebedyan. Later, Zamyatin wrote in his autobiography that he remembered "a light crystal August morning and distant transparent bells ringing in the monastery." The first bright impression of his early childhood was that of someone bringing some snow on a plate to show to the child. Zamyatin described it later as "something strange, sparkling—and oh, miracle—this white is suddenly disappearing into nowhere before my eyes. On the plate—a piece of unknown ... outer universe ... and this wonderful snow is still in my mind."

His mother was a gifted amateur piano player, and maybe that is the reason why Zamyatin's narrative seems so melodious. After finishing high school, his favorite subject was literature and among his favorite readings were Feodor Dostoevsky and Nikolai Gogol; he nevertheless entered the Ship Building Department of St. Petersburg Polytechnic Institute. As a student, Zamyatin was involved in revolutionary activities and was arrested. Later, the writer remembered that period as his "being in love with revolution."

In spite of it all, Zamyatin graduated, and as a talented engineer-shipbuilder was hired by the Polytechnic Institute as a faculty member. At the same time, Zamyatin tried writing, and his first literary success came in 1913. At that time, he started to develop his own original style combining, according

184

to literary critics, realist and modernist influences in his narrative prose. That style, used by the group of young writers—Zamyatin's contemporaries—was called "neo-realism." Later, he wrote about the essence of that style as a combination of "fantasy and the real life."

At the same time, in his narrative, Zamyatin was always distant from the events and the characters—typical for a folklore stylization—and showed a slightly ironical attitude. In an excerpt from one of Zamyatin's letters of October 1923 he complains about the gloomy, rainy weather of the cily's autumn. This message to his friend, the poet Maksimilian Voloshin, gives a sample of his original "fantasy" style: "I have already been in St. Petersburg for three weeks, and every day I watch through my window how some gray lizard-like belly has been creeping on the very roofs. It never turns out well when the sky forgets its place and tries to settle on the ground: it turns only into slush. And one feels somehow soaked inside and all people walk stooping—hanging their heads... as if they are afraid to bump the crowns against the sky." This abundance of comparisons, unexpected images, parallels, and especially—different bright metaphors—became the recognizable features of his magical style.

Another example displays Zamyatin's "narrative painting." In a description of London there are the lines "London was sailing—does not matter where. Light columns of Druids' temples—the yesterday's factory chimneys .... Curved necks of antediluvian-huge black swans-cranes: as if they were diving for the catch to the bottom." This magical style contains so many outlandish images and metaphors that his fiction sometimes reminds one of the abstractionists' canvases. Zamyatin himself revealed some of the secrets of his writing during his lectures on literature. He explained that the narrative should be organized as a musical piece with its rhythm, and that even different letters could be associated with artistic images. For example, "R" clearly tells me about something loud, bright, red, hot, fast; "L"—about something pale, light-blue, cold, smooth, light..." And this is true: while reading

Zamyatin's stories, one feels this music of each sentence, created as an embroidery of different colored threads. Each para-
graph, rhyming with another, becomes a part of a harmonious
music-like sequence.

Zamyatin's popularity as a writer was growing, but he continued his engineering career. In 1916, he was on a business
trip to Great Britain as an expert on icebreaker building.
However, in 1917, feeling nostalgic, Zamyatin came back to
Russia and actively took part in the literary life of the new
socialist country. He gave lectures on literature, worked at
publishing houses, and wrote fiction and plays. Zamyatin's
impressions of the post-revolutionary motherland were reflected in numerous stories, in which he pointed out the vio-
lence, unjustified cruelty, and the horrors of the Civil War and
the "Military Communism" period of 1918 to 1921.

The best writing of that period was his anti-utopia *We*,
a depressing parody of the future Communist society in which
a human being becomes a "number," a small part of a soulless
social mechanism. That novel brought its creator much trouble; when it was published abroad, Zamyatin lost his member-
ship in the Unit of the Soviet Writers and, as a result, could no
longer publish. In desperation, the writer sent a letter to Stalin
asking for permission to emigrate. He wrote that he "was not
able to work in the atmosphere of ... intensifying persecution," and he had realized that he had a "very inconvenient
habit of saying not what is profitable at a moment, but what
is truthful." The request was granted, and the writer left
Russia for good, dying in exile in France.

As a result of that decision, Zamyatin's name was prohibited in the Soviet Union, and he was considered a traitor. The
critics wrote that he did not understand the real essence and
value of the revolutionary events, as he depicted the post-
revolutionary period as a return to an anti-human, savage
type of relations, suggesting a new Stone Age.

The story "Dragon" depicts the horrible times in Petrograd,
when human life and the human civilization itself were bal-
ancing on a thread, expressed so eloquently by Shakespeare:

"The time is out of joint." A similar image of a catastrophe can be found in Osip Mandelstam's famous lines:
"My Age, my beast,
Who will dare look into your eyes?
Who will glue with their own blood
The vertebra of two centuries?"
The heartless, bloody, cruel reality of death all around, as in Francisco Goya's *Caprichos*, creates a phantasmagoria of fairy tale beasts. Those creatures sometimes, miraculously, could turn into human beings, diving out of that fourth dimension of the evil kingdom where they exist.

ЕВГЕНИЙ ИВАНОВИЧ ЗАМЯТИН

Дракон

Люто замороженный, Петербург горел и бредил. Было ясно: невидимые за туманной занавесью, поскрипывая, пошаркивая, на цыпочках бредут вон жёлтые и красные колонны, шпили и седые решётки. Горячечное, небывалое, ледяное солнце в тумане — слева, справа, вверху, внизу — голубь над загоревшимся домом. Из бредового, туманного мира выныривали в земной мир драконо-люди, изрыгали туман, слышимый в туманном мире как слова, но здесь — белые, круглые дымки; выныривали и тонули в тумане. И со скрежетом неслись в неизвестное вон из земного мира трамваи.

На трамвайной площадке временно существовал дракон с винтовкой, несясь в неизвестное. Картуз налезал на нос и, конечно, проглотил бы голову дракона, если б не уши: на оттопыренных ушах картуз засел. Шинель болталась до полу; рукава свисали; носки сапог загибались кверху — пустые. И дыра в тумане: рот.

Это было уже в соскочившем, несущемся мире, и здесь изрыгаемый драконом лютый туман был видим и слышим:

— ...Веду его: морда интилигентная — просто глядеть противно. И ещё разговаривает, стервь, а? Разговаривает!

— Ну, и что же — довёл?

— Довёл: без пересадки — в Царствие Небесное. Штычком.

Дыра в тумане заросла: был только пустой картуз,

YEVGENY IVANOVICH ZAMYATIN

Dragon

Brutally frozen, Petersburg was feverish and delirious. It was clear: unseen behind the misty veil, the yellow and red columns, steeples, and snowy-gray railings were walking away crunching, shuffling and tiptoeing. The icy sun in the fog, feverish and surreal—on the left, on the right, above and below,—a dove above the house on fire. From the delirious, foggy world, the dragon-like-people were surfacing, belching out the fog,—a sound of a language in the foggy world, but here,—just white round puffs; were emerging and sinking back into the fog. And the metallic grinding trams were rushing along into the unknown, away from the earthly world.

By the rear door of the tram, a rifle bearing dragon made a temporary home for himself, while rushing along into the unknown. The peaked cap was coming down his nose, and certainly would have swallowed the dragon's head if it were not for his ears; the cap seemed to be sitting on top of his protruding ears. The soldier's overcoat was hanging loosely to the floor; the sleeves were dangling; the empty boot tips were turned up. And there was a hole in the fog—his mouth.

But that was a sight from the vantage point of the world that jumped out of the tram, of the world that was now rapidly retreating. And over here, the brutal fog spewed out by the dragon was seen and heard.

"...I was bringing him under escort: he had that educated mugshot,—it's simply disgusting to look at. And he even dared to talk—son of a bitch, isn't he! He talked!"

"So, did you bring him anywhere?"

"Yes, I did: straight through—to the Kingdom of Heaven. With my darling bayonet."

пустые сапоги, пустая шинель. Скрежетал и нёсся вон из мира трамвай.

И вдруг — из пустых рукавов — из глубины — выросли красные, драконьи лапы. Пустая шинель присела к полу — и в лапах серенькое, холодное, материализованное из лютого тумана.

— Мать ты моя! Воробьёныш замёрз, а? Ну скажи ты на милость!

Дракон сбил назад картуз — и в тумане два глаза — две щёлочки из бредового в человечий мир.

Дракон изо всех сил дул ртом в красные лапы, и это были, явно, слова воробьёнышу, но их — в бредовом мире — не было слышно. Скрежетал трамвай.

— Стервь этакая: будто трепыхнулся, а? Нет ещё? А ведь отойдёт, ей-Бо... Ну ска-жи ты!

Изо всех сил дул. Винтовка валялась на полу. И в предписанный судьбою момент, в предписанной точке пространства серый воробьёныш дрыгнул, ещё дрыгнул — и спорхнул с красных драконьих лап в неизвестное.

Дракон оскалил до ушей тумано-пыхающую пасть. Медленно картузом захлопнулись щёлочки в человечий мир. Картуз осел на оттопыренных ушах. Проводник в Царствие Небесное поднял винтовку.

Скрежетал зубами и нёсся в неизвестное, вон из человеческого мира, трамвай.

The hole in the fog disappeared: it was only an empty peaked cap, empty boots, and the empty greatcoat. The tram was metallically grinding and rushing away from this world.

And suddenly, from the empty sleeves, from the void, red dragon's paws emerged. The empty greatcoat squatted to the floor—and a cold gray tiny creature materialized from the bitter freezing fog in his paws.

"Holy Mother! The sparrow chick got frozen, eh? For Heaven's sake!"

The dragon pushed back his cap—and two eyes appeared in the fog—two chinks from the delirium world into the human one.

The dragon was blowing into his red paws as hard as he could, and those were obviously words to the sparrow chick, but they were not heard in the delirium world. The tram was grinding.

"Such son of a bitch: it looks as if it flapped its wings, eh? Not yet? It's for sure, he will recover, I swear to God... Well, tell me!"

He was blowing as hard as he could. His rifle was lying on the tram floor. And at the moment, as fate willed, at the fate-decreed point of the Universe, the gray sparrow chick jerked, then again, and took wing off the red dragon's paws into the unknown.

The dragon grinned from ear to ear, baring his teeth inside the foggy flaming jaws. Slowly the chinks to the human world got closed by the peaked cap. It got stuck on the protruding ears. The Guide to the Kingdom of Heaven picked up his rifle.

Grinding its teeth, the tram was rushing away into the unknown, away from the human world.

Mikhail Afanasievich Bulgakov
Псалом / Psalm

Кузьма Сергеевич Петров-Водкин (1878–1939). За самоваром. 1926.
[Третьяковская галерея. Москва]

K. Petrov-Vodkin. *By the Samovar*. 1926.
[The State Tretyakov Gallery. Moscow]

MIKHAIL AFANASIEVICH BULGAKOV

1891–1940

Bulgakov was born in Kiev, in the Ukraine, to the family of a professor of the Ecclesiastical Academy. His parents gave their first son the name of the patron saint of Kiev, Archangel Michael. Until the end of his life, Bulgakov loved the beautiful ancient city where he spent his childhood and his younger years, as later described it in his narratives and plays, such as the novel *The White Guard*.

Bulgakov was educated in Kiev. At first, he studied at the First Alexandrovskaya Gymnasium, known for its high-quality, rigorous education; and the year of his high school graduation was a time of loss, as well as love. In 1907, his father died. That same year, Bulgakov fell in love with Tatiana Lappa, who later would become his wife. The following year, Bulgakov entered the Medical Department of Kiev University. Unfortunately, his student years coincided with the beginning of World War I. The young doctor, even before graduation, began to work at military hospitals, and after gaining experience as an army doctor, he was sent to work in a small village in the provinces. It was at that time that Bulgakov tried to write his first fiction. Then he returned to his native city. During the Civil War his forced "adventures" began, when different military parties mobilized him as a physician and he had to participate in the war against his will. After a few stormy years of medical activity in opposing armies, Bulgakov decided to end his medical career and devoted his energies to becoming a writer. Living in the Caucasus, he began to pro-

duce satirical essays, stories, and plays, and tried to write a novel.

He continued this activity when the family moved to Moscow, where the Bulgakovs experienced a great deal of hardship and had many troubles due to the housing crisis after the Civil War. They had to live in communal apartments, later described by the writer in detail. In Moscow, Bulgakov actively collaborated with different newspapers and published his first fiction. There, his literary fame began to grow. It was in this city that he wrote his brilliant, courageous satire *The Dog's Heart*, aiming against the Communist ideology; his magical *The Master and Margarita*, his partly autobiographical novel *The White Guard*, and a number of excellent plays.

Due to Bulgakov's independent nature and his unwillingness to bend his neck to the authorities, many of his narratives were created without any hope of reaching a reader, and many of his plays were prohibited. He always had problems with his job and was needy and in a desperate state because the leaders of the Communist regime did not like his writings, and Soviet censorship was hard on him, treating him horribly for his nonconformism. The informants infiltrating Moscow's literary circles reported constantly on Bulgakov's "counterrevolutionary speeches" and writings. As a result, the secret police searched the writer's apartment, confiscated his manuscripts and his diary, and required that he explain his behavior at interrogations. Once, during that questioning, he said, "I write things, which sometimes probably offend the public-communist circles. I always write with a clear conscience and I write how I see things..."

In this atmosphere of permanent persecution, Bulgakov started thinking about emigration and wrote to Joseph Stalin, asking for permission to leave. However, the Communist Party did not give permission, and the authorities continued to keep him on a short leash, from time to time giving more freedom and then taking it away. In that torturous cycle, the writer continued to work, creating marvelous profound fiction, high-quality dramas, librettos, and scripts.

In the late 1930s, Bulgakov's health was declining—from his father, the writer inherited a severe form of nephrosclerosis, and he began to lose his eyesight. However, the Soviet government did not let him go abroad for medical treatment. Bulgakov died in 1940; his last words were: 'I wanted to serve my people... I did not harm anyone..."

The name of the writer and his writings were essentially prohibited in the USSR. His rich legacy was given to the readers only due to the efforts of his widow in the Sixties, and then in full during Perestroika.

On September 23, 1923, Bulgakov's story "Psalm" was published. The story is interesting not only for its background, which was the writer's experience in communal apartment living, but also because of its mixing of genres—as if it were on the verge of narrative and drama. The entire story is a conversation between the narrator and a little lisping boy and, later, with his mother—the woman with whom the narrator is in love. At the same time, the writing is filled with music, not only because of its "singing" animated objects in the room playing the roles of minor characters—witnesses of the romance—but also due to the insertion in the plot of the popular romance by Aleksandr Vertinsky:

"I will buy a dog for myself on Saturday,
I will be singing a Psalm at night,
I will order shoes for my tailcoat...
I will somehow survive... It's all right."

That, all together, creates an exciting impression of the beginning of a tender love affair and the development of passion, as if Bulgakov's characters were standing on the threshold of a new hope.

МИХАИЛ АФАНАСЬЕВИЧ БУЛГАКОВ

Псалом

Первоначально кажется, что это крыса царапается в дверь. Но слышен очень вежливый человеческий голос:

— Мозно зайти?

— Можно, пожалуйте.

Поют дверные петли.

— Иди и садись на диван!

(От двери.) — А как я по паркету пойду?

— А ты тихонечко иди и не катайся. Ну-с, что новенького?

— Нициво.

— Позвольте, а кто сегодня утром ревел в коридоре?

(Тягостная пауза.) — Я ревел.

— Почему?

— Меня мама наслёпала.

— За что?

(Напряжённейшая пауза.) — Я Сурке ухо укусил.

— Однако.

— Мама говорит, Сурка — негодяй. Он дразнит меня, копейки поотнимал.

— Всё равно, таких декретов нет, чтоб из-за копеек уши людям кусать. Ты, выходит, глупый мальчик.

(Обида.) — Я с тобой не возусь.

— И не надо.

(Пауза.) — Папа приедет, я ему сказу. (Пауза.) — Он тебя застрелит.

— Ах, так. Ну, тогда я чай не буду делать. К чему? Раз меня застрелят…

— Нет, ты цай делай.

MIKHAIL AFANASIEVICH BULGAKOV

Psalm

At first, you would think there was a rat scratching on the door. But you hear a very polite lisping human voice:

"May I come in?"

"You may, welcome."

The door sings on its hinges.

"Go and sit down on the sofa!"

(From the door) "And how can I walk on the parquet?"

"You walk slowly and don't slide. Well, what's new?"

"Nussing."

"Allow me to ask, but who was howling in the hallway today?"

(Oppressive silence) "I was howling."

"Why?"

"My mudder thpanked me."

"For what?"

(After a tense silence) "I bit Shurka's ear."

"You don't say!"

"My mother says: 'Shurka is a rascal'. He teases me, took my kopecks."

"Anyway, there are no such decrees to bite people's ears because of kopecks. So, it appears that you are a stupid boy."

(Offence) "I am not playing wit you anymore."

"Don't."

(Pause) "My fadder will come, and I will tell him. (Pause) He will shoot you."

"So that's what you are up to! Then I will not make tea. For what? If he shoots me..."

"No, do make tea."

— А ты выпьешь со мной?

— С конфетами? Да?

— Непременно.

— Я выпью.

На корточках два человеческих тела — большое и маленькое. Музыкальным звоном кипит чайник, и конус жаркого света лежит на странице Джерома Джерома.

— Стихи-то ты, наверное, забыл?

— Нет, не забыл.

— Ну, читай.

— Ку...куплю я себе туфли...

— К фраку.

— К фраку, и буду петь по ноцам...

— Псалом.

— Псалом... и заведу... себе собаку...

— Ни...

— Ни-ци-во-о...

— Как-нибудь проживём.

— Нибудь как. Пра-зи-вё-ём.

— Вот именно. Чай закипит, выпьем. Проживём. (Глубокий вздох.) — Пра-зи-вё-ём.

Звон. Джером. Пар. Конус. Лоснится паркет.

— Ты одинокий.

Джером падает на паркет. Страница угасает. (Пауза.) — Это кто же тебе говорил? (Безмятежная ясность.) — Мама.

— Когда?

— Тебе пуговицу когда присивала. Присивала. Присивает, присивает и говорит Натаске...

— Так-с. Погоди, погоди, не вертись, а то я тебя обварю... Ух!..

— Горяций, ух!

— Конфету какую хочешь, такую и бери.

— Вот я эту больсую хоцу.

— Подуй, подуй и ногами не болтай. (Женский голос за сценой.) — Славка!

Стучит дверь. Петли поют приятно.

"Will you drink with me?"

"With candies? Yes?"

"Certainly."

"I will drink."

Two human bodies, a big and a small one squatting. The kettle boils ringing musically, and a cone of bright light is shining on Jerome Jerome's page.

"You, probably, forgot the verse?"

"No, I did not forget."

"Well, then tell me."

"*I...I will buy shoes...*"

"*For the tailcoat.*"

"*For the tailcoat and I'll be thinging at nights...*"

"*The Psalm.*"

"*The Psalm... And I will get... myself a dog...*"

"*It...*"

"*It does not ma...madder...*"

"*Somehow we'll survive.*"

"*Thomehow, we'll thur...vi...ve.*"

"Exactly. When the water boils, we will have tea. *We'll survive.*"

(Deep sigh) "*We'll thur...v...ve.*"

Ringing. Jerome. Steam. The cone of light. The parquet is shining.

"You are lonely."

Jerome is falling down on the parquet. The page is fading away.

(Silence) "Who on earth said that to you?"

(Serene frankness) "Mom."

"When?"

"When she was thewing on a button for you. Was thewing. She was thewing, thewing and saying to Nataska..."

"Well, mister. Wait, wait, don't fidget, or I may scald you... Ooh!.."

"It's hot, ooh!"

"Take any candy you want."

"I want dis big one."

"Blow on the tea, blow, and don't dangle your legs."

(Women's voice behind the stage) "Slavka!"

— Опять он у вас. Славка, иди домой!

— Нет, нет, мы с ним чай пьём.

— Он же недавно пил.

(Тихая откровенность.) — Я... не пил.

— Вера Ивановна. Идите чай пить.

— Спасибо, я недавно...

— Идите, идите, я вас не пущу...

— Руки мокрые... Бельё я вешаю...

(Непрошеный заступник.) — Не смей мою маму тянуть.

— Ну, хорошо, не буду тянуть... Вера Ивановна, садитесь...

— Погодите, я бельё повешу, тогда приду.

— Великолепно. Я не буду тушить керосинку.

— А ты, Славка, выпьешь, иди к себе. Спать. Он вам мешает.

— Я не месаю. Я не салю.

Петли поют неприятно. Конусы в разные стороны. Чайник безмолвен.

— Ты уже спать хочешь?

— Нет, я не хоцу. Ты мне сказку расскази.

— А у тебя уже глаза маленькие.

— Нет. Не маленькие. Расскази.

— Ну, иди сюда, ко мне. Голову клади. Так. Сказку? Какую же тебе сказку рассказать? А?

— Про мальчика, про того...

— Про мальчика? Это, брат, трудная сказка. Ну, для тебя, так и быть...

Ну-с, так вот, жил, стало быть, на свете мальчик. Да-с. Маленький, лет так приблизительно четырёх. В Москве. С мамой. И звали этого мальчика Славка.

— Как меня?

— ...Довольно красивый, но был он, к величайшему сожалению, драчун. И дрался он чем ни попало — кулаками, и ногами, и даже калошами. А однажды на лестнице девочку из 8-го номера, славная такая девочка, тихая, красавица, а он её по морде книжкой ударил.

There is a knock on the door. The door hinges are pleasantly singing.

"He is again with you. Slavka, go home!"

"No, no, but we are drinking tea with him!"

"He recently had tea."

(Quietly frankly confessing) "I... did not drink."

"Vera Ivanovna, do have tea with us."

"Thank you, I recently..."

"Join us, join us, I will not let you go..."

"My hands are wet... I am hanging the laundry..."

(Uninvited defender) "Don't dare to pull my mother's hand."

"All right, I won't pull... Vera Ivanovna, sit down..."

"Wait, I will hang the laundry and then will come back."

"Wonderful. I will not turn off the kerosene stove then."

"And you, Slavka, finish your tea and go home. To sleep. He bothers you."

"I'm not boddering him. I'm behaving."

The hinges are singing unpleasantly. The light cones are flying into all directions. The kettle keeps silence.

"Do you already want to sleep?"

"Not I do not want. You tell me de fairy tale."

"But your eyes are already getting small."

"No. No, they're not thmall. Tell."

"Well, mister, come here, to me. Rest your head here. Well, sir. Fairy tale? What fairy tale you want me to tell you? Eh?"

"About the boy, that one..."

"About that boy? This is, my dear, a difficult tale. Well, only for you, so be it, then...

Well, so once upon a time, lived a boy. Yes. A small one, about four years old. In Moscow. With his mother. And they called him Slavka.

"Like me?"

"...Quite handsome, but he was, to my greatest regret, a pugnacious fellow. And he fought with whatever his fancy would choose: with his fists, his feet and even with his galoshes. And, once on the staircase, he hit the girl, such a nice girl,

— Она сама дерётся…

— Погоди. Это не о тебе речь идёт.

— Другой Славка?

— Совершенно другой. На чём бишь я остановился? Да… Ну, натурально, пороли этого Славку каждый день, потому что нельзя же, в самом деле, драки позволять. А Славка всё-таки не унимался. И дошло дело до того, что в один прекрасный день Славка поссорился с Шуркой, тоже мальчик такой был, и, недолго думая, хвать его зубами за ухо, и пол-уха как не бывало. Гвалт тут поднялся. Шурка орёт. Славку порют, он тоже орёт… Кой-как приклеили Шуркино ухо синдетиконом. Славку, конечно, в угол поставили… И вдруг — звонок… И является совершенно неизвестный господин с огромной рыжей бородой и в синих очках и спрашивает басом: «А позвольте узнать, кто здесь будет Славка?» Славка отвечает: «Это я Славка». — «Ну, вот что, — говорит, — Славка, я — надзиратель над всеми драчунами, и придётся мне тебя, уважаемый Славка, удалить из Москвы. В Туркестан». Видит Славка, дело плохо, и чистосердечно раскаялся. «Признаюсь, — говорит, — что дрался, я и на лестнице играл в копейки, а маме бессовестно наврал, сказал, что не играл… Но больше этого не будет, потому что я начинаю новую жизнь». — «Ну, — говорит надзиратель, — это другое дело. Тогда тебе следует награда за чистосердечное твоё раскаяние». И немедленно повёл Славку в наградной раздаточный склад. И видит Славка, что там видимо-невидимо разных вещей. Тут и воздушные шары, и автомобили, и аэропланы, и полосатые мячики, и велосипеды, и барабаны. И говорит надзиратель: «Выбирай, чего твоя душа хочет». А вот что Славка выбрал, я и забыл…

(Сладкий, сонный бас.) — Велосипет?

— Да, да, вспомнил — велосипед. И сел немедленно Славка на велосипед и покатил прямо на Кузнецкий мост. Катит и в рожок трубит, а публика стоит на тротуаре, удивляется: «Ну и замечательный же человек

a quiet and a beautiful one, from the apartment number 8,—
with a book in her face."

"It is she who fights..."

"Hold on. It is not about you."

"Another Slavka?"

"Absolutely there was another one. Where was I, now? Yes...
Well, naturally, Slavka was spanked every day, because, one
should not allow fights, after all. And Slavka still could not stop.
And it came to the point when one fine day, Slavka quarreled with
Shurka, who was also a boy, and without long hesitation, he
snapped his ear with his teeth, and half an ear – without a trace. It
caused a hullaballoo. Shurka screams. Slavka is spanked, and he
screams too... Somehow they attached Shurka's ear with
Syndetikon. Slavka, of course, was put into the corner... Suddenly,
the doorbell rings. An absolutely unknown gentleman comes in,
with a huge red beard and in blue glasses and asks in a bass voice,
'Could you please tell me which of them is Slavka?' Slavka replies,
'It is I, Slavka.' 'So, listen, Slavka, I am an overseer of all pugnacious
fellows, and I will have to move you, dear Slavka, away from
Moscow. To Turkestan.' Slavka can see that things are turning
badly for him, and he open-heartedly repents. 'I admit,' he says,
'that I fought, and I gambled on the staircase with kopecks, and I
lied unashamedly to my mother, I said, that I had not gambled...
But I won't do this again, because I will start a new life.' 'Well,' the
overseer said, 'this is what I like to hear. Then, you should be
rewarded for your openhearted confession.' And he immediately
brought Slavka to the reward-distribution department. And Slavka
can see that there is countless number of different things. There are
balloons, toy cars and planes, and striped balls and bicycles and
drums. The overseer says, 'Choose, whatever you like.'

And what Slavka chose, I do not remember..."

(Sweet, sleepy bass) "A bicycle?"

"Yes, yes, now I remember – a bicycle." And Slavka sat
immediately on the bicycle, and started rolling away to Kuznetsky
Most. He rides, and blows the horn, and the passers-by stand on the
sidewalk and wonder, 'What a remarkable person that Slavka is!
And how can he manage not to be hit by a car?' And Slavka honks

этот Славка. И как он под автомобиль не попадёт?» А Славка сигналы даёт и кричит извозчикам: «Право держи!» Извозчики летят, машины летят, Славка нажаривает, и идут солдаты и марш играют, так что в ушах звенит…

— Уже?..

Петли поют. Коридор. Дверь. Белые руки, обнажённые по локоть.

— Боже мой. Давайте, я его раздену.

— Приходите же. Я жду.

— Поздно…

— Нет, нет… И слышать не хочу…

— Ну, хорошо.

Конусы света. Начинает звенеть. Выше фитили. Джером не нужен — лежит на полу. В слюдяном окне керосинки маленький радостный ад. Буду петь по ночам псалом. Как-нибудь проживём. Да, я одинокий. Псалом печален. Я не умею жить. Мучительнее всего в жизни — пуговицы. Они отваливаются, как будто отгнивают. Отлетела на жилете вчера одна. Сегодня одна на пиджаке и одна на брюках сзади. Я не умею жить с пуговицами, но я всё вижу и всё понимаю. Он не приедет. Он меня не застрелит. Она говорила тогда в коридоре Наташке: «Скоро вернётся муж, и мы уедем в Петербург». Ничего он не вернётся. Он не вернётся, поверьте мне. Семь месяцев его нет, и три раза я видел случайно, как она плачет. Слёзы, знаете ли, не скроешь. Но только он очень много потерял от того, что бросил эти белые, тёплые руки. Это его дело, но я не понимаю, как же он мог Славку забыть…

Как радостно спели петли…

Конусов нет. В слюдяном окошке — чёрная мгла. Давно замолк чайник.

Свет лампы тысячью маленьких звуков глядит сквозь реденький сатинет.

— Пальцы у вас замечательные. Вам бы пианисткой быть.

— Вот поеду в Петербург, опять буду играть…

— Вы не поедете в Петербург. У Славки на шее такие же

and shouts to the cabmen, 'Keep right!' The cabmen rush along, the cars tear along, Slavka flies like an arrow from a bow, and the soldiers go and play a march so that there is ringing in ears..."

"Already?.."

The hinges are singing. The hallway. The door. White arms bare up to elbows.

"My God! Let me take his clothes off."

"Please, do come back. I will be waiting."

"It's late..."

"No, no... I don't want to hear that..."

"All right then."

The cones of light. The ringing starts. The stove wicks are up. Jerome is not needed—it is lying on the floor. In the mica window of the kerosene stove, there is a tiny jolly hell. I'll be singing a Psalm at nights. We will survive somehow. Yes, I am lonely. The Psalm is sad. I do not know how to live. The most painful thing in life is buttons. They fall off as if they get rotten. One flew away from my vest yesterday. Today, one fell off the jacket, and another did from the back of my pants. I cannot cooperate with the buttons, but I see everything and understand everything. He will not come back. He will not shoot me. That time, in the hallway, she said to Natashka, 'My husband will come back soon, and we will go to Petersburg.' He will never be back. He won't be back, believe me. He has not been here for seven months, and three times, by chance, I have seen her crying. One cannot hide tears, you know. But he lost a lot because he left these white warm arms. This is his business, but I do not understand how, on earth, he was able to forget Slavka...

How jolly the hinges have just sung...

There are no light cones. The black darkness is in the stove mica window. The kettle lapsed long ago.

The light of the lamp is looking through the flimsy satinette with a thousand tiny notes.

"You have wonderful fingers. You could have become a piano player."

"When I go to Petersburg, I will start playing again..."

"You will not go to Petersburg. Slavka has the same locks on his neck like yours. And I feel sadness, you know. It is so

завитки, как и у вас. А у меня тоска, знаете ли. Скучно так, чрезвычайно как-то. Жить невозможно. Кругом пуговицы, пуговицы, пуго...

— Не целуйте меня... Не целуйте... Мне нужно уходить... Поздно...

— Вы не уйдёте. Вы там начнёте плакать. У вас есть эта привычка.

— Неправда. Я не плачу. Кто вам сказал?

— Я сам знаю. Я сам вижу. Вы будете плакать, а у меня тоска... тоска...

— Что я делаю... что вы делаете...

Конусов нет. Не светит лампа сквозь реденький сатинет. Мгла. Мгла.

Пуговиц нет. Я куплю Славке велосипед. Не куплю себе туфли к фраку, не буду петь по ночам псалом. Ничего, как-нибудь проживём.

incredibly dreary! It is impossible to live. Around only buttons, buttons, butto..."

"Don't kiss me... Don't kiss... I need to go... It is late..."

"You will not go. You will start crying there. You have this habit."

"It is not true. I don't cry. Who told you that?"

"I know it by myself. I can see this by myself. You will be crying, and I feel sadness... sadness..."

"What am I doing?... What are you doing?..."

The light cones went out. The lamp is not shining anymore through the flimsy satinette. Haze. Haze.

There are no buttons anymore. I will buy a bicycle for Slavka. I will not buy myself shoes for the tailcoat, and I will not be singing the Psalm at nights. It does not matter—somehow we will survive.

Ilya Ilf
(Ilya Arnoldovich Fainzilberg)

Рыболов стеклянного батальона /
Angler of the Glass Battalion

Кузьма Сергеевич Петров-Водкин (1878–1939). После боя. 1923.
[Центральный музей Вооруженных сил. Москва]

K. Petrov-Vodkin. *After the Battle.* 1923.
[The Central Museum of the Armed Forces. Moscow]

ILYA ILF
(ILYA ARNOLDOVICH FAINZILBERG)

1897–1937

The writer's real name was Iehiel Leib Fainzilberg; the pen name was created from the first letters of his name, patronymic, and last name. He was an extremely popular Soviet satirical writer, a successful journalist, and a scriptwriter.

Ilf was born and grew up in Odessa, in the south of Russia. This beautiful and romantic huge port-city on the Black Sea was the "nest" of a number of very gifted writers and poets. Ilf finished studying at the technical college there. He first worked in the drawing office, then in the telephone exchange, and finally at the military equipment plant. After the Revolution of 1917, Ilf worked as an accountant, a journalist, and an editor for humor magazines, mainly writing newspaper satires.

In his native city of Odessa, he began writing poetry. Unfortunately, this work did not survive, and only some fragments were remembered by his contemporaries. They noticed the unusual style of the young poet—original images and strange, elaborate metaphors suggesting painting: "The trussing of his soul is cracking under the heavy load of love... He attached his thoughts about her as wallpaper in his Room of Life. He even cleaned off the spots from the Sun to make it shine brighter for [her...]." That first experience in poetry was important for the writer because this dense and sophisticated manner of depiction later would influence his narrative style, becoming an integral part of Ilf's original manner.

As the fates decreed, in 1925, in Moscow, he met the writer Yevgeny Petrovich Kataev (pseudonym:Yevgeny Petrov), also from Odessa, and they decided to write together as a team. That ten-year long collaboration made Ilf and Petrov extremely popular after the publication of their two satirical novels, *The Twelve Chairs* and *The Golden Calf*. These books sparkle with humor, irony, and wit and are written in original, picturesque language. These novels became two of the most cited writings of the Soviet epoch; they are on everybody's bookshelf in Russian households and have been adapted for the screen many times. Together, in this fruitful cooperation, the writers created many tales, novellas, and scripts.

Ilf's fiction style is very original: spicy and humorous. It is mixed with the poetry he wrote in his younger years. According to his friends, the poems were blank verse filled with artistic images that reflect his creative vision of the world. Probably that gift was in the writer's family: his brothers were talented graphic artists, painters, and photographers. Ilf himself was a skilled amateur photographer who created an entire photo gallery; this collection was later published, long after his death from tuberculosis in 1937.

The story "The Angler of the Glass Battalion" was based on real events: at the time of the Civil War, Ilf was mobilized by the Red Army and participated in battles in the Russian South. The story was published in 1923 in the newspaper *Gudok*; Ilf worked for it as an editor and writer, developing his original style. The story is an unusual combination of irony and subtle humor, heroic content, and eccentric characters, with traces of melancholy and romanticism intertwined with elements of a painterly style of sunny southern Impressionism and a descriptive narrative saturated with bright images.

ИЛЬЯ ИЛЬФ

Рыболов стеклянного батальона

— Посмотрел я на эту рыбу...

Человеку, который это говорил, было тридцать лет. А мы валялись по углам вагона и старались не слушать.

— После рыбы хорошо пить чай, — продолжал голос.

Мы, это — первый взвод батальона. Никому не было известно, какого полка мы батальон. Числом мы тоже подходили: всего шестьдесят человек. Но нас называли батальоном.

— Стеклянный батальон! — сказал комендант Гранитной станции, когда нас увидел.

— Рвань! — добавил комендант. — Я думал, хороших ребят пришлют, а они все в очках!

Мы остались на охране Гранитной. Потом комендант переменил свое мнение, но кличка пошла в ход, и мы так и остались стеклянным батальоном.

— Посмотрел я на эту рыбу...

Никто даже не шевельнулся. От пылающего асфальтового перрона, шатаясь, брёл ветер. Горячий воздух сыпался как песок.

Это был девятнадцатый год.

Я поднялся и вышел. Лебедь пошёл за мной. Это он рассказывал про рыбу. Он всегда говорил о ней. Далась ему эта рыба.

Я пошёл на станцию. Лебедь двинулся в противоположную сторону, и я знал, куда он идёт.

Было очень скучно и очень жарко. Охрана станции — дело простое, а газеты не приходили уже вторую неделю.

ILYA ILF

Angler of the Glass Battalion

"I looked at that fish…"

The man who was speaking was thirty. And we were lying in the corners of the rail car and were trying not to listen.

"It is good to have tea after fish," the voice continued.

We were the first platoon of the battalion. Nobody knew to which regiment the battalion belonged. And our number matched too: in total, sixty people. But we were called a battalion.

"Glass Battalion!" said the commandant of Granitnaya station, when he saw us.

"Scamps!" the commandant added. "I thought they would send good guys, but all of them wear glasses!"

We were left for the protection of Granitnaya. Then the commandant changed his mind, but the nickname became popular, and we forever remained in memory as the Glass Battalion.

"I looked at that fish…"

Nobody even stirred. The wind was tottering from the flaming asphalt platform. Hot air was pouring like sand.

It was in the year 1919.

I got up and left. Lebed followed me. It was he who was telling us about the fish. He always talked about it. That fish gave him no rest!

I went to the station. Lebed started walking in the opposite direction, and I knew where he was going.

It was very boring and very hot. Guarding the station was a simple business, but newspapers had not been delivered already for the second week.

Разгорячённый асфальт обжигал подошвы, с неба, треща и всё разрушая, сыпалась жара.

У стенки, в тени, где стоял накрытый гимнастёркой пулемёт, я обернулся. Лебедь уже был далеко. Виднелась только его плывущая в пшенице голова.

— Куда пошёл? — закричал я.

Голова обернулась, что-то прокричала и унеслась дальше. Впрочем, я знал, куда пошёл Лебедь.

Ему было идти версты полторы. До пруда. Там он удил рыбу, о которой говорил.

— Всё к ней ходит? — спросил пулемётчик, зевая.

— Ходит, — сказал я. — А что слышно?

— Да ничего. Мохна, говорят, у Татарки стоит. Врут. Чего ему сюда идти? Не его район! А насчёт рыбы Лебедь, конечно, запарился. Мне стрелочник говорил. Никогда её там и не водилось.

Я ушёл.

История рыбы такая. Видел её в этом пруду один только Лебедь.

— Длинная и толстая. Вроде щуки.

Смеялись над ним сильно. Ну откуда же в пересохшей луже рыба? Де́ла нет, скучно — и пошёл смех, один раз вечером даже спектакль об этом устроили.

Первый акт. Сидит Лебедь и свою любовь к рыбе доказывает. Второй акт. Рыба свою любовь к Лебедю доказывает. Третий акт. Показывают ребёнка грудного, который от этих доказательств произошёл.

Совсем неостроумно. Ребёнка у сторожихи одалживали. Очень скучно уж было и жарко.

Однако Лебедя этим довели до каления. Сидит и только об одном:

— Посмотрел я на эту рыбу.

Просто бред. Поклялся Лебедь, что эту рыбу поймает и всё докажет.

Если человек захочет, то всё сможет. Из всякой дряни Лебедь сколотил себе удочку и днями сидел над своей помойницей-лужей.

The heated asphalt burnt the soles, and the crackling heat was pouring from the sky, destroying everything.

By the wall, in the shade, where the machine-gun was standing covered with a soldier's blouse, I looked back. Lebed was already far away. I could see only his head drifting in the wheat.

"Where are you going?" I shouted.

His head turned around; he shouted something back and sped away. Nevertheless, I knew where Lebed was heading.

He had about a mile to walk. To the pond. There he angled for that fish he told us about.

"He still goes to it?" the machine-gunner asked, yawning.

"He does," I said. "What is new?"

"Nothing. The Makhno's, they say, are by Tatarka. They lie. What does a Makhno need to come here for? It is not his territory! And about the fish, Lebed, obviously, is in a stew. There have never been any fish over there. The switchman told me."

I left.

The history of the fish is as follows. It was only Lebed who saw it in that pond.

"Long and fat. Like a pike."

We laughed at him a lot. Where could there be fish in that dried up puddle? We did not have anything to do, it was boring, the laughter started, and one night we even performed a play about that.

The First Act. Lebed sits and proves his love for that Fish. The Second Act. The Fish proves its love for him. The Third Act. A baby is shown who was born from those proofs.

Not ingenious at all. We even borrowed a baby from the watchman's wife for that. You know, it was too boring and too hot.

However, we made Lebed hopping mad with that. He sits and talks only about the same:

"I looked at that fish."

Pure nonsense. He swore that he would catch that fish and prove everything.

Where there is a will—there is a way. Lebed made a fishing rod from some trash, and all day long sat by his dirty puddle.

Комендант и рыболовом его называл и вообще крыл — не помогало. Дежурство кончит, о рыбке поговорит и сейчас же к ней на свидание. Удочку несёт и винтовку. Без винтовки нам отходить от станции не позволяли.

Солнце в беспамятстве катилось к закату. Телеграфные провода выли и свистели. Швыряя белый дым, вылез из-за поворота паровоз и снова ушёл за поворот. В пшенице кричала и плакала мелкая птичья сволочь. Солнце сжималось, становилось всё меньше и безостановочно падало. Луна пожелтела, и поднялся ветер.

Батальон вылез из тёмных углов, где прятался от жары. Семафор проснулся и открыл зелёный глаз.

Пришёл долгожданный вечер. Лебедя всё не было. Чёрные тени уцепились за станционные постройки и попадали на рельсы.

— Не рыбу он видел, а русалку! Сам же он говорил, что только хвост видел! Разве человек из-за рыбы станет, как головёшка? Рыба, рыба… У неё только хвост рыбий.

Комендант вышел из телеграфа, засовывая в карманы узенькие ленточки телеграмм, и сейчас же пошёл переполох. То, что казалось выдумкой днём, вечером сделалось правдой. В Татарке сидели банды.

Фонари шипя погасли. Гранитную захлопнуло темнотой. Первый взвод нахмурился и забросил за спину винтовки.

Первый взвод, мой взвод и взвод Лебедя, выступал в сторожевое охранение на версту в сторону Татарки.

— Где Лебедь? — кричал комендант. — Ну, я этому рыболову покажу! Никогда его на месте…

Комендант не кончил. Со стороны пруда грохнул и покатился выстрел. Потом ещё два. Остальное сделалось вмиг.

Первый взвод никуда не пошёл. Идти было уже некуда: шли к нам.

Пулемёт затарахтел по перрону и пошёл вбок. Я посмотрел в лицо залёгшего со мной рядом. Оно было жёлтое от света жёлтой луны. И сейчас же ударил пулемёт. Внезапная атака махновцам не удалась.

The commandant called him an angler, and even cursed at him, but it did not help. As soon as he finishes his duty, he tells about the fish and goes on a "date" with it. Carries both a fishing rod and a rifle. We were not allowed to leave the station without a rifle.

The sun, unconscious, was rolling down to the horizon. The telegraph poles were hauling and whistling. The locomotive, throwing white smoke, crawled from around the corner, turned and again disappeared. In the wheat, a rabble of tiny birds were shouting and crying. The sun was shrinking, getting smaller and steadily setting. The moon turned yellow, and the wind started blowing.

The battalion crawled out of the dark corners where we had been hiding from the heat. The semaphore woke up and opened its green eye.

The long-awaited evening came. But Lebed was not here yet. Black shades grasped at the station buildings and fell down on the rails.

"It was not a fish he saw, but a mermaid! He himself said that he had seen only a tail! A man will never get so crazy for a fish, will he? The fish, the fish... She has only a fish tail."

The commandant left the telegraph room, pushing into his pockets the narrow ribbons of telegrams, and immediately raised an alarm. What looked as a rumor in the afternoon, turned out to be truth in the evening. The gangs were in Tatarka.

The lamps went out hissing. Darkness fell down on Granitnaya station. The first platoon frowned and threw their rifles onto their shoulders.

The first platoon, my platoon and the platoon of Lebed, were going to move half a mile towards Tatarka to an outpost.

"Where is Lebed?" The commandant was shouting. "I will show him, this angler! He is never here..."

The commandant did not finish that. A shot thundered and rolled from the pond. Then two more. After that it all happened in a blink of an eye.

The first platoon was not going anywhere. There was nowhere to go: they were coming toward us.

The machine-gun rattled on the platform as it was dragged to the side. I looked at the face of the man laying by me. It was yellow from the yellow moonlight. Suddenly the machine-gun

Гранитная уже была предупреждена выстрелами с пруда.

Тишина пропала. Всё наполнилось звоном, грохотом и гулом. В чёрное лакированное небо полетели белые, розовые и зелёные ракеты. Из цепи брызгали залпами. Луна носилась по небу, как собака на цепи. Тишина пропала. Атака пропала. Они не дошли даже на триста шагов. Вслед резал пулемёт. Вслед в спину нагоняли пули. Атака была отбита.

Атака была отбита, но на другой день мы хоронили Лебедя.

— Я, товарищи, плохо такие речи говорю, — сказал комендант. — Что говорить? Не сиди он там у пруда вчера — ещё неизвестно, что было бы! Может, их сила была бы! Могли взять врасплох!

А стеклянный батальон кидал землю на могилу рыболова. Но в тех рассказах, которые шли потом, его больше рыболовом не называли. А сторожиха плакала даже.

struck. Makhnovtsy's surprise attack failed. Granitnaya station had already been alarmed by the shots from the pond.

Silence vanished. A clanging, roar and boom filled the air. White, pink and green flares flew up to the lacquer black sky. The skirmish line was splashing volleys. The moon was scampering through the sky like a chained dog. Silence vanished. The attack vanished. They could not approach closer than three hundred steps and ran. The machine gun was cutting them down, as they were retreating. The bullets were catching them in the backs. The attack was repelled.

The attack was repelled, but the next day we were burying Lebed.

"Comrades, I give such speeches badly," the commandant said. "What is to say? If he had not been sitting there by the pond the previous day, nobody knows what could have happened! Maybe, they would have won! They could have taken us by surprise!"

And the Glass Battalion was tossing earth on the angler's grave. Though, in the stories we told later, nobody called him an angler. And the watchman's wife was even crying.

Arkady Gaidar
(Arkady Petrovich Golikov)
Горячий камень / Hot Stone

Илья Ефимович Репин (1844–1930). Мужичок из робких. 1877.
[Государственный художественный музей. Нижний Новгород, Россия]

I. Repin. *A Shy Peasant*. 1877.
[The State Art Museum. Nizhni Novgorod, Russia]

ARKADY GAIDAR
(ARKADY PETROVICH GOLIKOV)

1904–1941

Born on January 9, 1904, in the small town of Lgov near Kursk, Arkady spent his childhood in Arzamas. When his father was mobilized and sent to the front during World War I, Arkady tried to run away from home to join the Russian army, but he was turned back. As a student, he kept a diary, and from it one can deduce that among his favorite readings were Twain's *The Adventures of Tom Sawyer*, Shakespeare, Gogol, Dostoevsky, and Tolstoy. Literature classes were among Gaidar's favorites, and he was fond of theater as well. In 1917, when answering a questionnaire, he wrote only one word when asked about his favorite activity: "Books."

In 1918, during the time of the Civil War, he joined the Reds, possibly following his family's influence. It is believed that the long-term support his parents were offering to the Communist movement played a role in his decision. Arkady volunteered for the Red Army and studied at different training courses for the commanding officers, and when he was sixteen he already was a commander of a regiment. He was wounded many times in battle. In 1924, after the Civil War, in spite of a strong desire to continue his career in the army, due to his state of health he had to retire.

Arkady started writing short essays for various newspapers. Even his first literary exercises showed that he was more of a writer than a journalist. Soon, his first fiction was published, and in the 1930s to '40s, Gaidar became a very successful

writer, reflecting in his incredibly popular stories his impressions of the Civil War. He depicted it as a romantic, heroic
struggle for a happy future for the country. And his fiction was
especially popular among teenagers, his tales earning him a
reputation as the best writer for the youth.

From his optimistic and sunny fiction, one could hardly guess
that Gaidar permanently struggled with serious psychological
traumas he had suffered during the bloody events of the Civil
War. Once, he wrote that he constantly had dreams about the
people "he had killed in his childhood," and as a result, he had
struggled with bouts of depression. There were rumors that
Gaidar tried to commit suicide. Even in his early poetry about
the war, together with a quite romantic "the wind is tearing off
the clouds" or "the wind is breathing with the smell of war,"
there also are lines of despair, such as "there are bloody streams
running on melted snow..." or "the iron death has started
howling" (from his poems of 1926 to 1927).

Possibly, that is why Gaidar dreamed of a spiritual balance
and peace in life that he was not able to reach. The only place
he could fulfill that goal was in the world of imagination that
he created in his books—sunny, warm, and happy, a world
filled with romanticism and the purity of childhood. He was
known for his childish behavior and a lot of boyish features in
his everyday life—likely an attempt to avoid the gloomy, depressing memories about the horrible experience of traumatiz-
ing war events.

At that time the writer took the pen name "Gaidar," and
there are a few explanations of the origin of his pseudonym.
One of them is that he created it using the first letter of his last
name, the first letter of his first name, and added the rest in
imitation of the characters of Alexander Dumas' French aristo-
cratic last names, similar to d'Artagnan from *Three Musketeers*,
which in the writer's case meant "from Arzamas."

This desire to linger in childhood made the writer an "eternal
child." This prolonged youth was partly responsible for
Gaidar's unique writing style—not entirely mature and adult,
but still boyish to a degree—and this made his vision of the

Civil War events express an innocent and pure schoolboy's vision. Among his best writings are "Timur and his Team" and the melancholy and poetical story "Blue Cup." His motto, no doubt, can be found in one of his best stories for children, "Chuk and Gek": "Everyone understood differently what happiness is. But everyone together knew and understood that we should live honestly, work a lot and love strongly and protect this happy huge land called the Soviet Country."

He wrote this in 1939; two years later, when World War II began, Gaidar began to work as a war correspondent. Soon circumstances brought him to one of the Soviet partisan units. Gaidar was killed by the Nazis on October 26, 1941.

Gaidar wrote the philosophical, fantastic tale "The Hot Stone" in April 1941, just before the beginning of World War II. It was the last work of fiction that he wrote for children. In spite of the potential young audience for the fiction, this parable contains a great deal of philosophical sophistication. It is clear that the writer expressed in this simple but profound tale some inner thoughts that might have tortured him, when he remembered his choices in life and his bitter war experience—exemplified by O. Henry in his tale "The Roads We Take": think of what you would do if you had a chance to start your life over from the beginning. Have you ever thought of it? What would you decide? Or, maybe one should leave his life the way it is so as to not regret the lost years?

АРКАДИЙ ГАЙДАР

Горячий камень

I

Жил на селе одинокий старик. Был он слаб, плёл корзины, подшивал валенки, сторожил от мальчишек колхозный сад и тем зарабатывал свой хлеб.

Он пришёл на село давно, издалека, но люди сразу поняли, что этот человек немало хватил горя. Был он хром, не по годам сед. От щеки его через губы пролёг кривой рваный шрам. И поэтому, даже когда он улыбался, лицо его казалось печальным и суровым.

II

Однажды мальчик Ивашка Кудряшкин полез в колхозный сад, чтобы набрать там яблок и тайно насытиться ими до отвала. Но, зацепив штаниной за гвоздь ограды, он свалился в колючий крыжовник, оцарапался, взвыл и тут же был сторожем схвачен.

Конечно, старик мог бы стегнуть Ивашку крапивой или, что ещё хуже, отвести его в школу и рассказать там, как было дело.

Но старик сжалился над Ивашкой. Руки у Ивашки были в ссадинах, позади, как овечий хвост, висел клок от штанины, а по красным щекам текли слёзы.

Молча вывел старик через калитку и отпустил перепуганного Ивашку восвояси, так и не дав ему ни одного тычка и даже не сказав вдогонку ни одного слова.

ARKADY GAIDAR

Hot Stone

I

One lonely old man lived in the village. He was weak; he wove baskets, mended winter boots, and earned his living also by guarding the collective farm garden and keeping the boys away.

He had come to the village long ago, from far away, but the people immediately understood that the man had seen a lot of troubles. He was lame, and had too much gray hair. A curved jagged scar ran across his cheek to his lips. That is why, even when he smiled, his face looked sad and harsh.

II

Once, the boy, Ivashka Kudryashkin, sneaked into the collective farm garden to pick some apples and stuffed himself with them to the point of bursting. But he caught his pants on the fence nail and fell down into the prickly gooseberry bush, scratched himself, howled and was caught by the watchman.

Certainly, the old man could have lashed him with a branch of stinging nettle, or, what would be even worse, he could have brought him to school, and told everyone what had happened.

But the old man took pity on Ivashka. Ivashka's hands were all in scratches, behind him a shred of his pants was hanging like a sheep's tail, and tears were streaming down his red face.

In silence, the old man took the boy out of the garden and set scared Ivashka free to run back home, without any clips on the back of his head, and without saying a single mean word after him.

III

От стыда и горя Ивашка забрёл в лес, заблудился и попал на болото. Наконец он устал. Опустился на торчавший из мха голубой камень, но тотчас же с воплем подскочил, так как ему показалось, что он сел на лесную пчелу и она его через дыру штанов больно ужалила.

Однако никакой пчелы на камне не было. Этот камень был, как уголь, горячий, и на плоской поверхности его проступали закрытые глиной буквы.

Ясно, что камень был волшебный, — это Ивашка смекнул сразу! Он сбросил башмак и торопливо начал оббивать каблуком с надписей глину.

И вот он прочёл такую надпись:

КТО СНЕСЁТ ЭТОТ КАМЕНЬ НА ГОРУ И ТАМ РАЗОБЬЁТ ЕГО НА ЧАСТИ, ТОТ ВЕРНЁТ СВОЮ МОЛОДОСТЬ И НАЧНЁТ ЖИТЬ СНАЧАЛА.

Ниже стояла печать, но не простая, круглая, как в сельсовете, и не такая, треугольником, как на талонах в кооперативе, а похитрее: два креста, три хвоста, дырка с палочкой и четыре запятые.

Тут Ивашка Кудряшкин огорчился. Ему было всего восемь лет — девятый. И жить начинать сначала, то есть опять на второй год оставаться в первом классе, ему не хотелось вовсе.

Вот если бы через этот камень, не уча заданных в школе уроков, можно было из первого класса перескакивать сразу в третий — это другое дело!

Но всем и давно уже известно, что такого могущества даже у самых волшебных камней никогда не бывает.

IV

Проходя мимо сада, опечаленный Ивашка опять увидел старика, который, кашляя, часто останавливаясь и передыхая, нёс ведро известки, а на плече держал палку с мочальной кистью.

Тогда Ивашка, который был по натуре мальчиком добрым, подумал: «Вот идёт человек, который очень

III

Because of shame and grief, Ivashka strayed to the forest, lost his way, and found himself in the swamp. Finally, he got tired. He sat down on a blue stone jutting out of the moss, but immediately jumped off the stone howling, because he felt that he was sitting down on a forest bee, and it badly stung him through the hole in his pants.

However, there was no bee on the stone. The rock was as hot as a coal, and on its flat surface some letters were showing through a layer of clay.

It was clear, the stone was magic; this is what Ivashka realized right away! He took off his shoe and hurriedly began to beat off the clay with its heel, as fast as he could.

And finally he read the inscription:

THAT MAN WHO BRINGS THIS STONE UP THE MOUNTAIN, AND BREAKS IT INTO PIECES THERE, WILL RETURN TO HIS YOUTH AND START LIVING FROM THE BEGINNING.

Underneath it there was a seal, but not a simple one like in the collective farm office, not like a triangle, similar to coupons in the cooperative, but more sophisticated; two crosses, two tails, a circle with a stick and four commas.

Here Ivashka Kudryashkin got upset. He was only a little past his eighth birthday—going on the ninth, and to start his life from the beginning, that would mean to repeat his first year in school, which he was not eager to do at all.

But if, by using the stone, he could jump over every other year at school, without doing his homework—that would be another matter!

But everyone knows since long ago, that even the most magic stones never have such might.

IV

Walking by the garden, sad Ivashka saw the old man again who was coughing, often stopping for rest, he was carrying a bucket full of lime, and was holding a stick with a fiber brush on his shoulder.

Then Ivashka, who was a kind-hearted boy, thought, "Here, this man could have lashed me with a branch of stinging nettle

свободно мог хлестнуть меня крапивой. Но он пожалел меня. Дай-ка теперь я его пожалею и верну ему молодость, чтобы он не кашлял, не хромал и не дышал так тяжко».

Вот с какими хорошими мыслями подошёл к старику благородный Ивашка и прямо объяснил ему, в чём дело.

Старик сурово поблагодарил Ивашку, но уйти с караула на болото отказался, потому что были ещё на свете такие люди, которые, очень просто, могли бы за это время колхозный сад от фруктов очистить.

И старик приказал Ивашке, чтобы тот сам выволок камень из болота в гору. А он потом придёт туда ненадолго и чем-нибудь скоренько по камню стукнет.

Очень огорчил Ивашку такой поворот дела.

Но рассердить старика отказом он не решился. На следующее утро, захватив крепкий мешок и холщовые рукавицы, чтобы не обжечь о камень руки, отправился Ивашка на болото.

V

Измазавшись грязью и глиной, с трудом вытянул Ивашка камень из болота и, высунув язык, лёг у подножия горы на сухую траву.

«Вот! — думал он. — Теперь вкачу я камень на гору, придёт хромой старик, разобьёт камень, помолодеет и начнёт жить сначала. Люди говорят, что хватил он немало горя. Он стар, одинок, избит, изранен и счастливой жизни, конечно, никогда не видел. А другие люди её видели». На что он, Ивашка, молод, а и то уже три раза он такую жизнь видел. Это — когда он опаздывал на урок и совсем незнакомый шофёр подвёз его на блестящей легковой машине от конюшни колхозной до самой школы. Это — когда весной голыми руками он поймал в канаве большую щуку. И, наконец, когда дядя Митрофан взял его с собой в город на весёлый праздник Первое мая.

«Так пусть же и несчастный старик хорошую жизнь увидит», — великодушно решил Ивашка.

Он встал и терпеливо потянул камень в гору.

right away. But he had mercy on me. It is my turn to feel sorry for him and return his youth to him, not to cough, not to limp, and not to breathe so heavily."

So, with these good ideas the noble Ivashka came to the old man and directly explained what the matter was. The old man dourly thanked him, but refused to leave his post for the marsh, because there were still people who were able to "clean out" with great agility the fruits of the community garden.

And the old man told Ivashka to drag that stone off the marsh up the mountain. And then he would come there for a little while, and quickly hit that stone with something.

Such a turn of events made Ivashka very upset.

But he did not dare make the old man angry with his refusal. The next morning, taking a strong sack and linen mittens, so he would not burn his hands on the stone, he went to the marsh.

V

Having gotten dirty with mud and clay, Ivashka pulled out the stone from the marsh with difficulty, and sticking out his tongue, he laid down on the dried grass by the foot of the mountain.

"Here it is!" He was thinking. "Now I will roll the stone up the hill, the lame old man will come there, break the stone, become young, and start living from the beginning. People say that he went through many troubles. He is old, lonely, beaten down, wounded, and certainly, has never seen a happy life. But other people have seen it." In spite of being young, Ivashka saw this kind of life already three times. Once it was when he was going to be late for class, and an unknown driver gave him a ride in a shining car all the way from the collective farm stable to the school. It was also then in the spring, when he caught with his own hands a big pike in a ditch. And, finally, a happy moment arrived when Uncle Mitrofan took him to the city to the jolly celebration of the holiday of May the 1st.

"So let the unhappy old man see good life too," Ivashka made a decision generously.

He got up and patiently dragged the stone up the hill.

VI

И вот перед закатом к измученному и продрогшему Ивашке, который, съёжившись, сушил грязную, промокшую одежду возле горячего камня, пришёл на гору старик.

— Что же ты, дедушка, не принёс ни молотка, ни топора, ни лома? — вскричал удивлённый Ивашка. — Или ты надеешься разбить камень рукою?

— Нет, Ивашка, — отвечал старик, — Я не надеюсь разбить его рукой. Я совсем не буду разбивать камень, потому что я не хочу начинать жить сначала.

Тут старик подошёл к изумлённому Ивашке, погладил его по голове. Ивашка почувствовал, что тяжёлая ладонь старика вздрагивает.

— Ты, конечно, думал, что я стар, хром, уродлив и несчастен, — говорил старик Ивашке. — А на самом деле я самый счастливый человек на свете.

Ударом бревна мне переломило ногу, но это тогда, когда мы — ещё неумело — валили заборы и строили баррикады, поднимали восстание против царя, которого ты видел только на картинке.

Мне вышибли зубы, но это тогда, когда, брошенные в тюрьмы, мы дружно пели революционные песни. Шашкой в бою мне рассекли лицо, но это тогда, когда первые народные полки уже били и громили белую вражескую армию.

На соломе, в низком холодном бараке метался я в бреду, больной тифом. И грозней смерти звучали надо мной слова о том, что наша страна в кольце и вражья сила нас одолевает. Но, очнувшись вместе с первым лучом вновь сверкнувшего солнца, узнавал я, что враг опять разбит и что мы опять наступаем.

И, счастливые, с койки на койку протягивали мы друг другу костлявые руки и робко мечтали тогда о том, что пусть хоть не при нас, а после нас наша страна будет такой вот, какая она сейчас, — могучей и великой. Это ли ещё, глупый Ивашка, не счастье?! И на что мне иная жизнь?

VI

And finally, before the sunset, the old man came to the mountain to the exhausted and cold Ivashka, who was drying his dirty wet clothes by the hot stone.

"Grandpa, why didn't you bring either a hammer or an axe, or a crowbar?" Ivashka shouted in surprise. "Or do you hope to break the stone with your hand?"

"Not at all, Ivashka," the old man replied. "I do not hope to break it with my hand. I am not going to break it at all, because I do not want to start living my life from the beginning."

Then the old man came to the astonished Ivashka, and patted him on the head. Ivashka felt that the heavy palm of the old man was shaking.

"You, of course, have thought that I am old, lame, ugly and unhappy," the old man said to Ivashka, "But I am the happiest man in the world."

"A log broke my leg, and it happened way back when we unskillfully broke down fences to build barricades, in the uprising against the tsar, whom you saw only in the pictures."

"My teeth were knocked out, but it happened when we were thrown into prisons, we sang the revolutionary songs together. My face was cut with a saber in a battle, but it was when the people's armies already were fighting and defeating the hostile White Army."

"In the low-ceilinged, cold hospital barrack, I was tossing and turning in delirium on the straw, sick with typhus. And more horrifying than death for me were the words that our country was besieged, and our enemy was defeating us. But, waking up together with the first sparkling ray of sun, I again learned that the enemy had been defeated and that we were attacking again."

"And, happily, we were stretching our bony hands to each other, and were shyly dreaming that even if not in our lifetime, but after us, our country would nevertheless be like now: great and mighty. Is it not already happiness, silly Ivashka? Why do

Другая молодость? Когда и моя прошла трудно, но ясно и честно!

Тут старик замолчал, достал трубку и закурил.

— Да, дедушка! — тихо сказал тогда Ивашка. — Но раз так, то зачем же я старался и тащил этот камень в гору, когда он очень спокойно мог бы лежать на своем болоте?

— Пусть лежит на виду, — сказал старик, — и ты посмотришь, Ивашка, что из этого будет.

VII

С тех пор прошло много лет, но камень тот так и лежит на той горе неразбитым.

И много около него народу побывало. Подойдут, посмотрят, подумают, качнут головой и идут восвояси.

Был на той горе и я однажды. Что-то у меня была неспокойная совесть, плохое настроение. «А что, — думаю, — дай-ка я по камню стукну и начну жить сначала!»

Однако постоял-постоял и вовремя одумался.

«Э-э! — думаю, скажут, увидав меня помолодевшим, соседи. — Вот идёт молодой дурак! Не сумел он, видно, одну жизнь прожить так, как надо, не разглядел своего счастья и теперь хочет то же начинать сначала».

Скрутил я тогда табачную цигарку. Прикурил, чтобы не тратить спичек, от горячего камня. И пошёл прочь — своей дорогой.

I need another life? Another youth? I spent mine in difficulties, but purely and honestly!"

Here the old man stopped, took his pipe and started smoking.

"Yes, grandpa," Ivashka said quietly. "But if it is so, why did I work hard and drag this stone up the mountain, when it could have just as well remained there in its marsh?"

"Let it lay in full view," the old man said. "You will see what will happen."

VII

A lot of time has passed since, but the stone is still lying on that mountain, unbroken.

And a lot of people stopped by it. They came, looked at it, thought, shook their heads and went away.

Once I was on that mountain, too. That day I had a sick conscience and was in a bad mood. "And what if I hit the stone and start living from the beginning!" I thought.

However, I was standing and standing by the stone and, finally, changed my mind in time.

"Hey, hey!" I thought, "My neighbors would say seeing me younger: 'Here comes a young fool! It is clear that he was not able to live through one life the way he should have lived, he did not recognize his happiness, and now he wants to start the same from the very beginning.'"

Then I rolled a cigarette. I lit it up from the hot stone to save a match. And I went away—on my own road.

Vasily Grossman

Из окна автобуса /
From the Bus Window

Илья Николаевич Занковский (Заньковский) (1832–1919).
Боржомское ущелье. [Национальный музей Грузии]

Ilya Nikolaevich Zankovsky. *Borzhomi Canyon.*
[National Museum of Georgia]

VASILY GROSSMAN

1905–1964

Iosif Solomonovich Grossman (Vasily Grossman) was a prominent writer, a gifted journalist, and a talented war correspondent. He was born in Berdichev (now Ukraine), to an educated middle-class family. His father, an engineer, attended school in Switzerland, and his mother was educated in France. As a child, Grossman's name, Iosif, was transformed into a diminutive form, Iosya, close to the Russian name Vasya, which later became Vasily.

Like his father, Grossman wanted to become an engineer, and, in 1929, he graduated from Moscow University and worked as a chemical engineer in the coal mines. His first publications appeared in the 1930s. He wrote about the life of miners as well as the Civil War, which he described in one of his best early short stories, "In the Town of Berdichev." This plot later became the foundation for an outstanding film version by Alexander Askoldov (*Commissar*, 1967).

The success of his first narrative encouraged Grossman to become a professional writer. When World War II began, he worked as a war correspondent. Showing great personal courage, he experienced the entire war, including the Battle for Stalingrad.

With his novels and tales dedicated to the heroism of the people at war, Grossman also was one of the first to touch upon the subject of the Holocaust, and he wrote many bitter truths about it. However, those books could not be published during the era of the Soviet Union for a number of reasons.

241

One of these was that the Communist Party policy prohibited any emphasis on the suffering of a specific nationality, because a writer was expected to depict the suffering of all Soviet people equally. The same reason caused the destruction of Grossman's (as co-author with I. Erenburg) *Black Book*, a documentary collection about the annihilation of the Jews by the Nazis on Soviet territory. The surviving manuscript wasn't published until 1980, in Jerusalem. The Holocaust was an especially painful subject for the writer because his mother was killed in Berdichev's Jewish ghetto.

After the war, Grossman worked on two related novels—*In the Good Cause* and *Life and Fate*—dealing with the Battle of Stalingrad. He wrote these in Leo Tolstoy's traditional epic style. However, his work was severely criticized by the Party ideologues and even by some colleagues for being "ideologically harmful." Grossman had to edit the first book, taking into account that criticism. The second part of his work met even stronger opposition due to its anti-totalitarianism content. In 1961, the KGB confiscated the manuscript, and Grossman wrote to the leader of the country, Nikita Khrushchev, asking him to "return freedom" to the "imprisoned" book. The author said, "I think that I wrote the truth, that I was writing it out of love for people, being compassionate to people and believing in people." Eventually, one of the top Party officials told Grossman that the book could be published in the USSR—in two or three hundred years. The other copy of the manuscript was saved and brought to the West by Grossman's friends after his death. It was published in 1980, but it was available in Russia only during Perestroika. According to many literary critics, Grossman's *Life and Fate* is one of the best novels of the twentieth century.

Robert Chandler, the translator of the epic novel *Life and Fate*, called it a "brave and wise book... written with Chekhovian subtlety." This also is true of some of Grossman's shorter writings. The story "From the Bus Window," chosen for this collection, is a miniature philosophical sketch without a real plot. However, it contains—like the inside of a many-

faceted crystal—the refracted light of Grossman's style, so well described by Chandler. It is close to a wise, subtle vision of the "stream of life" presented by Chekhov. In the almost biblical landscape of the rocks and the sea, Grossman shows how the magnificent world around us also is "closed" and remote to us, recalling Alexander Pushkin's expression of the "indifferent nature sparkling with eternal beauty." "From the Bus Window" is a fragment of everyday life and its routines, an observation of one's surroundings and a ritual of repeated motions and actions. At the same time, we can observe the writer's ability to see the "blue infinity" of a "distant, high and eternal sky," to quote Leo Tolstoy's *War and Peace*. We feel how fragile a human being's life is, and how transient our existence is—a fleeting moment in comparison with the eternal Universe. At the very end of Grossman's story, one can feel the "echo" of eternal questions important to all great minds, all writers and poets of all times, and to all of us, the readers. How often, like Heinrich Heine's young man appealing to the waves, do we ask, walking on our life path: "What is a man? Where has he come from? Where will he go? And who is living there on the stars above us?" And we, like Heine's man, await an answer in vain.

ВАСИЛИЙ ГРОССМАН

Из окна автобуса

Автобус подали после завтрака к подъезду дома отдыха Академии наук.

На турбазе для поездки учёных выделили лучшего работника — образованного и умного человека.

Как приятен перед поездкой этот миг неподвижности — люди уселись, притихли, глядят на пыльные пальмы у входа в столовую, на местных франтов в чёрных костюмах, на городские часы, показывающие неизменно абсолютное время — шесть минут четвёртого.

Водитель оглянулся — все ли уселись. Его коричневые руки лежат на баранке.

Ну, поехали...

И вот мир открылся перед людьми: справа пустынное море — не то, оставшееся за спиной, море купальщиков и прогулочных катеров, а море без берега, море беды и войны, море рыбаков, боцманов и адмиралов.

А слева, среди пальм, бананов, среди мушмулы и магнолий, домики, обвитые виноградом, каменные заборы, огородики, и вдруг пустынные холмы, кусты, осыпанные красными ягодами шиповника, дикий хмель в голубоватом, туманном пуху, библейские кроткие овцы и дьяволы — козлы на жёлтых афро-азиатских осыпях — и снова сады, домики, чинары, хурма...

А справа одно лишь море.

И вот автобус круто сворачивает, дорога вьётся рядом с рекой, река вьётся в узкой долине, горы её зажали с двух сторон. Как хороша эта дорога! Можно ли передать

VASILY GROSSMAN

From the Bus Window

After breakfast, they brought the bus to the entrance of the Academy of Sciences spa hotel.

The recreation office selected the best guide—an educated and wise man to accompany the scientists on the tour.

How pleasant this moment of quiet before departure: people sat down, silent, and began looking at the dusty palms at the entrance to the cafeteria, at the local dandies in black suits, at the town clock immutably stuck at the absolute, eternal time—six past three.

The driver looked back—did everyone sit down? His suntanned hands rested on the steering wheel.

Well, let us go...

The world opened before the peoples' eyes: on the right, the empty ocean—not the one that vanished behind, the ocean of bathers, and pleasure boats—but an ocean without a shore, an ocean of woe and war, an ocean of fishermen, boatswains and admirals.

And on the left, among palms, banana trees, among medlars and magnolias, houses were twined around with grape vines, stone fences, kitchen gardens and suddenly deserted hillocks and bushes covered in red berries of wild roses, wild hopes in a cloud of bluish misty fuzz, biblical-like meek sheep; devilish goats were on the yellow Afro-Asiatic crumbled mounds—and again gardens, small houses, sycamore and persimmon trees...

And on the right—just the ocean...

And then the bus is turning sharply, the road is winding by the river, the river is winding within a narrow valley that the mountains are gripping from both sides. What a wonderful

огромный размах земной высоты и земной глубины, это соединение: рвущийся вверх мёртвый гранит и мутный, зеленоватый сумрак в ущелье, застывшая тишина и рядом звон, плеск горной реки.

Каждый новый виток дороги открывает по-новому красоту мира. Нежный солнечный свет легко лежит на голубоватом асфальте, на полукруглой воде, скользящей по круглым камням. У каждого пятна света своя отдельная жизнь, со своим теплом, смыслом, формой.

И то ли постепенно, то ли вдруг, душа человека наполняется своим светом, ощущает самоё себя, видит себя в этом мире с пустынным морем, с садами, с горным ущельем, с пятнами солнца; этот мир — она и не она, — она его видит, то ли не видит, она полна сама в себе покоя, мыслит и не мыслит, прозревает глубины жизни и близоруко, слепо дремлет. Она не думает ни о чём, но она погружена в глубину бо́льшую, чем та, в которую может проникнуть межзвёздный корабль.

Дивное состояние, подобное счастью ящерицы, дремлющей на горячем камне вблизи моря, кожей познающей солёное тепло воздуха, тень облаков. Мудрость, равная счастью паучка, застывшего на нити, протянутой между двумя травинками. Чувство познания жизненного чуда теми, кто ползает и летает.

Время от времени автобус останавливался, и Иван Петрович, экскурсовод, негромко, словно боясь помешать кому-то в горах, рассказывал о геологической истории абхазской земли, о первых древнейших поселениях людей.

Участники экскурсии спрашивали Ивана Петровича о множестве вещей — он рассказывал и о нравах горной форели, и о храмах шестого века, и о проекте горной электростанции, и о партизанах времён Гражданской войны, об альпийской растительности, о бортничестве и овцеводстве.

Ивана Петровича чем-то тревожил один пожилой человек — во время остановок он стоял поодаль от всех и не слушал объяснений. Иван Петрович заметил, что все

road! It is impossible to express the earth's enormous heights and its depth, the interconnection of solid dead granite jutting upward and the muddy greenish darkness in the ravine, the frozen silence and then the jingling and splashing of the mountain river.

Each new winding of the road reveals again the beauty of the world. The sun's tender rays are resting on the bluish asphalt and on nearly round puddles of water sliding over the rounded boulders. Each spot of light has its own life with its warmth, meaning and shape.

Gradually, or suddenly, the soul of a man fills with its own glow. It perceives itself, and sees itself in this world with the deserted ocean, with gardens, the ravine with spots of sunny light. Be it an actual soul or not, whether it sees anything or not, it is itself full of tranquility. And whether a soul thinks or not, it penetrates the profound meaning of life, and it is short-sightedly and blindly dozing. It does not think about anything, but it is immersed in an abyss, which even a spaceship could not penetrate.

It is an amazing feeling, resembling the happiness of a lizard dreaming on a hot stone by the sea with its skin absorbing the salty heated air and the shade of passing clouds. It is wisdom equal to the happiness of a spider hanging on a thread spanning between two blades of grass. It is a feeling of being initiated to the mystery of life by those who crawl and fly.

From time to time, the bus stopped, and the guide Ivan Petrovich, not loud, as if being afraid to disturb someone in the mountains, was explaining the geological history of Abkhazia, and was telling about the ancient human settlements.

The members of the tourist group asked Ivan Petrovich about many subjects—he talked about the habits of the mountain trout, about the temples of the sixth century, about the project to build a power station in the mountains, about the partisan-fighters of the Civil War, about the Alpine flora, about bee keeping, and sheep breeding.

There was one elderly man who worried Ivan Petrovich. During the stops he had been standing on the side, away from the rest of the group and did not listen to his explanations. Ivan

путешественники часто поглядывают на этого пожилого, неряшливого человека.

Экскурсовод спросил:

— Кто сей дядя?

Ему шёпотом назвали знаменитое имя. Ивану Петровичу стало приятно — исследователь сложнейших вопросов теоретической физики, создатель нового взгляда на происхождение Вселенной участвует в его экскурсионной группе. В то же время ему было обидно: знаменитый учёный, в одной статье его назвали великим мыслителем, не задавал Ивану Петровичу вопросов и, казалось, не слушал его объяснений.

Когда экскурсия вернулась в курортный городок, одна учёная женщина сказала:

— Поездка чудесно удалась, и в этом немалая заслуга нашего замечательного экскурсовода.

Все поддержали её.

— Надо написать отзыв, и все мы подпишем его! — предложил кто-то.

Через несколько дней Иван Петрович столкнулся на улице со знаменитым учёным. «Наверное, не узнает меня», — подумал Иван Петрович.

Но учёный подошёл к Ивану Петровичу и сказал:

— Я вас всей, всей душой благодарю.

— За что же? — удивился Иван Петрович. — Вы не задали мне ни единого вопроса и даже не слушали моих объяснений.

— Да, да, нет, нет, ну что вы, — сказал учёный. — Вы мне помогли ответить на самый важный вопрос. Ведь и я экскурсовод вот в этом автобусе, — и он показал на небо и землю, — и я был очень счастлив в этой поездке, как никогда в жизни. Но я не слушал ваших объяснений. Мы, экскурсоводы, не очень нужны. Мне даже показалось, что мы мешаем.

Petrovich noticed that the other members of the tour frequently looked at that elderly, sloppily dressed man.

The guide asked members of the tour:

"Who is that man?"

In a whisper, they mentioned a famous name. It was pleasant for Ivan Petrovich to hear it—a researcher of the most complicated theoretical problems in physics, a founder of a new approach to the genesis of the Universe, was a part of his tourist group. At the same time, he was offended: that man, a famous scientist, called a great thinker in one of the articles, did not ask Ivan Petrovich any questions and seemingly did not listen to his explanations.

When the group returned to the resort, a learned lady said— "The trip certainly was a wonderful success, thanks to our outstanding tour guide."

All seconded her.

"We should write a positive review and we all will sign it!"— someone proposed.

After a few days, Ivan Petrovich ran into the famous scientist. "He surely won't recognize me," he thought.

However, the scientist approached Ivan Petrovich and said: "I thank you from the bottom of my heart."

"For what?" asked Ivan Petrovich with astonishment. "You did not ask me a single question, and even did not listen to my explanations."

"Yes, yes, no, no, that is not so"—said the scientist. "You helped me to answer the most fundamental question. I am also a tour guide on a vehicle,"—and here he pointed to the sky and earth, "I was very happy on that trip, like never in my life. However, I did not listen to your comments. It even occurred to me that we, as guides, only distract."

NOTES

"The Orphan." Maxim Gorky.

Сирота. Максим Горький. Полное собрание сочинений в 25-ти томах. Т. 5. Трое. Рассказы. Наброски. 1899–1901. М., Наука, 1970. С. 338–342.

First published in the newspaper *The Nizhegorodsky Listok*, #272, October, 1899.

Четвертак — 25 kopecks.

Мать — in the Russian tradition the priest's wife is called "мать, матушка"—"mother."

Пятиалтынный — 15 kopecks.

Ко́злы — a coach box in the front part of a carriage.

Баранка — baranka, a ring-shaped white flour biscuit, similar to a bagel. In Russia there is an old tradition of almsgiving (money or food) to poor people during the 40-day period after the burial.

Двугривенный — 20 kopecks.

Ряса — cassock.

Ай матушки! — this exclamation is equivalent to phrases like "Oh, Lord!"

Пролётка — light, open, four-wheel, one-horse carriage; a cab.

Дьякон — deacon, an assistant to a priest.

Псаломщик — a psalm reader.

Петрунька — Petrunka—from the name "Пётр" (Peter).

Показывать нос — to tease; to show a derisive gesture (one spreads a hand putting a thumb on the top of nose, wagging the fingers).

"On Christmastide." Anton Pavlovich Chekhov.

На Святках. Антон Павлович Чехов. Собрание сочинений в 12-ти томах. Т. 8. Повести и рассказы. 1895–1903. М., Государственное издательство художественной литературы, 1962. С. 406–410.

First published in *The Peterburgskaya Gazeta*, 1900, #1, January 1. There is an opinion that the female character Yefimia was modeled after the Chekhovs' housemaid, who was forced to marry against her will.

Святки — Christmastide, the festive winter two-week period from Christmas Eve (in Russia Christmas is celebrated on January 7) until Epiphany Day (January 19).

Пятиалтынный — 15 kopeks.

Yegor is citing (shown in italics in the text) mistakes made in an approximate text from the "Code of Laws of the Russian Empire"; Volume 4, Book 1 ("Code of Regulations on the Army Service"); Chapter 17 of the Code tells about the punishments.

"Пользовать" — means "лечить."

Клирос — choir, the part of the church where the choir sings; can be either on the right or on the left part from the iconostasis; on the eminence; or, sometimes, on a special balcony.

Душ Шарко — Charcot shower, a special high-pressure shower designed by the French doctor Jean Martin Charcot (1825–1893), one of the founders of medical neurology. In water spas this shower became very popular in the late nineteenth to early twentieth centuries for body massage and the treatment of cellulite.

"The Present." Leonid Nikolaevich Andreev.

Гостинец. Леонид Андреев. Повести и рассказы в двух томах. Т. 1. 1898–1906. М., Художественная литература, 1971. С. 220–226.

First published in the newspaper *The Kurier*, 1901, April 1, #90.

Ослобониться — освободиться.

Гусли — psaltery.

Бабки — knucklebones.

Кон — the place where knucklebones are placed by the players.

Гривенник — ten-kopeck coin.

Участок — police station.

Гармоника (гармонь, гармошка) — a small diatonic button accordion, a popular Russian musical instrument used in the past usually to perform folklore music.

Каёмчатый — with a border.

Орёл — Orel, an old Russian city (founded in the sixteenth century) where the story takes place. It is situated about 230 miles to the southwest of Moscow, by the River Oka and its tributary, the Orlik River. Orel was well known to the writer, who was born there; he described it in many stories.

Допрежде — сначала.

Как-с, когда же-с — letter "с" used at the end of a word substituted for the omitted original form from "сударь" (Mr.) or "сударыня" (Mrs.). Usually it was applied when talking to someone of higher position.

Мертвецкая — морг.

Прощевай — прощай.

Пар — fallow.

"Icarus." Skitalets.

Икар. Скиталец. Повести и рассказы. Воспоминания. М., Московский рабочий, 1960. С. 214–217.

"Икар" — Icarus. It is possible that the porcelain composition described in the story was a copy of the popular canvas "The Lament for Icarus" by Herbert James Draper. The artist depicted dead Icarus surrounded by lamenting nymphs. The canvas was awarded a gold medal at Paris World Fair in 1900. Icarus, in Greek mythology, was the son of Daedalus, a gifted

craftsman. To escape from Crete, where they both were forced to remain, he made wings using feathers held together wax. In spite of his father's warning, Icarus approached the sun too close and the wax melted. Icarus fell into the sea and drowned.

Вечный двигатель — an "eternal engine," a perpetuum mobile, a perpetual motion machine—existing only in theory, a machine, designed to produce more energy then it consumes.

Целковый — one ruble.

Кафтан — peasant's clothes similar to an overcoat.

Попритчиться — случиться.

"Marble Head." Valery Yakovlevich Bryusov.

Мраморная головка (Рассказ бродяги). В.Я. Брюсов. Избранная проза. М., Современник, 1989. С. 54–57. ISBN-5-270-00103-9

First published in the newspaper *The Russky Listok*, 1905, #5, January 6. Included in Bryusov's collection *Zemnaya Os. Stories and Dramas* (1901–1906). Moscow: Skorpion, 1907.

Хитровка, Хитров рынок — Khitrov Market (Khitrovka), an area in the central part of Moscow. In the nineteenth to early twentieth centuries it was a place where the outcasts of society congregated and lived; a place of cheap flophouses and taverns; the area where unskilled workers could find a job; a place infamous for its beggars and criminals (from pickpockets to the serious criminals-fugitives from Siberian convict camps).

Атлантида — Atlantis, a legendary island mentioned by Plato that sank into the ocean as a result either of an earthquake or of a flood.

"Trataton." Dmitry Narkisovich Mamin-Sibiryak.

Трататон. Д.Н. Мамин-Сибиряк. Собрание сочинений в 2-х томах. Т. 2. М., Русская книга, 1999. С. 313–323. ISBN-5-268-01022-0 (т. 2)

First published in the newspaper *Russkiye Vedomosti*, St. Petersburg, 1906, #271.

Трататон — Trataton, the old residents of Tobolskaya Guberniya called "tratatons" the migrants from southern Russia for their habit of speaking quickly (taratorit, tratatonit). According to the commentaries by E.N. Evstafieva to the Russian edition (p. 410), Trataton is from the Finnish "tratatus," which means "jolly" or "cheerful."

Finland was a part of the Russian Empire from 1809 until 1917, and being close to the capital city, St. Petersburg, it was a popular place for summer holidays among the Russian middle class.

Дача — a country house owned or rented for the summer by big city dwellers. Traditionally, there were many dachas around St. Petersburg and Moscow, inhabited mainly by the middle class.

Чухонский — Finnish.

Чухна — Finns.

Кулик — a surfbird.

"Пасынок природы" — "step-son of nature," a quotation from Alexander Pushkin's poem "The Bronze Horseman": "...Finnish fisherman, a sad step-son of Nature."

Вейка — Finnish or Estonian cabman and/or his cab.

Тобольская губерния — Tobolskaya Guberniya, a guberniya, a province, an administrative unit, existing during the times of the Russian Empire in Siberia and the Urals until 1919, with its center in the city Tobolsk.

Московская губерния — Moskovskaya Guberniya, a guberniya, an administrative unit of the Russian Empire and Russian Federation existing until 1929, with its center in Moscow.

"Немшоная" Сибирь — from the "moss" ("мох")—the name used to tease the people living in Siberia, because they did not interleave their log houses with moss.

Угодник — saint.

Питер — Piter, a popular, informal, shorter version of the name St. Petersburg.

Дураков — Durakov—from Russian word "дурак," which means "stupid, dummy."

Преосвященный — bishop.

Остяки — the Ostyaks, a Siberian indigenous people living in western Siberia, along the Ob River; they belong to the Finno-Ugric ethnic group.

Омморошный — a dialect curse word (adjective) in the Urals and Siberia. (from: S.K.Bulich. Materialy dlya Russkogo Slovarya, pp. 294–334: Otdeleniye Russkogo yazyka i slovesnosti, Emperor's Academy of Science, St. Petersburg, 1896, Vol. 1, Book 2, p. 313).

Становой — local police superintendent of a certain "stan" (a local police district); a police position existing in Russia from 1837 to 1917.

Земство — Zemstvo—elected district council, a self-governance institution in pre-revolutionary Russia, in existence since 1864.

Заседатель — assessor, in Siberia—the member of the district police department appointed by the government, sometimes in remote areas, performing functions of the head of the police department.

Обь — the Ob River, the longest river in Western Siberia, about 3361 miles long.

Осётр — sturgeon.

Нельма — Nelma, *Stenodus Leucichthys*, Siberian white salmon, inconnu.

Стерлядь — Sterlet, *Acipenser ruthenus*, a Eurasian species of sturgeon.

Моксун — Moksun (muksun), *Coregonus Muksun*, a type of whitefish found in Siberia.

Пуд — pud, a unit of weight; 1 pud was equal to 16.38 kg or 36.112 pounds.

Верста — versta, an old Russian unit of length, equal to about 0.663 miles.

Лычаги (from "лычага") — a rope made of thin wooden fiber.

Целковый — a silver coin of one ruble.

Двугривенный — a coin of 20 kopecks.

Тверской — from Tver, the city on the Volga River about 183 miles to the northwest from Moscow.

Квас — kvas, a fermented beverage made of rye bread.

Оглобля — a shaft.

Война — Russo-Japanese War, the war between Russia and Japan (1904–1905) for the control of Korea and Manchuria.

The following list gives the Russian equivalents for the Siberian dialect used by Trataton, as well as the pronunciation of some Russian words by local Finns.

Расейский — российский

Особь статья — особое дело, исключение

Расея — Россия

Выворотился — вернулся

Далёконько — далеко

Сперва — сначала

Вымерли — умерли

Протчее — другое

Не чета — не сравнить с, в сравнение не идёт с

Звание — название

Бабья — женская

Орудия — орудие, инструмент

Кожей наоборот выходит — совсем другой

Малоёмный — слабый

Корневище — корень

Точно руками — как руками

Подгнить — стать гнилым у основания

Пререда — природа

Всё от характера — всё от характера

Величать — называть

Малым делом — немного

В черепушке — в голове, в мозгу

Пустым-пусто — совсем пусто

Без малого произошёл — почти всю [реку Обь] прошёл

Не видать — не видно

Нехристи — язычники, неверующие

Пряменько сказать — по правде сказать

А вот что касаемо — что касается

Не выкупиться — не отдать долги

Великая в ём сила — великая в нём сила

Плепорция — соотношение, пропорция

Отличный от расейских — отличается от российских; другой, по сравнению с российскими

С бору да с сосенки набрались — отовсюду понемножку приехали

В свою голову — самопроизвольно, сами по себе, независимо

Наработал — заработал

Велик в перьях — очень важный

Кто ежели с умом — если кто с умом

Вольных местов неочерпаемо — вольных мест неисчерпаемо

Нигде не сыщешь — нигде не найдёшь

Лиха беда — несчастье

Здря — зря

Уксуском обольёшь — уксусом обольёшь

Настоящего скусу не понимают — настоящего вкуса не понимают

Тыщи три пудов — тысячи три пудов

Всё одно, как — похоже, как

Разберут по сословиям — разберут по сортам

Уважить — оказать уважение, доставить удовольствие

Лют — лютый

Характерный — характерный

Малый делом — совсем немного

Верстов с пять осетром плыл — верст пять плыл, как осётр

Своим средствием поучили — своими средствами поучили

Дом с мензелином — дом с мезонином

Приспособил хороминку — построил дом

Минюрненькая — миниатюрненькая, маленькая

Наладил — построил

Со всякой всячиной — с разными начинками

Водки трёкнулся — водки выпил

Попадейка — попадья

Порох порохом — как порох

Вынь да положь — чтобы было сейчас

Всё с срыву — всё очень эмоционально

Напиваться «вдребезги» — сильно напиваться

Рипа — рыба

Чука — щука

Али — или

Ежовые головы — недалёкие, глуповатые люди

Кузов — корзина

Ни из кузова, ни в кузов, как козьи рога — a saying about stubborn people

Куда похитрее — намного хитрее

Живёт справно — живёт хорошо

Потрафляешь — угождаешь

Шайка — деревянная ёмкость, ведро с ручками

Большак — старший брат

Промышлять — зарабатывать

Брюхо — живот

Из-за хлеба на квас — hardly making ends meet

Назад оглобли поворотят — возвращаются

Первым делом — сначала

Красный товар станет — самый лучший товар не будет продаваться

Недород — неурожай

Век — жизнь

Что касаемо — что касается

Всё одно — всё равно

Бабочка убивается — баба, женщина страдает

Свет тебе клином [сошёлся] — нет выхода

Силы в ём настоящей нету — силы в нём настоящей нет

Рылом в молоко тыкать — мордой в молоко тыкать (which means to point at something obvious)

В черепушке — в черепе

Возгордился — стал гордым, стал гордиться

И конец тому делу — и всё

Вперёд не гордись — больше не гордись

Превознёсся — высоко ценил себя, возвеличивал себя

По шапке — прогнали

Завсегда — всегда

Ежели бы — если бы

Человеки — люди

Промежду — между

Агромадный — громадный

Понастроены — построены

Целую жисть — целую жизнь

Не ропщу — не жалуюсь

Жисть прожил — жизнь прожил

"Electricity." Lydia Dmitrievna Zinovieva-Annibal.

Электричество. Лидия Дмитриевна Зиновьева-Аннибал. Тридцать три урода. М., Аграф, 1999. С. 190–192. ISBN-5-7784-0062-4

First published in *Belye Nochi. Peterburgsky Almanakh.* St. Petersburg, 1907.

Вирный — from "вир," "vir," whirlpool.

Электрическая рыба — either an electric ray or a Gymnotus.

"Like a Family." Aleksandr Ivanovich Kuprin.

По-семейному. Александр Куприн. Собрание сочинений в 6-ти томах. Т. 4. Произведения 1905–1914. М., Государственное издательство художественной литературы, 1958. С. 392–399.

First published in the newspaper *The Utro Rossii*, #126, April 18, 1910.

The first version of the same plot was published in 1897 under the title "Natashka" in Kiev. In 1910, Kuprin returned to the story and developed the plot, enriching it with additional characters and details.

Подол — Podol, the old Kiev district in the lowland, on the right bank of the Dnieper River.

Александровская горка — Alexandrovskaya Street, more often called Alexandrovsky (Vladimirsky) Slope, a hilly street going down the slope, connecting the Kiev downtown and Podol area.

Дендрология — dendrology, a branch of botany studying wooden plants.

Септаккорд — a septa chord, seventh-chord (a triad with the seventh added).

Доминанта — dominant, basic key in music.

Полесье — Polesie, a geographical area located over the

territory of four countries: Ukraine, Byelorussia, Poland, and Russia, known for its forests and many large swamps.

Элиз Геклю — Jean Jacques Élisée Reclus (1830–1905), French geographer, historian, and sociologist.

Черниговский берег — Chernigov is a city in the North of Ukraine, situated by the left branch of Dnieper, the Desna River.

Похристосоваться — exchange of a triple kiss as an Easter salutation, the old Russian tradition on Easter Day.

Коридорный — a bellboy.

Пасха — Easter Day. Also, the name of a traditional sweet Easter dessert made of pressed cottage cheese, raisins, butter, and other ingredients in the shape of a pyramid with a cross on its side.

Разговеться — to break one's fast. It is traditional in the Russian Orthodox Church to fast before the Easter Day celebration; and believers are allowed to eat only after the Easter church service is finished.

"Свячёная пасха" — Blessed paskha—Christian believers bring the ritual meals (painted eggs, paskha, and kulich) to the church either on the Saturday evening before Easter Day, or on Easter Day to be blessed by the priest after the service, which lasts the entire night. The priest reads the prayers, sprinkling the meals with blessed water. Usually this takes place outside of the churches after the morning service.

"Лупетки" — in slang, "eyes" (or, "bulging" eyes).

"Тенериф" — "Tenerife," wine produced on Tenerife Island.

Братство — Bratstvo, Bratsky Epiphany Monastery in Kiev Podol district, the part of Kievo-Mogilyanskaya Ecclesiastical Academy.

Заутреня — matins.

Кулич — kulich, the ritual traditional Easter cake made of white flour, eggs, raisins, dried apricots, and nuts, glazed on top. Usually the believers bring them to the church in the morning to be blessed after the Easter service.

Цветы «сон» — "dream" flower, *Pulsatilla patens*, a plant with blue-purple flowers; blooms in April and May.

Ж...кой — means "with its butt," i.e. the dull end of an egg. Here Zoya describes an ancient Russian tradition traced to pagan beliefs (later it turned into a gamelike ritual) to find whose boiled and painted Easter egg is stronger; the owner of the "weak" egg had to give it to the person with stronger egg.

"The Fugitive." Vladimir Alekseevich Gilyarovsky.

Беглый. Владимир Алексеевич Гиляровский. Сочинения в 2-х тт. Калуга, Золотая аллея, 1994, Т. 2. С. 201–205. ISBN-7111-0105-6 (т.2), ISBN-5-7111-0107-2

Халат (арестантский) — a gray robe, the clothes of prisoners and state convicts.

Шапка без козырька — a hat the prisoners had to wear as a part of the uniform.

Золотые "зайки" — flashes of reflected sunlight.

Кеньги — special winter boots (can be leather, with fur inside, or made of pressed wool-like galoshes) worn by a sentry in cold weather.

Тайга — taiga, dense Siberian forest.

В подземельях — in mines. The fact that the fugitive thinks about the work in mines tells us that he most likely was a state convict of the first category, sentenced either to life imprisonment, or to more than twelve years.

"Life Granted." Aleksandr Grin. (1915)

Подаренная жизнь. Александр Грин. Из памятной книжки сыщика. Детективные истории. Феодосия–Москва: Коктебель, 2009. С. 59-63. ISBN 978-966-1500-00-5

First published under the title "Gambler. Petersburg's Story" in the newspaper *The Birzhevye Vedomosti*, 1915, #18, December 19, and later, under the title "Life Granted," it was published in the *Siny Zhurnal*, 1918, #19.

In 1930, Grin wrote "The Green Lamp," the story in which he returned to the motif of the mysterious beauty of human anatomy, which suddenly changed a man's life. In this piece of writing, Grin told the story of a poor young man who first played a role in two rich men's practical joke. But when he became fascinated by the mysteries and beauty of the human body in an anatomical atlas found by chance, he decided to become a doctor. And, Grin wrote, "if one desires something passionately, there soon will be a result"—it changed the man's life and helped him to fulfill his dream.

"Джонка" — a hat in a shape of a "junk"—Chinese boat.

Пришить — in criminal slang, it means "to kill, to do in."

Лопух — *Arctium*, burdock, a plant with big leaves.

"Биоскоп" — "Bioskop," one of the typical names of movie theaters in pre-revolutionary Russia. The owners often organized concerts, performances, and exhibitions in the same building to attract the public.

Заводь — dialect word: "art," "industry," "mechanism."

Амба — in criminal slang, it means "kaput," "it's all over"; a dead end, no-way-out situation.

"Dragon." Yevgeny Ivanovich Zamyatin. (1918)

Дракон. Евгений Замятин. Сочинения. Т. 3. Повести и рассказы. Мы. Биографические очерки. West Germany: A. Neimanis Buchvertrieb und Verlag, 1986. C. 68–69.

The writer describes the Civil War times in Petrograd. St. Petersburg was renamed Petrograd after the beginning of World War I, as a reflection of anti-German sentiment in the society, because the new name, the City of Peter (the Great) sounded more Russian. In 1918 to 1923, the Soviet leaders called for the "Red Terror" against the social enemies and "counter-revolution," which resulted in a series of cruel mass executions.

"Psalm." Mikhail Afanasievich Bulgakov. (1923)

Псалом. Михаил Булгаков. Собрание сочинений в 5-ти томах. Т. 2. М., Художественная литература, 1989. С. 335–338. ISBN-5-280-007161-7 (т.2); ISBN-5-280-00760-9

First published in the newspaper *Nakanune*, September 23, 1923.

The writer's first wife later recollected that in the story, Bulgakov appeared to be describing life in the communal apartment, in which he and his wife lived in Moscow (10 Bolshaya Sadovaya St., Apt. 34).

The writer used the verses of the popular romance by A. Vertinsky, "This is All You Left" (1918).

«Куплю себе туфли к фраку,
И буду петь по ночам Псалом.
И заведу себе собаку.
Ничего. Как-нибудь проживём».

"I'll order the shoes to match my tailcoat,
I will start singing the Psalm at night,
I will buy a dog on Saturday,
It's OK. Somehow… We'll survive."

Джером — Jerome K. Jerome (1859–1927), a British author of humorous novels ("Three Men in a Boat," "Three Men on the Bummel").

Синдетикон — Syndetikon, a type of glue for paper and cardboard.

Кузнецкий мост — Kuznetsky Most, an old street in Moscow's downtown. From the eighteenth century until 1917, it was the center of trade and fashion, with many clothing stores, tailors' boutiques, bookstores, publishing houses, and restaurants. Traditionally there has always been heavy traffic and crowds of pedestrians on the street.

Слюдяное окно — mica window, a small window on the side of old models of kerosene stoves covered with a mica plate to watch the wicks.

Сатинет — satinette, thin satin fabric.

"The Angler of the Glass Battalion." Iliya Ilf. (1923)

Рыболов Стеклянного батальона. Илья Ильф. Евгений Петров. Собрание сочинений в 5-ти томах. Т. 5. М., Художественная литература, 1996. С. 19–21. ISBN-5-280-02842-8 (т. 5); ISBN-5-280-02838-X

First published in the newspaper *Gudok*, #1064, December 1, 1923.

"В очках" — in glasses—a long-lasting negative stereotype in Soviet times referring to the people of the intellectual, educated circle. It symbolized belonging to a different social layer of society, unfriendly to the Soviet power and the Communist regime. This stereotype was mentioned many times in Isaac Babel's collection of stories about the Civil War, "The Red Cavalry."

Верста — versta, an old Russian unit of measurement of length, distance, one versta equals 0.663 miles.

Мохна — from Nestor Makhno (1889–1934), an anarchist and the leader of the counter-revolutionary movement in Ukraine from 1918 to 1921; during the Civil War, he organized the Peoples Insurgent Army of Ukraine. At first, he fought against the German army occupying Ukraine, the White Army, temporary collaborating with the Red Army, and then from the summer of 1919, against the Red Army (Lev Trotsky proclaimed him an outlaw), though in the autumn of 1920 he again became an ally of the Bolsheviks. In 1921, Makhno (his army regiments at that time were called "gangs") was fighting against the Red Army, and after a number of defeats managed to escape abroad.

Махновцы — Makhnovtsy, the soldiers of the Makhno's Army.

Татарка — Tatarka; the author probably meant the village of Tatarka in Stavropolsky Krai in the southern Russia.

"Hot Stone." Arkady Gaidar.

Горячий камень. Аркадий Гайдар. Собрание сочинений в 4-х томах. Т. 3. М., Детская литература, 1964. С. 232–237.

This tale was first published in 1941, at the time of World War II, in the magazine *Murzilka*, 1941, #8–9. At that time Gaidar was already on the front lines.

Валенки — valenki, traditional Russian winter tall felt boots; they are made of dried pressed wool, and because their bottom wears out fast, they are often soled with leather.

Сельсовет — a village council during Soviet times.

Мочальная кисть — a fiber brush made of thin layers of the inner part of tree bark (usually the linden tree) and used in painting and gardening.

Праздник Первое Мая — May 1 holiday, an important state holiday in Soviet times called the Day of International Solidarity of All Working People. From 1918 on, that day has been celebrated with military parades and peaceful mass demonstrations.

Цигарка — a handmade cigarette.

"From the Bus Window." Vasily Grossman.

Из окна автобуса. Василий Гроссман. Несколько печальных дней. М, Современник, 1989. С. 304–306. ISBN-5-270-00033-4

Дом отдыха (dom otdykha, literally a "house for rest") — this is a type of a health resort where people can rest during their vacation. These houses were maintained by ministries, trade unions, and institutions. An employee could get a referral from a trade union for a two-week rest at dom otdykha, with a physician in attendance; the employee often shared the room with a few other people and enjoyed meals, scheduled physical exercises, and so-called "cultural programs," including movies, concerts, lectures, and bus tours. The most desirable and popular places were located in the south of the USSR—at the Black Sea shore, in the Crimea, and in the Caucasus. The Academy of Sciences of the Soviet Union mentioned by V. Grossman, a big institution with many employees, also owned a number of "houses for rest."

For further information on the authors and their stories, please consult:

Terras, Victor. *Handbook of Russian Literature*. New Haven and London: Yale University Press, 1985.